ABOUT THE AUTHOR

Kirk Lake is a writer and musician. He has contributed
articles to the *Guardian, Observer, Dazed and Confused,
The Idler*, the *NME*, and numerous other publications
around the world. He lives in London.

There Will Be
RAINBOWS

There Will Be

RAINBOWS

A Biography of
RUFUS
WAINWRIGHT

KIRK LAKE

itbooks

AN IMPRINT OF HARPERCOLLINS *PUBLISHERS*

*it***books**

Originally published in Great Britain in 2009 by Orion Books, an imprint of the Orion Publishing Group Ltd.

FIRST U.S. EDITION

Library of Congress Cataloging-in-Publication Data is available upon request.

ISBN 978-0-06-198846-2

10 11 12 13 14   /RRD   10 9 8 7 6 5 4 3 2 1

For Anne and Ruby, as ever . . .

CONTENTS

SIENNA MILLER: 'I can't imagine how proud your parents must be with kids like you and your sister.'
RUFUS WAINWRIGHT: 'They're quite proud. But sometimes they just wish we had No. 1 hits!'

Interview magazine, June 2007

They fuck you up your mum and dad.
They may not mean to, but they do.
They fill you with the faults they had
And add some extra just for you.

Philip Larkin, from *This Be The Verse*, 1971

There Will Be

RAINBOWS

PRELUDE

The guy across the cramped little picnic table is wearing a T-shirt with Rufus Wainwright's head printed on it. Rufus' face and features are whited out like in late Andy Warhol portraits and he's wearing a fedora and a smear of red lipstick. Arcing across the top of his image are multi-coloured balloon-shaped letters that spell out 'There Will be Rainbows'. The guy next to him is wearing a sky-blue T-shirt with a naked Rufus on the front. Later they tell me that nude Rufus is a Marc Jacobs limited edition and Rainbow Rufus has been home-made (and later still I discover it is a misquote, but with its implication of triumph over adversity and sunshine after the rain, it's so much more apposite than the actual lyric).

Rufus Wainwright is a few hundred feet away from us on stage at the Hollywood Bowl, bidding a relieved farewell to the Judy Garland show he has been performing intermittently over the previous year and a half. His voice deserts him every now and then, and he croaks at the end of a line, gasping after notes he cannot reach. On occasion he looks defeated and downcast, as if he can't wait to hang up his ruby slippers.

His sister Martha Wainwright has already received a standing ovation for her coruscating rendition of 'Stormy Weather'. The following night at a tiny club show at the Hotel Café, she'll know how it feels for a family member to pull the rug from under the main attraction when mother Kate McGarrigle slips some Jerry Lee Lewis-like glissandi into the usually restrained piano accompaniment of her song 'Factory', leaving Martha to gently curse, 'Oh, Mother. You're always trying to one-up me . . . '

But on this night Kate teeters across the vast stage and sits demurely at the piano. The Hollywood Bowl's concentric concrete circles ring subdued blue light over the stage and Rufus is spotlit alone on the runway that cuts into the garden terrace seating. For such an established and experienced performer, he looks like a little boy lost. Eyes closed, the glass brooch on his waistcoat sparkling, he starts to sing . . . 'Somewhere over the rainbow way up high . . .'

Hollywood is a great place to go to become somebody else. Norma Jeane Baker came to Hollywood and transformed herself from factory worker into the most famous movie actress there will ever be because she 'dreamed harder' than every other aspiring star. Halfway through the night's signature song something extra-ordinary happens: what had threatened to remain a disappointingly anti-climatic evening, in which Rufus failed to raise his head above the parapet of Garland's recreated ruins, is transformed by a tran-scendent Hollywood moment. Through the artifice, through the bloated conceit of the entire enterprise, Rufus suddenly connects with the 13,000-strong crowd. By the end of the song, the blue lights are changing into reds and yellows and greens. We are all dreaming harder. There will be rainbows indeed.

ACT 1

I will effuse egotism and show it underlying all, and I will be the bard of personality.

Walt Whitman, *Starting From Paumanok*

'Folk songs? I don't know what they is. I guess all songs is folk songs. I never heard no horse sing 'em.'

Big Bill Broonzy

1.1

In 1968 everybody was looking for a new Bob Dylan and every aspiring East Coast folk singer was making their way to Greenwich Village in New York City, hoping that they might be the ones to squeeze into Dylan's discarded motorcycle boots. In an area long favoured by musicians, artists, bohemians and poets, and as louche as it was intellectual, to play your songs in the clubs and coffee bars of MacDougal Street meant putting yourself up against legends. In every corner lurked an audience of hip, knowing ghosts ...

Imagine James Dean hanging out at Rienzi's, James Baldwin waiting tables at the Calypso, the spirits of Jackson Pollock and Dylan Thomas drunk and swaying on the chequerboard floor of the San Remo. John Cage throwing the I Ching in one of the booths. On MacDougal Street, Tallulah Bankhead had appeared at the Provincetown Playhouse, where Bette Davis had made her stage debut. It was a street that embraced strong women. Eve Addams ran Eve's Hangout, a lesbian bar ('Men admitted but not welcome' said the sign), before being deported in 1926 for publishing pornography. Later Anaïs Nin self-published her own early books by way of a printer further along the road and, years before that,

Louisa May Alcott wrote at least a little of *Little Women* in a house belonging to her uncle.

Bob Dylan loved the street. He had played his earliest New York shows at the Cafe Wha? and the Village Gaslight, but it was his extended stay at the latter club in 1962 that saw him begin his transition from talented interpreter of traditional music to mercurial folk poet and reconfirm the club's position as the hippest bar on the block. Recordings of these shows, known simply as 'The Gaslight Tapes', would become among the most famous bootlegs in rock history.

The Gaslight had been founded in 1958 by John Mitchell. He opened it as a coffeehouse in an undeveloped cellar with a low ceiling, so low that Mitchell had had to lower the floor in order to create enough space to enable patrons to stand up. Trouble was, he was going against planning rules so he'd had to dig out the cellar floor himself and distribute the bags of soil along the Greenwich Village streets like the 'penguins' did for the escaping POWs in *The Wooden Horse*.

The club soon became the most important place for poetry readings and a focal point for the East Coast beat movement. Allen Ginsberg, Gregory Corso and Lawrence Ferlinghetti all read at the Gaslight. There's a famous Fred McDarrah photograph of Diane DiPrima reading there in 1959, perched on top of a piano next to an oil lamp and a mantle clock. The place looks cramped and smoky. The walls are wooden panels, like a reinforced escape tunnel from straightsville. Indeed, the police were always trying to close them down, citing the club for hygiene violation or excessive noise. When applause drifted up from the pavement grating and caused the neighbours to complain, the audience took to snapping their fingers in quiet appreciation instead.

Under new ownership in 1960, the poets had been gradually overcome by a gentle folk wave that saw more and more acoustic guitars carried down the steps until Dylan's breakout success led to a stampede of hopeful troubadours. With Dylan's sales leading the way, the folk movement, despite its simple roots in protest singing, working-men's blues and provincial story-telling, had become ripe for exploitation by the record labels. By the mid-Sixties, even though Dylan had long since moved on, gone electric and become a star, record-label bosses still scouring the New York folk circuit looking for somebody to follow him into the charts would always be sure to check on whoever was playing at the Gaslight. As with Dylan, the other early Sixties regulars like Phil Ochs, Richie Havens, Mississippi John Hurt and Joan Baez had quickly outgrown the tiny venue but every night there were always a dozen other hopefuls waiting at the top of the stairs with their weathered six strings.

In 1968, one of these aspiring Dylans was Loudon Wainwright III, 22 years old, raised mostly in the affluent New York suburb of Westchester County after itinerant childhood stints in places including North Carolina, Los Angeles and Long Island, courtesy of his father, Loudon Wainwright Jr's, work as a columnist and editor at *Life* magazine. He had a set of songs that he had written himself and that he would deliver in a style quite unlike the other performers on the circuit. Later *Rolling Stone* would liken him to 'Charlie Chaplin through the eyes of Antonin Artaud', an acoustic comedy of cruelty, but for now his nervous tics and flitting tongue had the Gaslight crowd enthralled.

When his father had temporarily taken charge of the LA office of *Life*, the seven-year-old Loudon had found himself living on Hutton Drive in the heart of Beverly Hills and at school with the sons and daughters of the Hollywood elite. He'd have tea parties with Liza Minnelli at her mother Judy Garland's house. He'd find himself visiting film sets for his schoolfriend's birthday parties, where the children could play under the spotlights in imagined rooms or artificial landscapes – experiences that he would credit for getting him interested in a career in showbusiness in the first place.

This childhood ambition was the reason he chose to study acting at Carnegie Mellon University in Pittsburgh, where fellow students included future *Cheers* star Ted Danson. But before he could finish his studies, he was bored and dropped out to go where the action seemed to be – Haight Ashbury, San Francisco. A spell of hitch-hiking around the country living the hippie life ended with him arrested for smoking pot and spending five days in an Oklahoma jail. 'The only thing I learned in jail was that I wanted to get out,' he ruefully admitted. His furious father had to fly in from England to bail him out.

Loudon had played his first guitar when he was ten, a cheap acoustic given him by his father.[1] He hadn't kept up with the lessons that had been offered at school and although he had kept a guitar with him through his college years his playing was self-taught and rudimentary. Strumming songs wasn't really something he did that much and he'd ended up happily swapping his own guitar for yoga lessons in San Francisco. After another stint bumming around the country he wound up staying with a friend in Cambridge, Massachusetts. Like a lot of people in Joan Baez country, this friend had an acoustic guitar and one day Loudon picked it up and started writing a song. He remembered the song in an interview with *Folk Roots* magazine: 'I had been working in a boatyard in Rhode Island and I wrote a song about the lobster fishermen I'd met. It was a kind of saccharine oversimplified view of the common man, but it was . . . a song!'[2]

Although he would later describe his early songs as lousy, Loudon persevered until he had enough material to start playing shows. And for one man and a guitar, if you were going to venture out and play to anybody other than your stoned friends in your front room, New York City was the only place to be. Loudon hit the Greenwich Village clubs, playing anywhere he could and sleeping on people's floors. 'I did a kind of bohemian starving artist routine in a very dilettantish manner,' he recalled in a 1974 *Los Angeles Times* interview. 'If things got heavy, I just got on a train and went up to Westchester to my parents.'

His parents' record collection was a bigger influence on his songs than the folk scene of which he was striving to become a part. 'What I do is not really rooted in any kind of folk tradition apart from the

1. According to Lenny Kaye's April 1971 Loudon Wainwright feature in *Rolling Stone*, Loudon's first guitar had been a gift to his father from the folk singer Terry Gilkyson. Gilkyson was the writer of the song 'Marianne', which had been a 1950s hit for both his own group the Easy Riders and a bigger hit for the Hilltoppers. He subsequently went on to work extensively with Disney Studios and in 1968 would be Academy Award-nominated for 'The Bare Necessities' from Walt Disney's *Jungle Book*, the only one of his songs for the picture that Walt Disney retained after deciding the other material he had provided was too 'dark'. That Disney then employed Van Dyke Parks as arranger for 'The Bare Necessities' and Parks eventually worked with both Rufus and Loudon is a tenuous but pleasingly circular link.
2. The song 'Nanny' from Loudon's 2005 album *Here Come the Choppers* explains how his grandmother took him in after he was busted for drugs and found him a job at the boatyard.

fact that I happen to play a guitar and write songs,' he later told the *Melody Maker* before elaborating that his parents' tastes, encompassing musicals like *My Fair Lady*, *Guys and Dolls* and Doris Day in the *Pajama Game*, were the songs he could remember singing along to as a ten-year-old.

By mixing the influence of Broadway songs and musical humorists like Stan Freberg, Allan Sherman and Tom Lehrer with the more contemporary folk art of Dylan or his Dylanesque acolytes, Loudon hit on a winning formula. He stood out even more by wearing his hair unfashionably short and by wearing smart Brooks Brothers shirts and suit jackets. (In early photos, like the one used for his first album, he looks like a proto-NY punk rocker leaning mean against a brick wall, although this phase seemed to pass quickly with subsequent explosions of facial hair by the time of the third album.)

He took his drama-school training on stage with him to combat stage fright, a performing style that *Rolling Stone* noted was 'somewhat bizarre' and which the *Melody Maker* described as ranging from 'Quasimodo-like derelict to raving lunatic' (and this in otherwise completely complimentary reviews).

As Loudon told it: 'I physicalised my fear into strange, spastic body gyrations, replete with leg lifts, facial grimaces and lots of tongue-wagging. I made sure people noticed me.'

Working as a cook at the Paradox, a macrobiotic restaurant on the Lower East Side, and then for a while as a janitor at the famous Orson Welles Cinema back in Cambridge, he kept playing around the folk circuit, building a set, picking up fans. Sometimes he'd have to wait three hours just to get on a tiny stage and play three songs with a dozen other guitarists waiting behind him to take over. Often there were more ambitious performers hanging around than there were paying punters. But people were beginning to take notice of him. After impressing the bookers with a series of support slots and open mike nights, the prestigious Gaslight offered him five weeks straight as the resident act.

Milton Kramer, an enterprising music publisher looking to find a protégé, saw a couple of Loudon's shows and offered to manage him and try to secure a record deal. A number of labels immediately showed an interest, including Columbia Records' legendary John Hammond Snr, who'd signed Billie Holiday back in 1933, 'discovered' Count Basie while randomly tuning his radio one night, and had helped to launch the 'old' Bob Dylan. Loudon signed instead to Atlantic Records because another music business legend, Nesuhi Ertegun, was prepared to offer more money and because Loudon was excited at the prospect of being able to put out a record that had the same paper label on it as records he had loved by Ray Charles and Aretha Franklin.

Loudon wanted the album to be just him and an acoustic guitar. Although this replicated the sets he had been playing in the clubs, it was a sound that was beginning to seem a little dated by contemporary standards. It was a long time since Dylan had electrocuted the unsuspecting folk scene at Newport in 1965 and by now, even die-hard folkies had begun to experiment with augmented instrumentation.

Indeed, Atlantic wanted Loudon to record with other musicians, even enlisting the production skills of Arif Mardin to supervise. Mardin had produced Aretha Franklin and had just co-produced Dusty Springfield's career redefining *Dusty in Memphis* album (Dusty would thank him by suggesting that Atlantic sign a band of her acquaintance called Led Zeppelin). But whatever they tried, they just couldn't get these sessions to work.

Unlike a lot of young musicians, Loudon hadn't grown up playing rock'n'roll in garage bands. The only bands Loudon had been in were jug bands. He'd been in a Kingston Trio-style folk group called The Highlanders, then there was The Triaca Company, named after the Baltimore distillers whose name was written on the side of the actual jug they played, and then there was The Alumicron Fab-Tabs, a band he started at drama school that played songs by his favourite group the Jim Kweskin Jug band along with some Elvis and a few of his friends' songs. Nothing serious. (Jug band music is vaudevillian folk music, goofy good-time comedy songs that were generally taken as seriously as music made by blowing into a large jug could expect to be. It was certainly not rock'n'roll.)

Being asked to play with other musicians, even to experiment with strings, was not a success. 'We tried three different studios,' said Loudon. 'We could never seem to pull it together. I would listen to it and hear all these little faults and I would think, "Yeah, that's the part they're going to pick out and hear. That's the one." I could never see it in any kind of perspective.'

The failure of the first recordings finally convinced the record label that he should be allowed to record alone and he entered another New York studio with just his manager to help produce the tracks.

If Loudon Wainwright's authenticity as a 'genuine' folk singer depended mostly on the definition once put forward by Big Bill Broonzy,[3] then other Greenwich Village performers had come from far purer folk traditions.

Canadian Kate McGarrigle and her friend Roma Baran had arrived in the New York coffeehouses after playing the north-east folk scene around the Canadian and US border. Initially wary of getting on stage in the big city, Kate was unimpressed by a lot of the performers she saw and soon realised that she and Roma were easily good enough to hold their own. They really knew and understood folk music having been fully immersed in playing it live since the early part of the decade. Before that even, Kate had been brought up in a house that was always full of music.

Kate McGarrigle had been born in Montreal, Quebec, into an English-speaking family steeped in traditional music forms. Her grandfather had run the first commercial cinema exhibitions, hiring out small halls in the province of New Brunswick in the early 1900s, and her father Frank McGarrigle and his sister had been brought up singing parlour songs and the American folk songs of Stephen Foster.

Her mother, Gabrielle Latremouille, known to her family as Gaby, had once played violin in the Bell Telephone Orchestra on NBC radio and was as keen as her husband to teach her family a full repertoire of standards and music hall hits.

In their home in the small town of St Sauveur-des-Mont, north of Montreal, father Frank would play the songs on the family's 1883 Steinway and Kate and her older sisters Jane and Anna would

---

3. Big Bill Broonzy's quote refers to his disgust at his albums being referred to as 'folk' and is quoted, unsourced, in his *Time* magazine obituary of 1 September 1958. This predates the earliest use of the quote by Louis Armstrong by at least a decade, although the quote is still usually credited to the more famous Armstrong.

learn to sing and harmonise. As well as the piano, the family had instruments like a zither and a banjo lying around the house and by the age of ten Kate's father was helping her with guitar chords. All the girls were expected to take piano lessons from the sisters at their small church school.

'Our father played by ear,' remembered Anna in a 1986 interview. 'He was the life of the party. He taught us to sing when we were very young.'

Whenever possible Kate and Anna listened to the pop music and late 1950s rock'n'roll that they could occasionally pick up on a weak radio signal from WWVA, West Virginia, music that ghosted across the border on nights when the skies were clear. When eldest sister Jane returned from boarding school, she brought contemporary folk music and country blues records into the house and the sisters discovered there were even more styles of music to get excited by.

After seeing Pete Seeger in concert in the early 1960s, Kate and Anna decided to start their own folk group with a friend from school. They played the coffeehouse circuit in Montreal, including an appearance at the Finjan Club, where Bob Dylan would play an influential show in 1962.

There is a recording of the Dylan show on 2 July 1962 that has circulated for years, originally misidentified as being part of the Gaslight Tapes mentioned earlier. It's an inestimable document of both pre-superstar Dylan and the Canadian folk-club scene itself. In its unedited form, the tape runs from before the start of the set to when the recorder is clicked off after Dylan finishes with a particularly plaintive 'Muleskinner Blues' – all of the ambience and background noise are left intact. The recording was made by local fan Jack Nissenson, who at the time was a member of a Montreal folk group called the Pharisees.

Though the McGarrigles were still teenagers, Nissenson and fellow Pharisee Peter Weldon asked the sisters to join them in a new group called the Mountain City Four and they started playing the Montreal clubs like the Seventh Step on Stanley Street, performing a mix of standards, French-Canadian songs and more recent music from artists like the Carter Family. Kate thanks Nissenson and Weldon for introducing them to authentic folk styles and thereby helping them to develop their own unique sound: 'They introduced us to music at the sources and said forget about Joan Baez. Go to the sources at all times. "Don't copy styles, just learn the original music." We didn't try to imitate anyone, with the possible exception of Dylan, who everyone tried to imitate at one time or another.'

Kate and Anna played in the Mountain City Four while they studied at college. In 1966 the group were even asked to provide music for a Canadian Film Board travel documentary *Helicopter Canada*, which would be nominated for a Best Documentary Oscar and which caused Kate to flunk her chemistry final by ignoring her revision timetable to work on the film's soundtrack. But they had no ambitions to become professional musicians and even turned down an approach from a big New York promoter when he suggested that to get ahead they would need to smile more and take their hands out of their pockets.

After graduating from McGill University, Kate wanted to continue on the folk scene but Anna, who had studied painting at L'Ecole Beaux Arts, was less interested in performing and bowed out to take a job with social services in Montreal. The sisters shared a tiny garret on Evans Street and while Anna was happy to spend her free time working on her art at home, Kate formed a new duo with Roma Baran, who had herself been playing on the circuit for years with the well-respected Canadian singer Penny Lang. Baran's parents had given her an allowance and the use of a credit card so the pair began to play further afield, thinking nothing of driving thousands of miles just to play a $50 gig. Inevitably they gravitated towards New York where they played at clubs like Gerde's Folk City and the Gaslight.

One night at the Gaslight, Kate saw Loudon Wainwright III play. She was impressed enough to wait and speak to him afterwards. He was impressed enough to ask her out for a drink. 'She was very attractive,' said Loudon. 'I think every guy in the Village, they were all interested in Kate. When you heard her sing and play, you were knocked out. She was a wild and crazy swingin' folk chick.' Before too long, Kate and Loudon were a couple and they moved in together in Saratoga Springs.

Back in Montreal, Anna had started writing songs and the first of these was 'Heart like a Wheel', a deceptively simple, quite fragile love song. Both Kate and Anna had been slow to start writing their own material. 'Our circle of friends only thought a few people were good enough to be songwriters,' Anna later told the *New York Times*. 'Writing down lyrics seemed so final.' Undeterred, she sent a tape of her new song to Kate who immediately included it in her set.

The 1970 Philadelphia Folk Festival took place at the end of August. Over three days, 11,000 people watched acts like Fairport Convention, Bonnie Raitt and Luther Allison. Kate and Roma played on the last day. Jerry Jeff Walker, a fine folk performer who over time would evolve into an even finer country performer, saw them at the festival and was particularly impressed by Anna's song. Walker had been playing the circuit with Linda Ronstadt and they were always looking out for new material.

'"Heart like a Wheel" is one I just have never gotten over,' remembered Ronstadt in a *Rolling Stone* interview in 2002. 'Jerry Jeff Walker and I were playing at the Café Au Go Go in downtown New York and we would go out after the show ... just to have camaraderie and to find good songs and share experiences. We'd made the rounds that night. Just two sort of hunter-gatherers together. I remember the sun was coming up and we were in the back of this cab and stopping to let me out, he said, "You know there's a song I heard at the Philadelphia Folk Festival . . ." He sang me the chorus of it and it was so moving, the words just made me cry. I said, "I have to have that song."'

Walker contacted Kate and she sent him a reel-to-reel tape with a few songs on it. Alongside 'Heart Like A Wheel' was another song, 'Go Leave', which Ronstadt would eventually also cover. 'The McGarrigles are so much more into quality than glamour,' said Ronstadt. 'They forsake the glitz for gold dust in their writing. The tunes they compose are such beautiful parlour gems, carefully crafted songs meant for small audiences with big hearts.' Although Ohio folk-rockers McKendree Spring would actually release a cover of it first, Ronstadt's version of 'Heart Like A Wheel' appeared as the title track on the 1974 number one album that catapulted her to rock stardom.

It wasn't just Walker who had been impressed by Kate and Roma's set at Philadelphia. The *New York Times* singled them out in its review:

'[The day] . . . got off to a slow start with a succession of pedestrian performers. But after $2\frac{1}{2}$ hours the women took over and the atmosphere changed. The icebreakers were Kate McGarrigle and Roma Baron, a boisterously light-hearted pair who, between them, played fiddle, piano, guitar and cello while they shouted out duets in high, tight, country harmony.'

Although he sometimes said it was about the death of Janis Joplin, others are adamant that the song 'Saw Your Name in the Paper' was Loudon's particularly ungracious response to reading Kate's review. If correct, it was the first song he had written specifically about his new girlfriend and so began the continuing sequence of songs that would run like a director's commentary on Wainwright/McGarrigle family history over the next four decades, picked up on and extended by each generation as they began to make their own music.

It's easy to imagine Loudon spluttering his coffee over the page when he came to the review, reading through it green-eyed and seething. In the song he begrudgingly acknowledges Kate's talent but admits that the good review was 'quite a blow'. He warns her that success is fleeting and that the public's love will ultimately turn to hate before admitting that some of us 'really need it bad'. The song would appear on his second album. For now Loudon was preparing to release his first. And he would love to be getting those kind of reviews.

Loudon Wainwright III was released on Atlantic in November 1970. In the opening song 'School Days', in which he reminisces about his time at the St Andrews boarding school in Delaware (the same school that was used as a location for the 1989 film *Dead Poets Society*), he likens himself to James Dean, Marlon Brando, Buddha and Jesus Christ, establishing his style of simultaneous self-aggrandising, self-mocking, satirical songs for all those who had not yet seen him perform live. By 1970, at least in the eyes of outsiders, the folk troubadour ideal was pretty much interchangeable with the hippie movement that had peaked at Woodstock Festival a year earlier and was now dying a slow death. The rest of the album showed that alongside dismantling his own shortcomings, he wasn't afraid to rip into the hippie communities' own new age agenda. 'Bruno's Place' takes a dig at wholefoods and 'Glad To See You've Got Religion' ridicules affluent Western mysticism. And on 'Ode To Pittsburgh', a grateful tribute to the town where he'd studied acting, he demonstrated his command of the kind of blue-collar poetry for which Bruce Springsteen would later be lauded. The album was a witty set that stood apart from the more earnest, worthy records of the time.

With the Vietnam War dragging on and the demoralising assassinations of Martin Luther King and Bobby Kennedy in 1968, there had been a tangible shift from issue-based protest singing to songs about personal and emotional issues. Rioting in the streets in America and Europe hadn't really seemed to have achieved any fundamental change in society and the protestors and rebels had long since hung up their banners and taken off their army surplus clothing. The paving slabs were firmly back over the beach.

The folk traditionalists had hung their heads in sorrow when singers stopped singing 'we' and started singing 'I'. *Loudon Wainwright III* was all about the 'I' of Loudon Wainwright the man. And as such, it had more in common with the records of Leonard Cohen, Joni Mitchell or James Taylor than with any folk scene. In the early 1970s confessional singer-songwriters were where it was at. If anything, it was a new narcissism that fitted Loudon perfectly.

The critics loved the record. The *Melody Maker* suggested that he could finally be the 'New Bob Dylan' that everybody was supposedly needing to find. The only thing was the album didn't sell, a situation not helped by Loudon's apparent reticence to promote it. It was as if, after playing the circuit and creating a set from scratch (unusually for folk singers at the time, Loudon rarely played any cover versions) and being given a major label deal in a short space of time, he was afraid to take it further.

In later interviews he admitted to having had doubts about the album, although at the time he said he was pleased with how it had turned out. 'Well I was never surprised that it didn't sell,' he told *Rolling Stone* in 1971. 'I clearly didn't do anything to promote it. I was glad that people liked it and wrote about it, and played it on the radio.' Nevertheless, as he explained in the interview, right after its release he was playing less than ever. 'For some reason my judgement told me to lay low. I go periods of three months without

ever getting up on a stage. I've never been on tour. I've nev
to the West Coast ... much to the chagrin of my friends,
manager, and my record company. I suppose I just sort of dropped
it down about five levels.'

Instead of playing and promoting, Loudon started on his second
album. This time he went out of New York to a studio in Boston.
And this time he agreed to add a little piano and harmonica into the
mix as texture for the songs.

The new album would contain many of the songs that were part
of his set before the first album had been issued, but the standout
track was a newer song. 'Motel Blues' is an invocation of the loneliness of the long-distance solo musician. It's a desperate call-out for
companionship in another unknown town and it once got Loudon
into trouble with the station controller after playing it on a women's
liberation radio programme in Chicago. 'Come up to my hotel room
and save my life,' he sings but you know Loudon is only looking for
a girl to have sex with. It's a great performance bettered only by a
glacial cover version by Big Star from 1974 on which you can
believe that a bereft and desolate Alex Chilton is literally asking for
somebody to save his life.

On one of the other new songs, 'Be Careful There's A Baby in the
House', an ominous creeping blues warning of the disruptive power
of the newborn, Loudon makes a baby sound like a Midwich Cuckoo-
styled monster just getting ready to ruin everything and take over.
Whether this was a genuine fear or just one of Loudon's provocative
pokes at family mores, by the time *Album II* was released, Loudon
and Kate had discovered that they were going to have a baby of
their own.

As Kate was Canadian and they were living in the US, they
decided it would make things simpler in the long run if they got
married. After a wedding at the Wainwright family home in
Bedford, New York, they flew to Europe for their honeymoon.

Always a volatile pairing, Kate and Loudon managed to visit
Sweden, Denmark and Holland before having a major row, leading
Kate to fly on ahead to England on her own. After a few days of
stubbornly kicking his heels on his own, Loudon decided that he
should perhaps try to find his new wife, eventually arriving in
London in late 1971. Reunited, the couple stayed in an old vicarage

in Kennington, Loudon thrilled by the area's Charlie Chaplin connections. When Loudon wasn't following his own Chaplin trail along the streets of Lambeth and Walworth, they travelled across town to the Notting Hill area and busked on the Portobello Road with their friend Chaim Tannenbaum. Among the antique stalls, the bric-a-brac and the debris, Loudon and co. entertained the locals and the visitors who would come to the area for the market or to visit some of the last remaining hippie hang-outs in London. 'It was more for fun than money,' Loudon would later recall in a 1979 *New Musical Express* (better known now as *NME*) interview, 'but when the other buskers found out we were professional there was a lot of resentment. We didn't do it for the money but we took the money and we did well.'

When he realised that the reviews he had seen for his album in the UK press were because it had actually been released in the country rather than just being available as an import, he called Atlantic's London office to let them know he was in town. The label hastily arranged a London showcase for Loudon to perform for the UK journalists who had shown even more enthusiasm for his music than their American counterparts.

The venue was the Speakeasy, just off Regent Street in central London. In an earlier incarnation, the club had been owned by the Krays but since reopening in 1966 it had become a favourite after-hours music industry drinking hole and a venue for concerts by the likes of The Who and Jimi Hendrix. With celebrities like Robert Plant and John Entwhistle in attendance, there was a buzz about the special afternoon show before Loudon had even sung a note. The event was compered by the DJ John Peel, who had been regularly playing Loudon's music on the radio and who would continue to promote and support him at every opportunity for years to come (even, in the punk era, going so far as to suggest to him that he should change his name to Cat Sick in order to widen his appeal).

With the journalists and music business crowd already on his side, Loudon won over the initially dubious paying crowd. He was called back for three encores and even got some of the rock critics to join in on a new song that he had written and was playing for the first time. 'I'd like to do you a song that's just three days old,' he said from the stage. 'It's come to my mind that there's more roads in America than there is in England and for some reason there's a lot of skunks about this time of year. They walk over the road and they get killed and like every three miles you can smell a skunk. Now this is a sing-a-long song.' In 1971 he could never have guessed how often he would end up having to lead a crowd through the comedy song 'Dead Skunk'.

Loudon was far more keen to please the UK press and public than he had been in the US. He even offered to be interviewed hanging from the ceiling if that was what was asked for. He hung around in London but he still didn't play many shows. At only his second live appearance in the UK, a support slot for the Everly Brothers at the Albert Hall on 12 October, he had beer thrown at him and was booed off by drunken Teddy boys. At least the press were sympathetic, noting that it was a billing mismatch and no fault of Loudon's. In deference to sympathetic, or possibly sarcastic, cheers he had returned to the stage and played 'Dead Skunk'. As the *Melody Maker* put it: 'His least complex song went down the best.'

Loudon saw his role as that of an entertainer. 'I'm really nothing more than a comic,' he'd say. 'I get the most fun out of life when I know that everyone is having a good time. People singing along with me, well that's great. I'm just an entertainer, my idol is Jerry Lewis. THE Jerry Lewis. My idol, and the French intellectuals' idol.'

Professionally things were going well but domestically the situation was dire. Kate was devastated when she had a miscarriage and, due to complications, she was scared she would never have children. The couple argued constantly and although Loudon was enjoying the attention he was getting in the UK, he agreed to accompany Kate back to the US.

1.2

After his first two albums had failed to sell, Loudon found himself dropped by Atlantic. Fortunately Columbia still had an interest in him so his manager did what he could to revive that deal. Loudon stayed at home writing songs. 'I don't work on writing songs, they just materialise. It's a waiting game,' he said. 'The best songs I've written come out within a period of thirty minutes to an hour.'

He could and would write about anything. 'Red Guitar', which he would include on his next album, gives an insight into the often volatile atmosphere of the Wainwright/McGarrigle household. In the song he explains how he destroyed a guitar, making his wife cry. Kate recalled the incident in an interview for *Vanity Fair*: 'He got mad at the guitar. He took it – I guess Loudon has some kind of anger or something – he took the guitar and he started smashing it right by the fireplace, more and more angry, and he threw it in the fireplace and burned it.' In the song Loudon writes about how he goes into New York the next day to replace his guitar, but the way he sings about his new 'blond' leaves you wondering whether it's just a new guitar he's gone looking for.

After marrying Loudon and their extended stay in Europe, Kate had stopped playing as a duo with Roma Baron. (Baron would later find her own success as a music producer, including work on Laurie Anderson's debut album *Big Science*.) Back in the US, Kate played the occasional solo set, including a show at a club a friend ran in Ann Arbor, Michigan. While she was there she told her friend that she thought she might be pregnant. Years later, from the stage at the Ann Arbor Folk Festival, she recalled what happened next: 'She said, "Well I have a very good friend at the Planned Parenthood Clinic so let's check it out." So we go over to the place and I do the test and they come out and they say, "Mrs Wainwright, I hate to tell you this but you're going to have a baby." And I started dancing around the floor. And they said, "You're happy?" And I said, "I'm delighted." And they said, "You're the first happy face we've ever seen here." And they all came out of the office and said, "Look at her. She's smiling."'

Loudon was signed to Columbia Records and in January 1973 released his third album. The record had been made with the musicians from a band called White Cloud and he played a show with them in New York but soon realised he was happier solo. 'I felt uncomfortable doing it. I became almost just the lead singer in the band. I'm egocentrical enough so that I feel more relaxed and more in control when it's just myself. And you don't have to divide the money.' He went back out on the road alone.

Rolling Stone likened Loudon to Lou Reed in his ability to 'write on any subject and make it pertinent and funny'. Which makes a kind of sense when you remember that at the time Reed had just released the droll *Transformer* and had a hit with 'Walk On The Wild Side' (Reed would put a stop to any laughs by the end of the year by releasing the terrifying *Berlin*.) Indeed, *Album III* was lighter in tone than the bittersweet or just plain bitter songs of his first two records. It also included his one bona fide comedy song.

'Dead Skunk' had proved so popular in his live set that Columbia thought they might be able to turn the song into a hit. Gene Denonovich was the publicist for the south-west, working out of St Louis and he convinced Sonny Martin, the programme director at KAAY, a 50,000-watt radio station in Little Rock, Arkansas, to play the record and it instantly became the local number one song based on audience response. Steve Popovich, who was Columbia's Vice-President of Promotion, worked with his assistant Gene Brewer on concocting some promotions to help push the song at the radio station. 'We had contests to find the best painting, sculpture or carving of a dead skunk in the middle of the road,' remembers Popovich. 'The station picked it up and a month later Loudon was performing in front of thousands of fans in a stadium in Little Rock and judging the "best skunk" contest.

'A month later we spread the record out to Nashville with a similar contest and Loudon played at a promotional event at the River Gate Mall in Hendersonville, Tennessee.' Popovich rightly figured that if he could make the song a hit in one region then it could become a national hit. They continued to promote the record across the country, getting airplay on local and underground radio stations.

The strategy worked. After the song went to number one in Little Rock and stayed there for weeks, it went Top 20 on the national charts. The sing-a-long chorus could be heard all across America: 'Dead skunk in the middle of the road/Dead skunk in the middle of the road/Stinking to high heaven'. As poetry it wasn't a patch on almost every other song he had written but, as he'd discovered after the rain of beer at the ill-fated Everly Brothers show in London, sometimes the simplest songs are the most popular.

Loudon recalls doing almost everything he could to hinder the success of his runaway roadkill hit. He shaved his head (because he 'felt like being monk-like'), got drunk five or six nights a week and often just refused to play the song at all. 'I did a big TV show, *Midnight Special*, right after "Dead Skunk". They'd flown me out to LA to do my hit and I got there and said, "I don't want to do my hit" and they said, "Well, we paid your plane fare basically and you've got to do your hit." And I said, "I'm not gonna do my hit." And I didn't.'

As Popovich says, with the wisdom earned from decades dealing with mercurial musicians: 'Hits can do good things and hits can do bad things ...' Whatever the artistic merits of the song or of its nagging legacy – skunk becoming albatross – for the rest of Loudon's career 'Dead Skunk' was a genuine hit and its popularity helped push the sales of its parent LP. With Loudon reluctantly teetering on the brink of becoming a commercially successful musician and Kate happy to stay at home writing and singing songs just for herself, their son Rufus was born on 22 July 1973.

Within three weeks of the birth, the new family found themselves in Nashville where Loudon was preparing to record his next album. They stayed at the Roger Miller King of the Road Motel[4] and recorded at Ray Stevens' studio (Stevens was somebody who knew a thing or two about comedy records and would soon have a world-wide novelty smash of his own with 'The Streak' about the brief craze for athletic public nudity). For the first time, Kate appeared with Loudon on a couple of tracks. While his parents worked together in the studio Rufus slept in a guitar case.

The album was recorded and mixed in five days. Some of the tracks used were first takes and the album, again using backing musicians, has a rough, half-finished sound with Loudon's voice

---

4. Country singer Roger Miller had a huge hit with the song 'King of the Road' in 1965 and invested some of his money in his own Nashville hotel, unsurprisingly called 'Roger Miller's King of the Road Motel'. It was a favourite spot for visiting musicians and even had a club on the roof where many country legends played. The song that made his name is still regularly covered today and Rufus recorded it with Teddy Thompson for the soundtrack of *Brokeback Mountain* and performed it live with Thompson, and the aid of a lyric sheet, at his Kenwood House show in summer 2008, quite probably unaware of the song's link with his first few weeks of life.

way down in the mix. It seemed he was subconsciously sabotaging his new-found fame, looking to make a record that neither his old allies, the critics, nor his new-found public would like.

'It was almost like an attempt to obliterate that success. Success freaked me out,' he told the *NME* in 1979. 'Success is scary. Almost scarier than failing. Failing is frightening, but success is really frightening.

'I don't think I could assimilate or absorb the success of "Dead Skunk". I felt guilty about it. Almost apologetic about it. From a psychological point of view that probably explains the nature of the record that followed it. It was an abysmal failure. [It] died a death. It was more like an anti-record.'

Aside from a dubious Kubrick-inspired country-violence song 'Clockwork Chartreuse' and the featherweight 'Bell Bottom Pants', *Attempted Mustache* is an excellent album and it's hard to work out why it was so badly thought of at the time. Some 35 years on, when quickly recorded, slightly muffled 'motel room'-type recordings are often used as a signifier for musical 'authenticity', it sounds far less dated than his earlier records.

The album opens with 'Swimming Song', with Kate and Loudon on banjo (Loudon considered Kate's teaching him the instrument as one of the nicest things anybody had ever done for him). This would become one of Loudon's most loved songs and it was his immediate suggestion for a single but initially the record label wouldn't release it. They wanted another comedy song and they refused to countenance any single that wasn't about funny animals.

Kate contributes a beautiful song of her own, 'Come A Long Way' and there's the acapella song 'Liza' about Loudon's time as a child with Liza Minnelli in which he tells her she has caught the 'curse' of showbusiness. The bluesy 'Nocturnal Stumblebutt', on which Loudon performs a Mick Jaggeresque vocal that is so low down in the mix it sounds like he'd been locked out of the studio and was singing through the letterbox, and country rocker 'A.M. World' are both good songs that sound almost wilfully badly mixed, if in fact they were mixed at all.

The closest thing to old folk music was 'I Am The Way', basically a rewrite of the Woody Guthrie song 'New York Town' that Loudon had worked on during a cross-country car journey. He changed the title and the words but Guthrie was still given a credit as songwriter.[5]

The album closed with two tunes Loudon had written about his new son. 'Lullaby', one of Loudon's most exquisite songs, on the surface seems to be a rather callous plea from a father to get his grizzly child to stop crying ('Shut your mouth and button your lip/You're a late night faucet that's got a drip/All you're doing is merely complaining'). Rufus is even mentioned by name on the lyric sheet, though the line is not sung in the recording. But the subtext is that it is Loudon as father who is the worried one that cannot sleep. It's new-parent anxiety and restlessness being addressed, not a crying baby. Loudon is chastising himself for his constant complaining and is trying to sing himself to sleep.

'Dilated To Meet You' is a duet with Kate that poignantly captures the worries of prospective parents as they await the birth of their child, particularly, as in this case, a first child. A fragile vocal (in the sleeve-notes of the 1998 reissue, Loudon claims this was because they were tired) that aches with tenderness and ends on a wish: 'We really think you'll like it here/We hope that you like us.'

Loudon might have been doing his best to dismantle his music career but Kate soon found that hers was beginning to take off, courtesy of a musician who had made a strong impression on Loudon as far back as 1963.

'I was in love with Maria Muldaur,' Loudon joked in an *NME* interview. 'Maria Muldaur was something else. She was the first

---

5. Robbie Williams included slightly rewritten lines from Loudon Wainwright's song on his 1998 song 'Jesus In A Camper Van'. In the original song Guthrie sings 'Every good man gets a little hard luck sometimes'. Wainwright has this as 'Every Son of God gets a little hard luck sometimes, especially when he goes round saying he is the way.' While Williams' version runs 'I suppose even the Son of God gets it hard sometimes, especially when he goes round saying I am the way.' Wainwright was credited on the label, as was the original publisher, Ludlow Music. Wainwright made no claim on the copyright and Williams' record company EMI originally offered a 25 per cent share of the royalties from the track to Guthrie's publisher but they in turn demanded 50 per cent. When EMI released the track on the hit album *I've Been Expecting You* they held back a 25 per cent share of the track's royalties for Ludlow but as this had not been by prior agreement, Ludlow chose to sue them for 100 per cent of the royalty. In 2002 the High Court ruled that because the copyright infringement was not cynical or flagrant and the song had no particular 'staying power' EMI need not give up any more than the original 25 per cent offered, a sum reported to be £50,000.

woman I ever saw who didn't shave under her arms. I remember at the Newport Folk Festival 1963 looking up around the fence and seeing the Kweskin Jug Band. She was 23 years old. Had this shirt on with nothing up her arms and she kinda leaned up to scratch her head and I saw this ... incredible tuft of black hair. Aarrgh. Most erotic thing I ever saw in my life.'

Maria D'Amato had been part of the folk scene since the early 1960s, originally as a vocalist with Loudon's beloved Jim Kweskin Jug Band, then as a duo with her fellow jug-bander and temporary husband Geoff Muldaur. By 1973 she had split with Geoff and was starting a solo career. Her first solo album had been recorded in California and she had chosen to include one of Kate's songs, 'The Work Song', that she had picked up from one of the home-recorded demo reels that Kate had made with Anna.

The album, *Maria Muldaur*, went gold in the US, its lead single 'Midnight at the Oasis' hitting the top ten. The producer of the album was Joe Boyd, who was best known for his work on albums by British artists like Nick Drake and the Incredible String Band. However, his greatest legacy was his work with Fairport Convention and his role as the catalyst that enabled them to develop from an above-average English rock band to genuinely avant-garde electric-folk pioneers. In the space of two years and four albums, Boyd guided Fairport from simple Joni Mitchell cover versions to eight-minute-plus drone rock folk that could make an English traditional song like 'Matty Groves' sound like a Velvet Underground out-take (albeit without the feedback).

Boyd had loved the 'Work Song' demo tape and wanted to use similar harmonies on his recording with Muldaur for the follow-up album, *Waitress in the Donut Shop*. He told *Folk Roots* how he first got involved with the McGarrigles: 'We rang up Kate and asked her to come out to California and sing harmony. She said, "Can I bring my sister?" and we said, "Well, we don't know about that." There'd just been this tape of a couple of songs which we thought was just Kate overdubbing or something – we didn't know there was an Anna McGarrigle. We just thought she was wanted to hold Kate's hand or something!'

In fact, Anna had actually already released one single herself. With Kate away, she had begun occasionally collaborating with other writers and wound up being asked to record a tribute song to a Canadian ice-hockey player that she had written with the guitarist Richard Baker. Because the track was really nothing more than a novelty record, no thought had been put into what would be on the B-side until the night before they were due to record it. Anna stayed up late and put music to the lyrics of poet Philippe Tatartcheff's 'Complainte Pour Saint-Catherine' and the next day they recorded both songs at the studio of Andre Perry, who was famous for having recorded John and Yoko singing from their bed-in in Montreal. The single 'Hommage a Henri Richard' was released on the Pacha label in early 1974.

Muldaur had selected another song from the McGarrigle demo tape for the record, 'Cool River', a majestic and lachrymose suicide note, which would be rightly highlighted as the standout track in the album's *Rolling Stone* review. When Kate had flown out to the West Coast for the recording sessions, Boyd asked her to play the piano part and she admitted she didn't know it. She remembers him saying, 'What do you mean you don't know it? You wrote it.' But it was one of Anna's songs. Boyd soon realised that Anna was indeed an equal and integral part of the McGarrigle sound and arranged for her to fly down from Montreal to join them in the studio.

With the McGarrigles' growing reputation as songwriters, Joe Boyd recognised their potential as recording artists in their own right: 'When I heard these two girls singing these amazing harmonies, I thought Warner Brothers should do something.'

Lenny Waronker was co-producing the Muldaur album and as one of the heads of Warners, he too saw enough potential in the McGarrigles to offer them some recording time to see what they could come up with. Despite not having played together since their shows with the Mountain City Four, other than on the simple home demos, the sisters found that working on each other's songs came naturally. Kate would later say that it was in the Los Angeles demo studio in April 1974 that they became 'Kate and Anna McGarrigle'.

Waronker had helped to establish Warner Brothers' reputation for being an artist-friendly company that put music and musicians ahead of business. He had worked closely with singer-songwriter Randy Newman as well as the maverick musician Van Dyke Parks, neither of whom had been commercially successful. Years later he would become involved with Loudon and would ultimately be the person responsible for the heavy investment in Rufus Wainwright's career. But, in May of 1974, after hearing their demo, the first family members to be offered a contract by him were Kate and Anna.

1.3

It was mission accomplished as, unsurprisingly, Loudon's *Attempted Mustache* album failed to sell in any quantity. With imminent success averted, for the follow-up, *Unrequited*, he chose to split the album into half live and half studio. It could have been an inspired decision but the studio production was even worse than on the previous record, blunting any subtlety, and the material chosen for the live side consisted almost entirely of novelty songs without the substance, poignancy or lyrical wit of Loudon's earlier work. Though 'Unrequited to the Nth Degree' is fun, and in time would turn into a favourite audience participation laugh-a-long, 'On The Rocks' is predictable and dull, featuring casual violence, sexism and aural gurning. *Unrequited* ended with another song for his son. 'Rufus is a Tit Man', in which Loudon seems to begrudge his child's breastfeeding, his son like Blake's 'infant sorrow' sulking on his mother's breast with Loudon jealously trying to get his own head into 'Mamma's' shirt and, in a moment of erudite crudity, conjures up an image of pre-Roman suckers Romulus and Remus. As usual he could turn even the most fundamental human interaction between a mother and child into a humorous song in which he was the focus. On the cover Loudon is pictured with a feel-sorry-for-me tear running down his cheek.

Loudon had always been a favoured artist among the staff at Columbia, even if his sales figures did little to thrill the company accountant. Steve Popovich remembers him playing the annual staff convention and bringing the house down: 'We'd always appreciated his artistry even if he hadn't been a big seller,' recalls Popovich. But *Unrequited* didn't sell at all and received generally poor reviews, a double negative that was enough for Columbia, against the wishes of a good proportion of the label's office staff, to decide against taking up their option for another LP. Once again Loudon was dropped.

Loudon had always kept one eye out for opportunities to get into acting, which remained his first love. He'd managed to appear in three episodes of $M^*A^*S^*H$[6] as Capt. Calvin Spaulding during 1974/5 and had hoped his role would be expanded but nothing more came of it. He told *Melody Maker* of his disappointment: 'I was willing to do more but they didn't seem to want me. Not only didn't they use me in any other capacity other than that of a musician or only having to say "Yes Sir" two times but the songs I wrote for them . . . they could only use a verse or a few lines.' He would later joke that as a draft-dodger in the 1960s it had been a great opportunity to finally get a uniform on.

Temporarily without a record label, Loudon did what he could to push himself forward in acting circles but nothing was immediately forthcoming. Still, if nobody would cast him in a movie or a TV show at least there were still record labels out there who were prepared to sign him no matter how commercially unsuccessful he had proved to be. One such supporter was Clive Davis, who had originally brought Loudon to Columbia. When Davis left that label to work with Arista Records, he offered Loudon a two-album deal with the new label and work started immediately on what would become the sixth Loudon Wainwright III album, *T-Shirt*. Loudon was grateful to be working again but somewhat surprised: 'People keep letting me make these records. I've made six records in six years. Only one of them has paid for itself yet they keep letting me make them.'

He might have wondered why he'd bothered. He recorded *T-Shirt* with a full band augmented by numerous guest musicians, perhaps as a means to make something that sounded, if not commercial, then at least contemporary. He filled the record with a batch of new songs, some of which he was sure were as good as any he had written in a while and he even tried to go disco with the sexed-up but still rather awful 'At Both Ends'. He had high hopes for the album and was looking to pay back Davis' faith in him, but when *Rolling Stone*

---

6. The $M^*A^*S^*H$ episodes are 'Rainbow Bridge', 'There Is Nothing Like a Nurse' and 'Big Mac'. All are from the third series and aired in the US in 1974/5.

gave the record a pasting, he got so depressed that he stayed in bed for five days straight and became convinced that it was, after all, awful.

In 1975 Kate and Anna found themselves in Hollywood working on what would become their debut LP. Warner Brothers were prepared to risk a lot of money ($120,000 which, at the time, was a huge budget) on launching the pair, hiring top musicians and putting Anna, Kate and family in residence at the Chateau Marmont on Sunset Boulevard. Gaby McGarrigle came down from Canada to look after her grandson Rufus while the sisters spent their days in the studio.[7]

The recording was far from straightforward. Kate and Anna had strong ideas about what they wanted, as did the two producers that Warners had hired. Trouble was they couldn't usually agree: Greg Prestopino was looking to make it poppy and Joe Boyd wanted it to be more folk-rock based. And Warners thought they had signed a pair of Laura Nyro-styled soul singers.

'Early on they tried to get us to go without any folk stuff,' Kate told Jerry Gilbert of UK music paper *Sounds*. 'They were pretending that they would let us do these folk songs just to make us happy. In the end they found their way on to the album.'

Before Warners would agree to release the album, they wanted Kate and Anna to be performing with a band that was capable of seeing them through an extensive national tour. The record label hired musicians and sent the sisters up to Boston to play a three-week residency at the Inn Square Men's Bar to get them into shape. The shows were bringing in $250 dollars a week but it was costing $400 to keep them there. No expense was spared – Warners even arranged for a dress designer to meet with the sisters to work on their image.

---

7. On stage at the Hollywood Bowl during the 2007 Judy Garland show, Rufus told an anecdote about how he had fallen into the Chateau Marmont pool during his family's stay while Kate and Anna made their first album. A fellow resident dived in and rescued the two-year-old Rufus. Kate later told him that his saviour had been Betty Buckley, the Broadway singing star and TV actress. He went on to say that he heard that somebody had told this story to Betty Buckley and she had been unable to recall the incident but had soon proved to be ever the enterprising showbiz professional by incorporating the same anecdote into her own cabaret act by way of an introduction to her version of Rufus' 'Cigarettes and Chocolate Milk'.

'The terrible thing about this band was that they had a spokes-man,' said Kate, 'and he'd say, "We've decided we're not rehearsing this afternoon, we want to go to the zoo." It was awful. Warners were lavishing so much money on us. It was like "What do you need here? It's done."'

After they had listened to a tape of their set recorded live with the band, they decided they just couldn't carry on. They didn't like the way it sounded at all. Kate happened to be pregnant again and the sisters saw this as a perfect reason to cancel the entire tour.

'That could be why Warners didn't do anything to sell our records,' Kate said later. 'I guess it was very unprofessional of us but because of the way we had come up we had a strong feeling of the way to do things.'

By the time the album was released, Warners had virtually given up on the McGarrigles. *Kate and Anna McGarrigle* was begrudgingly released in the US in February 1976 and the only show that the sisters performed to promote it was a one-off in Montreal for which they rallied a group of old friends from their Mountain City Four days.

Kate and Anna McGarrigle is a truly timeless album. Although it begins with a fairly rambunctious folk-rocker, 'Kiss and Say Good-bye', featuring the guitar licks of Lowell George and a trademark tenor sax solo from Bobby Keys (who had played on all of the great Rolling Stones albums of the 1970s and was infamously captured on film helping Keith Richards throw a TV set off a hotel balcony in Robert Frank's *Cocksucker Blues*), the majority of the album consists of gentle, carefully crafted songs that have their roots in traditional folk, gospel and blues, yet manage to sound otherworldly and unique.

Songs like 'My Town', 'Blues In D' and '(Talk To Me Of) Men-docino' are taut, austere, and like the very best country music, exist at a kind of fulcrum of misery where the yearning for escape and the impossibility of leaving a lover or a loved place teeter. 'Closing my eyes I hear the sea/Must I wait?/Must I follow?' sings Kate as if she is being asked to step out into an unknown darkness beneath the waves.

The version of 'Heart like a Wheel', on which elder sister Jane joins on vocals and organ, is a bleak rendering of the song that reasserts its inherent hopelessness after Linda Ronstadt's comparatively upbeat cover. Even Loudon Wainwright's 'Swimming Song' sounds here more like a report from a repentant suicide than good-time aquatic japery and it's one of three songs dependent on water metaphors and suggestions of drowning. Imagine Virginia Woolf let loose in a recording studio.

On the rerecorded 'Complainte Pour Ste-Catherine' from Anna's novelty ice-hockey single, they sing with gusto in French over a slightly stilted cod-reggae backing. Although they'd often sung traditional French songs in their sets from the very beginning, they had rarely tried to play to the French-speaking audiences of Montreal and this was an early attempt to reach out to a crowd who had their own stars, often very different from those of the English speakers. In 1975, for instance, Roger Whittaker's French language recordings were hugely popular and yet, outside of cosy afternoon television shows, he barely registered elsewhere. 'Complainte Pour Ste-Catherine' would go on to be a minor hit in mainland Europe and become an enduring classic that is still covered today.

Kate contributed two songs that related directly to her marriage. 'Tell My Sister', in which she predicts that she'll be coming back to her mother's home alone, relates to the couple's tumultuous time in London. The devastating 'Go Leave', solo vocal with guitar, in which she suggests that the unnamed target of the song should leave her for another woman who might be 'better' than her is an incredibly raw performance and one in which Kate admitted to having cried real tears while recording. (Martha would later, melodramatically, suggest that you can actually hear a tear fall on the guitar strings at the end of the song.) That Loudon and his inability to stay faithful was the target was obvious to all. In fact, the song specifically concerned his involvement with performance artist and one-time Andy Warhol/Paul Morrissey film star Penny Arcade with whom he had had a brief fling.

None of this is to say it's a depressing album. Far from it. Whether by luck or judgement, the sisters managed to create a unique record that blended their naïve debutant charm with the versatile musicians under the adept, though divergent, guidance of Boyd and Prestopino. *Rolling Stone* likened the lyrics to the poetry of Emily Dickinson and said it was the only album 'in which total innocence and total sophistication seem to coincide'. An *NME* review said that the songs were 'presented in so real and so open a way that it is almost scary'.

The record maintains an ascetic purity quite at odds with the bloated excesses of much of the major label output of the mid-1970s. The critic John Rockwell, writing a year after the album had been released, claimed it to be a 'folk parallel to the punkish primitivism' of the punk rockers that would soon emerge, and an 'unconsciously feminist' record.

Indeed, the record received across the board compliments. It was the *Stereo Review* record of the year,[8] the *NME* had it in a dead-heat with *The Ramones* for best debut album of the year and the *New York Times* would declare it second only to Stevie Wonder's *Songs in the Key of Life* in their albums of the year list.

While the acclaim for her debut album undoubtedly pleased Kate, its success was overshadowed by her increasingly fragile marriage. Loudon gave a frank insight into their domestic situation in his song 'Reciprocity' which recounts unfaithfulness, duplicitous behaviour and flying ashtrays. He even suggests that, like a lion tamer, you'd need a chair and a whip to keep them apart. In a telling line that echoes a similar sentiment to Kate's 'Go Leave', Loudon sings how they were once lovers and best friends, although he inserts 'practically' before 'best friends' seemingly unable to commit, even retrospectively.

Loudon was miserable. Years later he would admit to believing that at the time he felt it was necessary to feel bad to be creative ('unless you were Johann Sebastian Bach'). By his own account he created conflict by staying away from home as often as he could, being drunk a lot or by sleeping with as many waitresses as possible.

Unable to accept his responsibilities as a husband and father, Loudon had fallen for the old Cyril Connolly line and it was Rufus' pram in the hall that he saw as the 'sombre enemy' of his art.[9] Worse

---

8. In the February 1986 issue of *Folk Roots* Kate McGarrigle recalls seeing James Taylor in an issue of *People* magazine being given a banquet by Warner Brothers for achieving the *Stereo Review* Record of the Year award. When she asked why they hadn't received so much as a letter of congratulations when they had won the same award the year before, she was told it was because they hadn't made a record yet. At the time the sisters were working on their third record, the implication being that uncommercial records didn't count.
9. Cyril Connolly, *Enemies of Promise*, Routledge, London 1938.

still for Loudon was the fact that Kate would be having another baby all too soon.

Among the anecdotes of drunk-driving associates and ill parents that make up Loudon's 1995 song 'That Hospital', a rumination on health and sickness with typically empathetic emphasis on his own, Loudon sings about visiting a hospital with Kate in 1976 for a 'D& C' (a euphemistic initialism for dilation and curettage – at the time, a common form of abortion). He sings about how Kate couldn't go through with it and how, at the time he wrote the song, he had just attended the resultant child's graduation. The girl who escaped 'that scrape with fate' was Martha, their second child, born on 8 May 1976 and named after his mother.

The response to *Kate and Anna McGarrigle* in England was sufficiently enthusiastic for the sisters to agree to cross the Atlantic to play a handful of shows. This time there was no money forthcoming from their record label other than basic travelling expenses. But at least that meant that they could work with musicians of their own choosing. They called some friends together and rehearsed a group of songs around the piano. The sisters knew that they were at their best when they were not bound by a rigorously rehearsed formal set. They had to maintain an element of surprise or at least the opportunity for the music to exist and unfold naturally. Theirs were songs that needed space to breathe.

Their first show in England was at a three-day folk festival in Lancashire. The Chorley July Wakes festival was notable for its on-site 24-hour swimming pool and a line-up that included the Chieftains, Alan Stivell and Bert Jansch. The McGarrigles played a mid-afternoon slot on the second day. They may have been under-rehearsed but they endeared themselves to the press and the public. Writing in the *Melody Maker* Colin Irwin suggested their 'disarrayed charm gave them an almost hillbilly appeal' and local photographer Roger Liptrot remembers how their 'eccentric stage presence made it feel like you were being treated to a concert in their own home and not from a stage in a field'.

By the next night they were playing their London debut at the Victoria Palace Theatre. Not having brought a drummer with them, they called in formidable session man and sometime Fairport

Convention member Dave Mattacks to sit in with them. Once more their appealing amateurism won over the audience.

In *The Times*, Richard Williams praised the 'ad hoc nature of their five-piece band whose members appeared to perform more by intuition than through prior knowledge gleaned from rehearsals'. He noted that 'here was something human and honest'. The *Melody Maker* was even more positive. Under the headline 'Shattering McGarrigles' the show was described as 'a holy marriage of strong sentiment and brilliant pure singing' in which 'their gaucheness, their blushing modesty and even their appearance in oddly ana-chronistic white tunics – like the Grecian figures in Victorian paint-ings – were charming and somehow touching'.

Loudon was in the country at the same time but pretty much did his own thing; after all, he had his own shows to play, his own crowds to please. He headlined the 1976 Cambridge Folk Festival where he led the singalong through a rousing encore of 'Dead Skunk' with Maddy Prior as guest vocalist.

He recorded a number of the shows on his UK tour, some of the recordings would be used later on the self-produced live 'best of' album, *A Live One*, on which he sounds confident, assured and funny as he plays through the highlights of his earlier records to appreciative audiences. In the UK he could generally count on good-sized crowds that were ready to sing and laugh along and who saw Loudon as being in the tradition of 'funny' folk acts like Billy Connolly or Mike Harding, part way between stand-up and serious music. Loudon relished the attention. The solo tour may have been a success but by the time he returned to the US in the autumn, the fraying knot of his strained marriage had come undone for good.

In 'Kitty Come Home', a new song that would appear on the next McGarrigles album, Anna implored her sister to leave Loudon, take the children and come home to where the 'birds in the trees call your name'. Finally sick of the arguments and Loudon's continuous philandering, this is exactly what she did. Rufus has said that one of his earliest memories is his mother packing up all of their possessions into a U-Haul trailer, dining table and all, and driving him and his sister away from their father and what had been their family home and into a new life in Canada.

ACT 2

'At every moment, behind the most efficient seeming adult exterior, the whole world of the person's childhood is being carefully held like a glass of water bulging above the brim.'

Ted Hughes [1986], letter to his son
Nicholas, *The Letters of Ted Hughes*, 2007

'Childhood is never history. Childhood is always there.'

Loudon Wainwright III (attributed)

2.1

With Kate and the children settled in Montreal, the sisters continued work on their second album for Warner Brothers using studios in New York and Quebec and, for the most part, their now regular group of Canadian musician friends. The album did feature guest appearances by Dave Mattacks and Pat Donaldson, an English bass player who was at the time best known for his work with Sandy Denny in Fotheringay, who were on tour with Joan Armatrading and happened to call into the studio. John Cale, who had worked with Boyd on the second Nick Drake album and with Donaldson on his own *Fear* and *Helen of Troy* records also dropped by and was drafted in to add organ and some fanciful marimba.

In many ways *Dancer With Bruised Knees* is a more traditional folk record than *Kate and Anna McGarrigle* and that is probably one of the reasons why it was looked upon as something of a failure. It is still a good record but somehow lacks the unique qualities that made its predecessor so exceptional. Its main problem is that it isn't different enough to stand apart from nor brave enough to step out of the debut album's long shadow and so it fails to bloom.

There are a couple of traditional songs which, while competent and assured, lack the spark that they would be given in a live performance and are here rendered as lifeless and dusty as a respected but unplayed song sheet on a library shelf. The performances are circumspect and scholarly rather than vibrant and alive, although lyrically the grim(m) fairy story of an imprisoned girl pretending to be dead rather than give herself to her captors is compelling.

For the most part, the McGarrigles' own lyrics are less cryptic, and less poetic. There is an immediacy about tracks such as 'Walking Song' and 'Be My Baby' which means that the more you listen to them, the less you get from them, in direct contrast to the ethereal, perplexing songs on the debut.

'Come A Long Way', which ends the record, suffers from an awkward pedestrian arrangement that detracts from the lyrics that stood proud like ancient wisdom on the drumless version on Loudon's *Attempted Mustache* album. Some of the other arrangements also seemed ill considered and smother the life out of the songs.

At one point Kate had been fooling around in the studio with a song called 'Never Had No Biscuits', which she had learned from a tape she'd been given more than a decade earlier by a friend of the family called Galt MacDermot. MacDermot was best known for having written the music to the Broadway hit *Hair* but this had been a tape of otherwise unrecorded songs.[1] Producer Joe Boyd suggested they put the song on the album.

'We did it there and then,' said Kate, 'with bass drums, harmonica . . . but that wasn't how we used to do it. We'd always performed it simply with four voices and one acoustic guitar.' Although the usual more basic arrangement may not have been enough to rescue it, here, as 'No Biscuit Blues', the song is redolent of a theme tune to an unloved sit-com and is not helped by its kitsch lyrics of childhood poverty.

The Dory Previn-esque track 'Southern Boys' is perhaps the

---

[1]. In an interview years later, Martha would moan about the number of times she had had to listen to McDermot's first LP on the family turntable. An ardent record collector, Kate was the proud owner of the very rare LP that he had released under the name Fergus Macroy on his own label. 'We were forced to listen to that fucking thing over and over again. It's very obscure. Nobody has it but Kate – and he sings really badly – but there are some great lyrics on it.' (Interview – Will Hodgkinson, *Guardian*, 18 March 2005).

strongest and strangest song on the album, a lilting country waltz with some asthmatic harmonica wheezing and a rippling wave of a chorus that ebbs away leaving the listener beached on the sand of the barren piano verses. Other high points are Kate's sweet song for Rufus, 'First Born', and Anna's song for Kate, the maudlin 'Kitty Come Home', on which the sisters harmonise so beautifully it's as if they were mythical sirens luring sailors to run aground.

The album was completed quickly but came as something of a disappointment to both the public and the sisters themselves. Both Kate and Anna were frank in their own appraisal of the record when they were interviewed by the *NME*, which had rightly noted that *Dancer With Bruised Knees* lacked the 'emotional depth charge' of the first album. In fact, the interviewer, Bob Woffinden, an ardent fan who had named the *Kate and Anna McGarrigle* record as his record of the year, had admitted that he had been plunged into such despair by the album that he hadn't initially been able to review it at all.

'(The album) was finished in a very short time,' said Kate. 'We could have improved on it because the songs were there. I just don't think enough care was put in at the end. Soundwise it doesn't hang together. The first record just flows beautifully and moves naturally from track to track. The second one doesn't.'

Anna explained how Joe Boyd had pushed them to get it finished. '(He) was banging us over the head saying if we didn't finish it quickly we'd have to cancel the European tour. The real reason was that he didn't want to run over budget although as it turns out we did anyway and lost the second part of our advance for the second year running.'

In fact, Boyd had been their second choice. The sisters had wanted to record the album with the other co-producer of their debut, Greg Prestopino, preferring his more meticulous production technique where everything was worked on over and over, in contrast to Boyd's more intuitive style. But as Prestopino had gone way over budget on an earlier project, the record company would only let him produce if the album was made in California, where they could keep an eye on things. Kate and Anna didn't want to go to California again. It would have meant another two months away and it would have meant using the same Los Angeles-based musicians that everybody else used. They had wanted to do it their own way.

With the album released, the sisters embarked on their first major tour. This included 13 dates throughout February in Ireland and the UK (to which an extra night was soon added as their first London date had quickly sold out).

They were their usual 'direct, uncomplicated' selves according to the *NME* review of the 19 February 1977 London concert. Not wholly positive, the review suggested that at times the audience were deflated by certain elements of 'bungling and boredom' which beset the evening and stated that the McGarrigles were far from a 'dynamic duo' being 'nervous and klutzy' between the songs and how they had needed Chaim Tannenbaum's singing to add 'pizzazz'. Though worried that the 'honeymoon might be over', the reviewer did admit to having been brought to tears by a 'highly strung and breathtaking' 'Heart like a Wheel'.

In truth the live set was, as ever, an endearing shambles, under-rehearsed and reliant on the McGarrigles charm and the general goodwill that the audience felt towards them to carry the evening through. Although Kate and Anna were quite capable of playing a show as a duo, the more musicians that were added into the mix the more likely it was that something would go wrong. Drummer Dave Mattacks walked off the tour in the middle of the London show after a disagreement with the rest of the band after one false start too many, much to the bemusement of Kate and Anna. They finished the set, and the remaining six dates of the tour, without any drums at all.

To satisfy their record label, they finally played a few shows in the US, including a return to Boston on 30 March, which marked their first American performance as recording artists proper after the debacle of their residency in 1976. The *New York Times* headlined a review of their New York debut at the Bottom Line as 'Magical McGarrigles' and noted that: 'There is something so fragile and wonderful about their present songwriting and performing that one would hate to jeopardise it by subjecting them to the rigours and cynicism of the road.'

This was an entirely accurate assessment and the sisters were pretty much in agreement. They had no inclination to step on to the standard record/tour/record treadmill. Kate had a young family to bring up and Anna, who had married the journalist Dane Lanken, also a guest vocalist on their two albums, had young children too. They decided that their families had to come first and withdrew from any more extensive promotional work, much to the exasperation of their record label. 'Anna and I are always one step behind the career that has been set up for us by the record company and the press,' said Kate.

The sisters were often uncomfortable with the way the music business operated: the pressures to conform to the wishes of others and the pointless extravagances offered by record labels that would entice and hook in performers who then found it hard to step away from that lifestyle. Anna had once been collected by limousine from a New York hotel to be driven to where they were due to play as part of the Philadelphia Folk Festival. She had made the driver stop well out of sight as she felt too embarrassed to be seen arriving in a limo. Kate was also the first to point out that at the end of the day, the bouquets of roses that might turn up as a gift from a grateful record label in the dressing room after a performance would, ultimately, be being paid for by the artist who was receiving them.

Kate and Anna had never been interested in being famous so it was easy for them to step away from the business whenever they felt like it, as Kate made clear: 'The only ambitions we've ever had is for what we do to be recognised as good.'

There's a line by Philip Larkin that goes 'the only way of getting shut of your family is to put your neck into the noose of another one'.[2] Shortly after Kate and the children had moved out of the house in New York, Loudon had moved another woman in. During the elongated break-up with Kate, he had become close to Suzzy Roche, a young folk performer who was herself part of a singing family. Kate remembered visiting Loudon not long after moving out to sort out a few last details and finding that Suzzy was already in residence.

Suzzy had just joined up with her older sisters Maggie and Terre who had been performing on the same folk club circuits as Loudon and Kate since the early 1970s. The Roches had changed from a duo

2. *Selected Letters of Philip Larkin* – ed. Anthony Thwaite, Faber, 1992, UK.

into a harmonising folk trio. As a duo, the sisters' main claim to fame was as backing singers on Paul Simon's *There Goes Rhymin' Simon* LP but they had released their own album, *Seductive Reasoning*, to no great success. With the addition of Suzzy, the sisters managed to create a more commercial sound that was closer in tone to American Spring than it was to the McGarrigles, although much to Kate and Anna's bemusement people saw enough surface similarities for the two sister acts to often be compared. Perhaps sensing that the Roches would have more of the requisite work ethic that was expected of a major label act, or at least be more compliant than the headstrong McGarrigles, Warner Brothers signed up Suzzy and her sisters and put them to work on their first LP.

Loudon's 1978 album *Final Exam* again featured the modestly uptempo full band approach that had rocked so unconvincingly on his previous album *T-Shirt*. Other than the slower more restrained songs like 'Pretty Little Martha', a simple song for his daughter that states that fate and the world are cruel and how he misses her and her brother, or the country trudge of 'Mr Guilty', it's a set that finds Loudon sounding hopelessly outdated and old-fashioned. The songs are still full of witty lines but many of them are just stand-alone gags, sporadically funny but lacking the resonance of his better work where his integrated rhyming and comic timing are more controlled and considered. On the cover Loudon is alone in a college lecture theatre. Though he is dressed more like a schoolteacher, it isn't difficult to imagine him as the last student left, a class clown forever gooning instead of studying, compelled to retake his finals when all of his classmates have long since graduated and moved on.

He could hardly have been seen to be competing directly with the likes of Patti Smith or Lou Reed, but they were among the artists who shared the same record label and released albums at the same time. Patti Smith's *Easter* was a huge success on the back of her breakthrough hit 'Because the Night' and Lou Reed had returned with the classic *Street Hassle* album after having lost his way with *Rock and Roll Heart* (that he would sour things again with the comically bad-tempered *Live: Take No Prisoners* later in the year is beside the point). Though Loudon was as entertaining and popular as ever on the live circuit, alongside a roster like this, *Final Exam* looked forlorn. There would be no more Loudon Wainwright III albums with Arista, and aside from his self-produced independent record *A Live One* (1979), no Loudon Wainwright III albums at all until 1983.

Although Kate and Anna had put their own musical aspirations aside to concentrate on bringing up their children, there was the small matter of their final record for Warner Brothers. By this point it seemed to be looked upon more as an obligation to the record company than the next step in a recording career. But Lenny Waronker thought that it was possible to get the McGarrigles to cross over from folk into pop in the same way that Maria Muldaur had. He asked David Nichtern, who had worked extensively with Muldaur as her producer and musical director, to try some demos with the sisters which led to him producing a whole album. As Nichtern and Muldaur had scored a big hit with his song 'Midnight at the Oasis', Warners might have hoped they could get some similar commercial success from the McGarrigles but it was not to be.

Pronto Monto (a pun on the French for 'grab your coat') is the least successful of all of their recordings. It's an uncomfortable blend of their signature harmonies with soft country-rock and pop embellishments. Nichtern remembers the sisters had wanted a record that crossed over into pop but one that came as a natural progression from their earlier work. It wasn't an attempt to sell out, more an experiment in a different way of working.

The record has its moments: the elemental love song 'Na Cl' – the romance of salt – puts Kate alongside Tom Lehrer in an elite band of (probably just the two) folk singers to have been inspired by the periodic table; Anna's 'Fixture in the Park', with its swelling old movie strings, is as archly desolate as ever and Kate's 'Stella By Artois' is another deft personal narrative about a birthday spent on the road that is far better than its awkward punning title would suggest.

Added to these is a cover of 'Trying to Get to You' that is virtually on its knees begging to be AM-radio-friendly, with its sprightly Jerry Donahue guitar break and disco-country percussion, and the confusing 'Side of Fries', which begins in spoken verse then meanders into a pointless saxophone and wah-wah nowhere. Another of Anna's songs, 'Dead Weight', with its love-gone-bad lyrics was perhaps better served by the urchin tough cover version by Julie Covington on her underrated Joe Boyd-produced album released in the same year – here it just fails to convince.

Nichtern was happy with the way the record turned out, although admits it wasn't a total success: 'It didn't really seem to be on the cards for this project to achieve that crossover. Certain things, like song choice and editing and arranging the songs to be more radio-friendly, weren't really followed up. So it's more of an "art" record than a commercial record. On a good day you can get both but perhaps on this outing, the two ideas, commerce/art, might have worked against each other.'

The record sleeve shows the sisters in soft focus, back-lit, their hair a halo, looking somewhere between sultry and sulky. The back cover image of Kate pulling a face and Anna snubbing her nose (blowing the staged grace of the angelic cover shot and puncturing its manufactured sophistication) was a typical self-effacing McGarrigles gesture but were they snubbing their noses at the record label or at the fans who had supported them? Either way, the pop makeover failed and the album has become the lost McGarrigles' record, never released on CD, never reissued at all.

Continuing the McGarrigle family tradition, both Kate and Anna encouraged their respective children to become involved with music at every opportunity. They sang songs together and there was always music playing around the house, whether on the family's collection of instruments or from Kate's comprehensive record collection. One day, when Rufus was only a few years old, Kate was singing 'Old MacDonald' to him and he joined in in the same key. As she progressed through the verses he followed her pitch as she modulated through the menagerie, matching her note for note. 'That's when it started,' remembered Rufus. 'Later on we learned to sing rounds, then to play the piano. All of which culminated in weekend variety shows for Grandma.'

Aside from preparing for the variety shows, Rufus could be found running around the house in a favourite apron he called his 'put-tit-on'[3] either as Dorothy in the Wizard of Oz dancing with the

---

3. 'Put-Tit-On' would later be used as the name for Rufus' music publishing company, replacing 'Rock and Roll Credit Card Music' from the Want Two album onwards.

stuffed lamb he called Toto, or if in a bad mood, pretending to be the Wicked Witch of the West and standing in Kate's shoes imagining he was melting. Other favourites were *That's Entertainment* or *Annie*. 'I had a real gut electric reaction to musicals,' said Rufus in a *Rolling Stone* interview. 'I'd listen to *Oliver!* but sped up really fast and sing and smash my head into the couch.'

Another musical he enjoyed was *The Sound of Music* but he was only allowed to sing along to 'Edelweiss'. 'It was the one song [from the film] that my mother would let me sing ... My mother's big mission in life was to exterminate Julie Andrews,' remembered Rufus.

She may have exerted some influence on his repertoire but Kate was always proud to have Rufus perform for guests. Although he'd later claim, perhaps with tongue in cheek, that he'd felt like a 'trained seal', it's not hard to imagine the five-year-old Rufus getting a kick from singing 'Over The Rainbow' at the end of a dinner party. Kate suspected even then that he was setting himself up to enter the family business. 'Nobody got up in the morning and put on a shirt and tie, so I didn't think he was going to become a banker,' she said.

Rufus made his stage debut at six, singing with Kate and Anna, and although they didn't play live with any frequency, a few years later he and Martha had become part of the show.

It was a bohemian household in a regular neighbourhood and the children felt a little different, a little bit special. Rufus would later comment: 'We were outsiders and as a family of musicians we were really considered odd.'

Pat Donaldson had moved into the house and would become Kate's long-term boyfriend. He took on fatherly duties and helped bring up the children without ever trying to take on a surrogate paternal role. 'He never sat you on his knee and said, "I'm your dad",' remembered Martha years later. Kate and her partner may have been professional musicians but they always ensured that the kids went to bed on time and got to school every day. 'It wasn't like there were people doing lines of coke off the piano at five in the morning as happened to a lot of people I know who had rock and roll parents,' said Martha, who remembers her childhood with fondness. 'It was a wonderful environment,' she says. 'We lived in an old Victorian house that was falling down. We had boho-chic up the ass!'

Kate and Anna were highly respected artists and occasionally other musicians would call up and ask just to meet with them. Martha recalls a time when The Police, who were recording their 'Every Little Thing She Does Is Magic' single at Le Studio in Morin Heights called the house and asked if Kate would like to come and see them at the studio. 'Kate and Anna had just roasted a chicken and I think there was something on the TV so they said "No". That was just like them.'

As the eldest child, Rufus did his best to boss around Martha and his cousins. When they played together in the park, he would be the all-powerful Zeus and he would designate the roles of lesser gods to them so that he could order them around with impunity. With typical fraternal meanness, he once told Martha that she wasn't Kate's child and that she was an alien and he would frequently tell her that he was far more beautiful than she was. He'd challenge her to tasks that he knew he would win – who could sing the longest? Who could sing the loudest? He did everything he could to outdo his sister and at bedtime they would hold more singing competitions which Rufus would always win even if he had to wait for Martha to fall asleep to do so.

Martha remembers Rufus creating his own world in which he was a prince and he would sometimes deign to allow others to enter his realm. Sometimes he would stare into the distance, lost in his own imagination. He had an alter ego named Bela and dreamed of living in another age.

According to his mother, Rufus was obsessed with drawing castles and beautiful horses, like a 'pre-teen goth without the make-up or the black outfits'. She also remembers him being strangely obedient to the extent that when she accidentally mixed up some bags in the kitchen and sent him to school with a pound of cheese in his lunch box, he just ate the whole thing up even though he admitted it was hard to swallow.

Loudon was hardly around at all. He would occasionally visit them in Canada but more often the children would stay with him in the holidays or visit when he was home in New York between tours. Rufus would remember when he was very young seeing his father playing in concert and shouting out a request for 'Rufus is a Tit Man' without really understanding the song. The fact that it was a song about him was enough. Or at least it was something, some link to his father.

Loudon seemed more able to communicate in song, as though he saw a song as a way of bundling up his emotions and feelings for someone, whether good or bad, and leaving the package in their lap for them to unwrap later while he was safely out of the way. It is not surprising that Kate, and later his children, would write songs directed at him as that seemed to be a language he understood, a dialogue in which he could engage.

Loudon wrote another song for Martha for her birthday in 1981. 'Five Years Old' describes a fun fifth birthday party, with pin-the-tail-on-the-donkey, party dresses and ice-cream. It was a party that Loudon hadn't attended; the song was sent in lieu of a personal appearance.

Talking about the situation years later, Rufus would admit to a long period of resentment of the fact that Loudon had written so much about him and his family: 'He certainly dealt on stage I think more directly with the anatomy of the family than any other performer I know. At the same time my father was very distant from us and very hard to get to at all.' Martha would prove to be even more hostile.

The fact that he rarely saw his father impacted in other ways on Rufus. He lacked a male role model and in fact had very little interaction with men at all. 'I remember pining for a brother desperately,' he would later say. 'I had these odd dreams about finding a little brother egg in the forest. I think there was a hole in myself that needed to be filled by men in general. I didn't know many.' Later he would identify these feelings as part of the reason for some of his more reckless behaviour.

2.2

In 1980 the call for Quebec and its majority French-speaking population to separate from the rest of Canada had grown to such an extent that a referendum was called. The separatists were defeated as 60 per cent of the electorate rejected the proposal. In this climate the McGarrigles were offered the chance to record an album in French for Kebec Records, an exclusively French-Canadian label. Its owner, Gilles Talbot, wanted to 'extend a hand of friendship to us and ask us as English-Canadians to produce a record for a French audience. It was a political gesture in a sense,' explained Kate.

Entre Lajeunesse et la Sagesse, literally 'between youth and wisdom', and a pun on a Montreal street name, is more commonly known as *The French Album*. It collects three of their French language songs from earlier albums (one rerecorded) and adds eight new songs, all but two of these co-written with long-time collaborator Philippe Tatartcheff.

In contrast to the various guests and session players who had graced their Warner Brothers records, *The French Album* was recorded using the local friends and musicians that they had always enjoyed playing with, their 'musical bedfellows' as the sleeve would have it. The sisters produced the album themselves with Chuck Gray engineering in a small local facility, Studio Six on St Antoine in Montreal. Elder sister Jane is credited as executive producer (for a time she would become Kate and Anna's first proper manager). All in all, it was a more intimate, more sustained collection of songs which evoked the McGarrigles' spirit of 'parlour singing' and folk simplicity.

Much of the record is concerned with the Canadian countryside, its tiny villages and frozen lakes or its snow and city cold. Yet there is a real warmth to these lyrical, expressive songs and even though there is only one traditional piece, the whole set sounds as if it has been passed down from generation to generation. They are time-worn songs with the patina and sheen of aged quality craftsmanship.

For non-French speakers there is also the option of listening to the sisters' voices as an instrument, there are no translations provided. Kate and Anna had often tempered the beauty of their singing with words of great sadness and this French-language record provided an opportunity to disregard the meaning of the words and give listeners a new way into the music. Many people found it to be the most uplifting and spiritual collection in the McGarrigles' discography.

In 1979 Kate and Anna had recorded a song with their old

Mountain City Four friends for a short film for the National Film Board of Canada (NFB). *La Valse du Maître Draveur* was an animated short about the logging industry directed by John Weldon. The song was written by Wade Hemsworth[4] (as 'The Log Driver's Waltz') and translated into French by Philippe Tatartcheff.

Derek Lamb, who was head of English animation at the NFB and the producer of the film, was a long-time admirer of Kate and Anna and was keen to produce a documentary about them. Lamb knew that his colleague, the acclaimed animator Caroline Leaf, whose films included the Mordecai Richler adaptation *The Street* (1976), which had been nominated for an Oscar, was looking to experiment with live-action filming and he offered her the chance to make a McGarrigles film.

Leaf, originally from Boston, Massachusetts, was aware of the McGarrigles' music and admired them as singers and songwriters. But there were other factors that encouraged her to make the film: 'I was interested in their ambivalence about being mainstream or remaining marginal but artistically independent,' she says. 'I think they accomplished both through writing and performing. This is a dilemma for many artists whose abilities let them go either way.'

The documentary, simply titled *Kate and Anna McGarrigle*, follows the sisters through rehearsals, photo-shoots (including an ill-advised shirt, tie, boxing gloves and drums sequence) and day-to-day living. It also gives a glimpse into how they worked on composing songs together and how they balanced their creative lives with bringing up the children. Anna is filmed saying that their other responsibilities sometimes account for occasional 'sloppiness' on stage. 'All the parts are really rehearsed; whether they all come together at the same time that night is happenstance.' A witty excuse right up there with Eric Morecambe's classic comedy performance

---

4. Wade Hemsworth (1916–2002) was an important figure in Canadian folk music. Although he would release just two albums (his second at the age of 79) and write less than 20 songs in his entire career, the sheer quality of this tiny output is extraordinary. The Mountain City Four had played many of his songs (he would occasionally join them on stage) and the McGarrigles included his sublime 'Foolish You' on their debut record. They continue to perform his songs to this day. Another animated short film using one of his songs, *Blackfly* (dir. Christopher Hinton) was made in 1991, on this Hemsworth sang lead with the McGarrigles on backing vocals.

as the inept concert pianist tackling Greig: 'I'm playing all the right notes, but not necessarily in the right order.'

Using a voiceover, Leaf mixed live action with innovative animation. She created sequences with drawings that she had made of the sisters and these animations provide a perfect way of exploring the otherworldliness of their music, sometimes moving in and out of the regular world. The film culminates in a successful performance at Carnegie Hall where they were supporting Rick Danko and Paul Butterfield. They almost didn't make the concert at all after realising at the last minute that they didn't actually have work permits. Anna had thought that they would be okay because they could use a cultural pass as they sang some songs in French but the rest of the band weren't so sure. In the end, when they got to the airport they pretended they didn't know each other and were all tourists. 'We're all working illegally,' announced Anna from the stage, fairly confident that there were no border guards in the audience.

In the film Rufus can be seen running around backstage after the show in a home-made red and blue jumper with a blond bowl haircut dodging in and out of the well-wishers. His grandmother Gaby is there too. When interviewed, she admits to having enjoyed the concert and, although obviously beaming with pride, is reluctant to overpraise her daughters: 'I'm their mother. I don't want to boast too much,' she says.

Leaf remembers the sisters being easy to work with and not uncomfortable being filmed. She wonders now if a different approach might have got them to open up even more. 'I wanted to get more feeling of their spontaneity and spirit than I thought I managed at the time. I wish I had known how to work with a more intimate, responsive crew, just camera and sound.'

Overall the film is an engaging portrait of artists who had sought to balance their commitment to art with dedication to their family. It brings an intelligent and refreshingly feminist perspective to the music documentary format. In fact, perhaps Leaf's greatest achievement with the film is having created a documentary of a family who happen to be musicians rather than the other way around.

After the success of *The French Album*, the sisters chose to produce their next album themselves at another local studio in Morin Heights. *Love Over and Over* was more pop-sounding, in effect a slightly more successful attempt at what *Pronto Monto* had been trying to achieve. Even so, it relied heavily on older material for its best moments including a recording of 'The Work Song' and an English version of 'On My Way to Town' from their preceding record. On the title track they invoke the Brontë sisters, as they had on 'Oh My Heart' on *Pronto Monto*. Lost on the moors, 'What could anyone know about love?' they ask, as guest guitarist Mark Knopfler noodles away.

When *Love Over and Over* was reissued on CD in 1985, it included a later song 'A Place in Your Heart', which was recorded for the charity compilation album *Feed the Folk*. For this recording Kate and Anna had called in their children to form part of a choir, so marking Rufus and Martha's first appearance on record.

Loudon continued to play live and was still chipping away at his acting career whenever an opportunity arose. In 1979, after a one-off bit part in a long-running sit-com, he appeared in a pilot for a sketch show put together by Rob Reiner, Christopher Guest and Harry Shearer. *The T.V. Show* failed to get commissioned for a series but at least Loudon could rightfully claim to have once been a member of Spinal Tap as he could be seen playing keyboards on 'Rock'n'roll Nightmare' in a sketch featuring an early outing for the mock-rockers.

He can also claim to have been the original musical sidekick for David Letterman when he hosted a daily afternoon comedy talk show for NBC in 1980. The show won two Emmys and was a critical success but the viewing figures were disappointing and it was cancelled. Unluckily for Loudon, when Letterman was moved to what would become his legendary late night slot, he chose to up the budget beyond one man with a guitar and brought in a whole band. Loudon must have cursed under his breath every time he switched on a hotel room TV after a show and Letterman's gap-tooth grin flashed across the screen.

When no further TV opportunities came his way, Loudon returned to his old standby and got back on the live circuit promoting the *A Live One* album that he had self-funded and licensed to independent labels in the UK and USA. In 1981 Suzzy and Loudon had a baby, Lucy Wainwright Roche, the birth coinciding with Suzzy and her sisters achieving success with their own albums. The ultra-competitive Loudon knew he needed to get back into the studio as, for the first time, he was firmly in the back seat while the Roches, and the McGarrigles, were driving on to critical and, at least in the Roches' case, commercial success.

After a brief break for a moderately successful stint in the Broadway musical *Pump Boys and Dinettes*, where he starred alongside Ronee Blakley, best known for her part in Robert Altman's *Nashville* (1975), Loudon headed back into the studio. *Fame and Wealth* was a back-to-basics return to form in which Loudon eschewed his rock band sound and returned to solo performances, accentuated by a pair of tracks that separately feature Richard Thompson's elliptical strumming and Mark Hardwick's saloon bar piano.

Lyrically the album returned to Loudon's usual preoccupations of family, past and present and, of course, himself. His song for Martha 'Five Years Old' was included and another song, 'Ingenue', in which the narrator seeks a younger naïve woman to take care of him, also directly addressed his personal life. By mentioning his previous wife's name in the lyric, Loudon virtually turns the song into an unflattering portrait of Suzzy, painting her as the unsophisticated girl of the title.

One of the best tracks is 'IDTTYWLM' an initialism for 'I Don't Think That Your Wife Likes Me' which has Loudon badmouthing his drinking buddy's wife because when she smiles at him it's 'forced' and wondering if it's because he's 'famous' that she has a problem with him. *Rolling Stone* likened this to Tom Waits, with its honky-tonking piano backing. Loudon had long expressed an admiration for Waits as a songwriter but if there is a similarity, it is to his 1970s albums like *Small Change* or *Foreign Affairs* rather than the 'sturm und clang!' direction change which Waits would imminently announce with *Swordfishtrombones*. In fact, it's the album's title track that's sonically closest to the Waits of 1983. It's almost a field-holler, just voice and solitary beating drum, a comically desperate plea for success in which Loudon offers his family and everything he owns, even pledging willing enslavement, in return for fame and wealth. Although it's obviously impossible to take too seriously, with Loudon's history you are left wondering if there isn't just a little kernel of truth hidden away in all the bluster.

In early 1985 Loudon was invited to be the resident singer-songwriter for an eight-week stint on comedian Jasper Carrott's prime-time BBC1 show in the UK. It would mean reaching an audience of 10 million viewers on a Saturday night. Surely fame and wealth were just around the corner. Loudon initially wrote and performed a new topical song on each show. After playing one about the Super Bowl which proved baffling to a British audience with no interest in or understanding of American football, he returned to live favourites like 'Nocturnal Stumblebutt' and 'Unrequited (to the Nth Degree)' for most of the rest of the series.

In the final show he played a new song, 'Harry's Wall', about a person who becomes just famous enough to have his 10 x 8 photograph hung on the wall of his local dry cleaners alongside the Three Degrees, Frankie Vaughan and Chas and Dave, but not famous enough for anybody to know exactly who he is.

Loudon had held high hopes for the show, thinking that it would perhaps lead to his own solo TV career when viewers saw how well he interacted with Carrott. As it panned out, his hopes for sidekick jinks with the popular comedian were scuppered as Carrott kept his distance and barely spoke to Loudon on screen or off, casting him adrift in his solo spot every week. Not only did Loudon not get an offer of his own show, he didn't even get the invite back for the second Jasper Carrott series. Once again the fame and household name status that he had continually craved proved to be out of reach. Like his character in the 'Harry's Wall' song, for millions of British viewers he remained 'Whatshisname', the guy they think they might have seen on TV but aren't quite sure.

2.3

By the time he was in his early teens, Rufus had started toying with writing his own songs and music. The first thing he remembers writing is a short piano piece called 'The Dancing Lady'. 'It was about some chick with castanets I used to hang out with at recess,' he said.

Rufus was occasionally hassled at school by some of the jocks but he'd counter their bullying by singing or by making sure he was always the best at school drama. 'I realised at a very young age with me not being the toughest guy or the meanest guy at school, that music or a talent can really protect you and be a power over others,' explained Rufus in a 1998 interview. 'People in the end really prize talent and art and people need it. Whether you're a jock footballer or a little art fag, everybody likes a nice song or a good play so I immediately went into that realm, partly to watch my back and also because people respect that in the end.' Though countless entertainers have spent their schooldays using future performing skills as a defence against school bullying, Rufus is probably unique in seeking to disarm his tormentors with a quick show tune.

By the time he was 13, Rufus knew that he was gay. He was comfortable with his sexuality and made no real attempt to hide it, but the spectre of AIDS loomed large in the mid-1980s and, like many who grew up during this period, he had a nagging sense of dread of what would become of him.

In those early days of AIDS, there was a grim, fatalistic prognosis that ominously overshadowed the gay community and sexually awakened young people of whatever persuasion. The spread of the disease was unprecedented and, by 1985, the media, often implicitly, focused on the fact that as infection was prevalent among homo-sexuals or drug-users, they had somehow brought the illness on themselves and should take all of the blame. The actor Rock Hudson became the first household name celebrity to admit to having AIDS (and in so doing outed himself, although in truth his homosexuality was so well known that if he was considered to have been in the closet, it was a closet that didn't have a door). In one of the first dramatic works to tackle the subject, the playwright Larry Kramer likened the situation to the gay community living through a war while those around them, even those in the same neighbourhoods, were living in peacetime.[5]

However, even those who had contracted the illness via a con-taminated blood transfusion or through a heterosexual partnership were treated with suspicion and disgust. Myths and scaremongering

5. Kramer, Larry, *The Normal Heart*, Plume, 1987, US.

were rife as scientists argued about how the disease could or could not be spread. In the UK, firemen were told not to administer the kiss of life and some Catholic churches curtailed the sharing of Communion wine.

By 1986 worried governments had embarked on a programme of awareness initiatives to help educate the public. Although many would argue that these were ineffectual and under-funded, the Surgeon General in the US did release an explicit report urging the education of schoolchildren on sexual health issues as a matter of urgency if there was to be a chance to slow the spread of AIDS. The coverage of the disease in the media was troubling, relentless and revealed little cause for optimism. As an example of the paranoia and general ignorance that lay at the heart of the initial attitude to the identification of the disease were stories like that of Ryan White, a haemophiliac. Ryan just 13 years old, banned from his American school and cast aside for having contracted the disease from a blood transfusion.[6] With children as young as himself already affected, Rufus couldn't help but be terrified at his own prospects for the future. Growing up in the mid-1980s was scary.

At the same time that Rufus was trying to come to terms with the fact that his sexuality, in effect his very essence, may sentence him

---

6. Ryan White became a symbol of the harsh reality of AIDS in the US, demonstrating clearly, and for many people for the first time, that the disease could affect anybody regardless of sexuality or age. After it was discovered that the 13-year-old had contracted the disease from an infected blood transfusion, he was banned from attending his school in Indiana, requiring his family to embark on a lengthy legal struggle to get him readmitted into the education system. His story was featured in many magazines and on numerous television stations and he became a media figurehead in the fight for understanding and equality in the treatment of those with AIDS.

The discussion of his story was a chance to explode many of the fallacies and rumours about the disease that had been spreading throughout the early 1980s (for instance, some people had refused to be included on White's paper round as they thought they might catch AIDS from the newspapers he delivered) and it was his story that brought the tragedy of AIDS into many homes, to people who would otherwise have felt it was something that would never affect them.

White and his family were always keen to make clear that he was not an 'innocent' victim as this would somehow lend credibility to the idea that homosexuals who had contracted the illness were culpable. This attitude helped to attack the barely disguised homophobia in much public discussion of AIDS.

When White died in 1990, Elton John, Michael Jackson and Barbara Bush were among the attendees at his funeral. After his death, Congress instigated the Ryan White CARE Act which to this day remains the largest government-funded treatment programme for American AIDS/HIV sufferers on low income and without health care insurance. (For more see www.ryanwhite.com.)

to a life of either virtual celibacy or inevitable infection, he had an epiphany. He had already discovered classical music and would spend hours listening to Chopin in Kate's bedroom and he had already investigated classical vocal records by the likes of Beniamo Gigli and Jussi Bjorling. One day Kate brought home a copy of Fritz Reiner's 1959 recording of Verdi's *Requiem* that featured Bjorling and Leontyne Price and it changed the way Rufus listened to music for ever. Almost instantly he became besotted with opera, relating its treatment of death and the drama of love with his own nascent sexuality and his fear of disease. 'It came at a junction in my life where I was completely hit simultaneously by different things. One that I was gay, two being that AIDS was on the scene. This thrilling, consoling music immediately hooked into all the emotions I was feeling,' he later explained.

After hearing Verdi, Rufus listened almost exclusively to opera, ignoring the Top 40 stations that Martha enjoyed and giving up on the likes of The Thompson Twins or the Eurythmics, whom he'd previously loved. He had 'bang-out battles' with Kate who he'd later say was furious that he'd become involved in this 'escapist, rather dark medium'. Rufus claimed that she would play him what he disparagingly called 'poor people's music' to demonstrate to him what he should be listening to, but he would counter by just playing more Verdi and turning up the volume.

Rufus started visiting the antique shops and cafés along St Laurent Boulevard, the road that separates Montreal into French and English sides. It was exciting to get out of the pretty but dull Westmount neighbourhood where he lived. Before long he had discovered Montreal's gay village around St Catherine Street and had begun sneaking out of the house and going down to the gay bars to hang out.

He admits to having been a Lolita-esque character, a 14-year-old boy who looked no older than his years, leaning at the bar, craving attention from adult men. He has said that although these jaunts into town were driven by a strong sexual yearning and a need to experiment, they were partly driven by a need to find a male role model in his life. He lived with his mother and sister and although he had a strong loving family he found that, with Loudon never present and Kate's boyfriend Pat Donaldson understandably reluctant to try and take his place, he lacked a real father figure and he sometimes confused the sexual attention of men with this need for male guidance and advice. 'There were drinking laws, but they obviously didn't enforce them,' he says. 'I was a young 14. I looked like an underdeveloped lizard.'

Although he did nothing to hide the fact that he was homosexual, Kate was in denial, even after she had found a gay porn magazine hidden under his bed. Loudon, ever the pragmatist, had flat out asked him if he preferred boys to girls. Although neither parent was especially homophobic, they still found it difficult to deal with. His father just tried to ignore the subject and let it play out over time, while his mother, in light of the AIDS crisis as much as anything, and fearing for the well-being of her son, chose to pretend it wasn't a real issue and wouldn't discuss it at all.

In 1986, while staying with Loudon in New York, Rufus was sent over to see his father's friend, the artist Penny Arcade, whom Loudon had briefly run off to Europe with in the early days of his marriage to Kate. Arcade had become a family friend and would subsequently exert an important influence on Rufus' artistic development. She had appeared in the Andy Warhol/Paul Morrissey film *Women in Revolt* (1971) and had subsequently gone on to write, produce and perform a series of cutting-edge shows and performance pieces that used sexuality and feminism to push the boundaries of experimental theatre and artistic confrontation. She was a well-connected figure in hip New York circles.[7]

'When Rufus was about 14, Loudon started to think he might be gay,' remembers Arcade. 'I had seen Rufus at a birthday party for Loudon when he'd been 12 and I'd realised he was gay then. Loudon called me and said, "If Rufus is gay then you are the best person for him to know." I understood some of the issues that would be created by Rufus being gay in that family at the time, clearly, as there would be for most families of young teens in the mid-1980s in the middle of the AIDS epidemic. So I took Loudon's call very seriously.'

---

7. Penny Arcade was born Susana Carmen Ventura and changed her name while high on LSD at 17 years of age. A fascinating artist, she has performed all over the world and alongside her own work has helped the careers of numerous well-known performers. There is not enough space here to do her career justice so I suggest you visit her website www.pennyarcade.tv.

From then on, whenever Rufus was in New York, he would visit Arcade and be introduced to her East Village associates. She would remain a confidant to Rufus for many years, taking a compassionate interest in his upbringing, acting as a kind of surrogate parent whenever he was in town. Indeed, Rufus would come to refer to her as his 'New York mother', and she supported him both artistically and emotionally (as later she would also counsel Martha). Arcade played a pivotal role in Rufus' development as an artist as she became a conduit to ideas and influences that were more challenging, more avant-garde and more appealing to Rufus than those of the artistic circle his parents had mixed in.

Arcade remembers Loudon and Rufus attending a party she was holding to celebrate New Year's Day 1987: 'There were many of my East Village circle there, including Quentin Crisp and Jack Smith. Rufus was introduced to Quentin that day but had little interest then so probably doesn't remember, after all Quentin was a very old man. Rufus was quite intrigued by Edgar Oliver, the writer and actor, who was a dandy and spoke French and drank a lot of red wine out of a Coke bottle, and his sister the painter Helen Oliver. They were very glamorous in a true East Village edgy 1980s bohemian way.'

It was important to Arcade that Rufus got to meet many of the hippest New York artists, including taking him to see Patti Smith with whom she had worked since the 1960s and Taylor Mead, the poet and sometime Warhol film star. She gave Loudon and Rufus tickets to see her shows, including a performance of her breakthrough work *Bitch! Dyke! Faghag! Whore!* at Performance Space 122, an experimental arts centre located in an abandoned school. The show featured male and female strippers and Arcade performed a burlesque striptease that she remembers horrified Loudon. Rufus absolutely loved it. Later it would go on to great acclaim at theatre festivals around the world.

If Rufus couldn't remember meeting Crisp at the party, he did later recall seeing him at Arcade's apartment. Far from being the recipient of any of Crisp's *bon mots*, Rufus can't recall ever being spoken to at all. Perhaps, though, Crisp's very being was enough to empower Rufus; after all, the Stately Homo had dealt with his own sexuality back in the more repressed 1930s by deciding that he would live his life 'not merely as a self-confessed homosexual, but a self-evident one'.[8]

Even though the Jasper Carrott show hadn't resulted in the hoped-for career boost, Loudon still hoped to secure more British TV work. By 1986 Loudon had moved to London, where the previous year he had recorded the *I'm Alright* album with Richard Thompson producing, a record that had been nominated for a Best Contemporary Folk Recording Grammy.

The album contained a collaborative song with Suzzy, one of the very few times Loudon has ever collaborated on any music, called 'Screaming Issue', directed at his younger daughter. In it he admits to not quite knowing what to do when she cried or how on earth he could help such a grizzly child. *I'm Alright* also included one of his best-known songs, 'One Man Guy'. It's a song that manages to balance narcissism and self-loathing, self-reliance and loneliness in equal measures. If it's anything, it's a brutally frank manifesto for the way that Loudon had lived his life: ultimately eschewing meditative calm or family responsibility for the sake of himself and the 'three cubic feet of bone, blood and meat' that is all he really loves or understands. Why would he know how to soothe a crying child when he had spent a lifetime concentrating on what was best for himself? As he sang in the title cut 'I'm alright without you' it seemed that the 'you' could stand for 'anybody'.

It could certainly stand for Suzzy and Lucy, who he left behind in New York, documenting the break-up on the poignant 'Your Mother and I' a song to Lucy that explains how her parents had come to be splitting up and telling her that he would visit her. Again Loudon managed to coat the bitterest of lyrics in the sweetest tune.

After the Grammy nomination, Loudon had hooked up with Richard Thompson again for the follow-up, *More Love Songs*. On the whole it's a more reflective album, alongside 'Your Mother and I', is the 'golf as life' parable 'The Back Nine' and the particularly brutal self-analysis of 'The Home Stretch', in which Loudon takes a long hard look at himself and doesn't like what he sees. The old Loudon is fully represented by the feminist baiting 'Man's World' and a rare

---

8. Crisp, Quentin, *The Naked Civil Servant*, Cape, 1968, UK.

political satirical song 'Hard Day on the Planet', which takes a brief dig at Bob Geldof, this the result of a long-held grudge caused by Geldof in his previous incarnation as a rock journalist for the Canadian music paper *Georgia Strait*, having annoyed Loudon to such an extent that he'd walked out of the interview. Perversely, after the success of the previous record, *More Love Songs* had difficulty even finding a distributor in the US and for a long time was only available as an import.

When Rufus went to stay with Loudon in London in the summer of 1988, it would result in the most traumatic experience of his life to date. Out wandering the streets on his own, Rufus had gone into a bar and started chatting to one of the customers. The man asked the 14-year-old if he would like to go for a walk around Hyde Park and Rufus, rather naïvely, thought that this would indeed be a pleasant enough end to the evening. When they got to the park the man attacked Rufus and raped him. He would later describe the man almost strangling him and how he had had to feign an epileptic fit in order to make his escape. He didn't feel able to tell his parents what had happened and he didn't admit it to anybody until many years later.[9]

Rufus was convinced that the assault would result in him contracting AIDS. When he got back to Montreal he stopped cruising the gay bars and stayed in his room worrying, listening to Verdi's *Requiem* over and over again. He abstained from sex at all for many years afterwards. Much later, when he realised that he had not contracted anything, he admitted that the rape may have saved him from an even worse fate. With hindsight, he admitted to having been too obsessed by sex as a 13- and 14-year-old and this negative experience had, in a way, steered him in a different, safer direction.

Unaware of his traumas and alarmed that their son just seemed to be moping around the house all day, listening to opera with the curtains drawn, Kate and Loudon decided to send him away to boarding school in an attempt to get him to pull himself together

---

9. On a number of occasions (including *Rolling Stone*, 10 June 1999) when recounting this episode, Rufus has said that his assailant asked him to the park so that he could see 'where the Mandela concert' had been. The 1988 Nelson Mandela tribute concert was actually held at Wembley Stadium.

and get his life in order. Against his wishes, he was packed off to the elite private school Millbrook[10] with Loudon doing what he could to become the dutiful, if distant, father by turning over a sizeable portion of the income he generated from his frequent touring into school fees.

It was at Millbrook that Rufus says he regained his innocence; its verdant, peaceful location a pleasant contrast to his previous inner-city high school. He thought of Millbrook as a kind of *Brideshead Revisited* environment and imagined himself as an aristocrat, spending much of his time in the chapel where the school piano was located. He got fully involved with the performing arts department and took the lead in school productions of *Godspell* and *Cabaret*, performing in front of both of his proud parents.

In Montreal Kate had split with her boyfriend Pat Donaldson, who would subsequently relocate to France and become a clown. With Rufus away at school she moved with Martha into a smaller apartment. Kate wrote a bleak, contemplative song about her situation. 'I Eat Dinner (When the Hunger's Gone)' sees her sat in silence with her 13–year-old daughter,[11] eating leftovers, counting grey hairs, with nobody to kiss her goodnight or even to turn out the light. When the song eventually appeared on the *Heartbeats Accelerating* record, the *New York Times* suggested it was as if Emily Dickinson had been reincarnated as a late twentieth-century songwriter. Kate's lyrics certainly conjure the gelidity of loneliness as readily as Dickinson's 'polar expiation'.[12]

At the time, Martha was moving out of her Prince, Tracy Chapman and Cyndi Lauper phase and into Leonard Cohen and Fleetwood Mac. She'd play *Rumours* repeatedly when she came in from school and Kate would scream at her to turn it off. Cohen's *I'm Your Man* had just been released and Martha listened to it on cassette but kept it secret from her school friends, who she thought would think it was weird. Even at 13, Cohen's precise lyrical skills, his virtual

---

10. Millbrook School was used as a location in the film *The World According to Garp* (dir. George Roy Hill 1992). It's not the school in *Dead Poets Society* as is often reported.
11. When the song was rerecorded by Rufus and Dido for the soundtrack to *Bridget Jones: The End of Reason* (dir. Beeban Kidron 2004), the lyrics were clumsily rewritten, replacing the lines about a daughter with ones about light fittings and television.
12. 'I tried to think a lonelier thing', Emily Dickinson circa 1862, reprinted Emily Dickinson, *The Complete Poems*, Faber and Faber, 1970, UK.

embodiment of Poe's definition of the poetry of words as rhythmic beauty,[13] appealed to her: '*I'm Your Man* was a revelation,' she says, 'because it was clear that the words are more important than the music. This is where it all started for me.'

Since they had worked with the National Film Board of Canada, the McGarrigles had made friends in the Canadian film business and through one of them were introduced to the film director Mike Rubbo. Rubbo was looking for some music for a children's feature film he was working on and he asked Kate if she would like to contribute.

Tommy Tricker and the Stamp Traveller is a delightful film about a lovable prankster, Tommy, who steals a rare stamp from one of his friends. His friend, Ralph, soon discovers that it's possible to travel across the world by magically shrinking yourself until you fit onto a stamp and getting somebody to post you. This leads to a globe-trotting adventure as the children try to find a stamp-collecting boy who has been lost in the post for 75 years. Some of the acting may be a little shaky but it's a film that's packed full of old-fashioned charm and innocent fun.

Rubbo says he originally came up with the idea after an East European entertainer called Klimbo told him a story at a party about a boy who flicked ink on to a world map and created a new island in the South Pacific that he eventually got to visit. Later he read a magazine story about a Chinese girl who wished she could post herself to her penfriends around the world. 'From these scraps I developed the idea of being able to miniaturise yourself on to a postage stamp,' explained Rubbo. 'I had always liked the idea of smallish kids being able to cleverly escape from under parental control and do amazing things.'

The film's producer Rock Demers was always keen on including songs in his movies. He saw a song as added value and something that could perhaps be released separately, and as he had managed to get future Canadian mega-star Celine Dion for Rubbo's previous film, he proved he had an ear for talent. With Kate working on the

---

13. 'I would define, in brief, the poetry of words as the rhythmical creation of beauty. Its sole arbiter is taste.' Edgar Allen Poe, *The Poetic Principle*, *Sartain's* magazine 1850, reprinted in *The Works of Edgar Allan Poe Vol. III*, Arcadia House, 1950, US.

soundtrack with Anna, Rubbo asked them if they could also include a song. Keen to get him involved, Kate suggested to Rufus that he might like to exercise his fledgling compositional skills by trying to write the song. Both Rubbo and Kate made it clear to him he could write whatever he wanted to; there was no particular brief other than that the director had given him an outline of what the story entailed.

The song Rufus came up with was 'I'm a Runnin'' an uptempo almost rock-a-billy number that's verging on Sun Records' era Elvis Presley.[14] Rubbo was so impressed that he found a way to get Rufus' song actually performed on screen rather than just heard in the film. 'It was a late addition to the script,' said Rubbo. 'I don't recall writing it into the early drafts but I was aware that his voice had a special quality that made it compelling. I'm kicking myself now that I did not bring Rufus more into the story!

'But Rufus was not a star of course in any way at that time, just a kid who sang superbly. I remember going to their apartment in Montreal and hearing the song as it progressed.'

Lois Siegel was in charge of casting the movie. Siegel was aware of the McGarrigles after having been given the sisters' first record by one of the directors at the NFB some years earlier. She auditioned Rufus when it was decided that he would be appearing on screen as well as on the soundtrack: 'I remember him being very quiet, but he still had a very strong presence. He wasn't lively and outgoing like most of the other kids. He stuck mainly to himself and focused on what he was doing. I was very impressed when I saw his band in the film. Even as a child, he had a riveting presence with strong character. And his music was terrific.'

Rufus has a few lines in the film, he turns down an offer of management from one of his classmates and is seen sitting on a step, tapping a pencil, working on the song, but he is best remembered for his live band performance at the Complexe Desjardins shopping

---

14. Although not the most immediately obvious influence, Rufus was as aware of Elvis as any broad-minded music enthusiast and even chose Elvis' Mystery Train as the first pick on 'Tracks of my Years' on Ken Bruce's BBC Radio 2 show in July 2007. His other choices were Kate and Anna's 'Talk to Me of Mendocino'; Dionne Warwick – 'Trains and Boats and Planes'; Bob Dylan – 'I Want You'; Serge Gainsbourg – '69 Annee Erotique; Roberta Flack – 'Will You Love Me Tomorrow'; Blondie – 'Heart of Glass'; Harold Arlen – 'Accentuate The Positive'; Bjork – 'Venus as a Boy'; Beach Boys – 'In My Room'.

mall in Montreal as the rest of the cast enact a slapstick chase sequence.

Kate and Anna's music was versatile enough to fit perfectly into the movie and the soundtrack contains some atypical but tremendous percussive instrumentals. Keeping it completely in the family, Martha, though barely even a teenager, got to perform a song, 'Tommy Come Home', over the end credits although she wasn't actually filmed. 'Another missed opportunity,' says Rubbo.

When the film was released in 1989, both Rufus' song and Mike Rubbo's script were nominated for a Genie, the Canadian Film Academy's annual award. Neither of them won and Rufus would later claim that he was happy he didn't win, saying it would have been too weird: 'You don't want to get too many awards and accolades when you're too young.' He also claimed that his experience at the ceremony where he was faced with a 'vast, unclapping void' caused his temporary disillusionment with pop and triggered a desire to eventually be a classical composer.

In 1990 he was also nominated for a Juno, the Canadian music industry award, but lost out in the 'Most Promising Male Vocalist' category to Daniel Lanois. If being a runner-up for the second successive ceremony was less easy to accept, he could take some solace in the fact that Lanois was more than 20 years older than he was. There was plenty of time to get awards.

Rufus was soon starting to write more songs. 'I'd always written stories, many of which were downright florid,' he says. 'Once I started writing songs it immediately helped me cut out a lot of bullshit.'

Kate was a fierce critic and she didn't believe in going soft on Rufus' early efforts. She wasn't afraid to tell him if she thought something he had written was awful, even if it meant listening through 20 songs and criticising every single one of them. It all helped him develop a thicker skin, be less precious and more self-critical. 'She wasn't just my mother. She was also my coach,' he said.

The first song that Rufus wrote that was wholeheartedly approved by Kate was actually one he had written especially for her. 'Beauty Mark' is a comparatively simple piano song. There is nothing florid about it, it positively barrels along. Lyrically it's a fine counterpoint between a son and mother contrasting the way that they grew up with Rufus appropriately pledging allegiance to the dramatic, expressive Maria Callas while linking Kate to the more elegant, restrained Paul Robeson. He also broaches the delicate subject of his sexuality by admitting that he 'may not be so manly' but he knows she will still love him whatever.

Kate and Anna were still writing and playing music, although they hadn't released a record for many years and didn't have a deal. After they had performed together on a Canadian radio show, they received a call out of the blue and an offer of a record contract from former Tangerine Dream keyboardist Peter Baumann. He had set up a new experimental record label called Private Music that encouraged musicians to work with electronics and synthesisers. Folk traditionalists they may have been but the McGarrigles were forward-thinking enough to see that this would be an interesting experiment.

Heartbeats Accelerating was made with producer Pierre Marchand who had worked with Daniel Lanois on his debut record *Acadie* (the record that had helped Lanois pip Rufus to the 'Most Promising Vocalist' prize the year before).

There are certainly strong songs on the album, including the aforementioned masterful 'I Eat Dinner (When the Hunger's Gone)' and the pleading ethereal title track. Kate's song, 'I'm Losing You', about a child growing up and moving out, gains added poignancy with Rufus singing the backing vocals and it's the first part of a powerful trio of thematically linked songs. On 'Mother, Mother' the anguish of letting go (or leaving) is even greater – it feels like a gothic story, a hint of horror – the singer is calling for a dog that bites and howls, and a starving bird of prey, for protection from some unnamed, perhaps imagined thing that stalks the world outside the childhood home. 'Help me, Someone's trying to hurt me' is the refrain. The theme returns in 'Leave Me Be' a murder ballad come fairy tale about a girl who ignores her father's advice, falls for the wrong man (his hair is like 'black gold' – you know the type), and is later found washed up on the Gulf of Mexico, face down in the sand 'like poor Pinocchio'.

The *New York Times* reviewer read the record as though it was a Henry James ghost story, 'the wind moans in the eaves, the floorboards creak', with the sisters cast as silent spinsters working on a tapestry in front of the fire. It's easy to understand the reviewer's enthusiasm; even now the actual material stands up well, the recording itself is completely of its time.

Perhaps if they had been more bold with the synthetic drum patterns and less free with the pre-set new-age swooshing, they could have created a kind of forerunner to the electro-folk stylings of bands like Goldfrapp and Beth Orton who would become popular almost 20 years later. Unfortunately the electronics and proto-funk bass playing today render much of the record hopelessly dated, in a similar way to how Leonard Cohen's antiquated synthesisers now diminish much of his *I'm Your Man* album. *Heartbeats Accelerating* is not avant-garde or innovative enough to have survived two decades without just becoming a period curio; it's interesting but ultimately unfulfilling as a whole album.

A side project provided more traditional fare for the McGarrigles. *Songs of the Civil War* was a stand-alone album and video featuring interpretations of civil war era songs by musicians such as Waylon Jennings, Hoyt Axton and Richie Havens. It acted as a musical companion piece to Ken Burns' epic PBS documentary on the American Civil War. The McGarrigles contributed three tracks, two of which featured their families on backing vocals. It was the kind of musical archaeology that the sisters both loved and excelled at.

2.4

Loudon had released his 11th album *Therapy* on the UK label Silvertone, a bizarre one-shot deal on a newly formed label that he shared with The Stone Roses, Sonic Boom (of the Spacemen 3) and John Lee Hooker. The record was of a typically high standard, including the superb dysfunctional family story 'Thanksgiving' that includes a reminiscence of Loudon's own childhood disguised as a dream in a section where he is lying down and looking at the stars. It could have been written by Raymond Carver. The album even had a single 'T.S.D.H.A.V. (This Song Don't Have A Video)', (as it happened it did, but it wasn't played anywhere), but by this stage Loudon was preaching to the converted. He was writing and recording some of the most assured music of his

career and his regular fans were more than appreciative of his
frequent live performances. He could sell out mid-size theatres in
almost any town but without the benefit of regular television or
radio exposure it was difficult to break new ground or nurture new
fans.

Silvertone concentrated on getting as much mileage as it could
from The Stone Roses, who were still riding high on the waves from
1988's 'second summer of love', and when the label secured some
surprise success with the rejuvenated bluesman Hooker, it left
Loudon even further down their list of priorities. He was soon
forgotten.

At 15, Martha spent a fractious year with her father in New York.
They argued constantly, with Martha understandably unhappy and
confused at her father's abandonment of her mother and the family.
She admits that she didn't know her father at all well and that they
had never had the opportunity to talk about a lot of the issues that
concerned their relationship. It was a difficult year for both of them.
Perhaps thinking that she might take the same approach to family
communication as he had, Loudon gave her a Sigma guitar which
she gradually taught herself to play.

That same year Rufus decided to come out to Kate in a straightforward, no-mistakes possible, unequivocal way. During a visit to
Paris, after a perfect day spent sightseeing and shopping together,
he confronted her with the statement she had made some years
earlier when she had told him that she couldn't love him if he was
gay.

'But Mother, you don't love me,' he said.

When she realised what he meant, she replied, 'Of course I love
you,' and they both burst into tears.

Kate admitted to being worried about what being gay would mean
to her son, worried that he would be oppressed, worried that he
would be beaten up, worried especially that he would get AIDS
and die. Although she was not particularly religious, Kate remembers going to church to look for guidance. 'I said, "Oh my God this
is horrible." So I went and said a big prayer. I went to Sacré Coeur
and said, "Oh what am I going to do?" and it was like a lightning
bolt hit me and said, "Do nothing. You don't try to change a person.
It's not a sickness. Don't treat it as one."' In the end she realised

that she would just treat him the same as she always had and worry about him as any mother worries about their child; the fact that he was gay could not alter that.

After finishing at Millbrook, Rufus headed to McGill University in Montreal to study music. He hated it. He wasn't disciplined enough to learn the piano by rote, he couldn't abide the relentless practising and he got bogged down by the technical aspects of studying music, learning to read it, dissecting fugues ... 'I was turned off by the factory aspect for turning out these cookie-cutter musical types,' he said, although he also admitted that he wanted to go back to regular songwriting because he found it easier than studying. Within a couple of years he had dropped out and was back at home, working on constructing a set of songs and getting them ready to play some shows of his own.

The death of Loudon's father in 1992 inspired him to write and record perhaps the best album of his career. *History* is an intensely personal collection that is haunted by a real sense of mortality, perhaps the one basic human concern that Loudon had previously only touched on in humorous ways.

Here the sadness is real, deep-felt and raw. For the most part, it is a reflective album and even the few 'funny' songs ('Talking New Bob Dylan' and 'The Doctor') are in their own way wistful and tinged with regret. 'The Picture' spins an entire family story of a brother and sister relationship, in this case Loudon and Sloan, from the description of a single family snapshot. He describes a card table, a shoebox of crayons and two young siblings drawing together. In the background of the snapshot is the fender of their old automobile and Loudon realises he can't now name the make of car but his dad would've been able to if only he could ask him. With just this tiny detail, Loudon reveals so much about what is lost when a close friend or relation dies, the ease of recall of a seemingly trivial shared fact that has now disappeared for ever representative of greater truths that also vanish.

The heart-breaking 'Sometimes I Forget' expands on this feeling with a desolate inventory of objects left behind in his father's house: the empty suitcase in the hall, his wallet, his watch, his ring. Like Tom Waits' 'Soldier's Things' or the Beatles' 'Junk' it is a masterpiece of the poetry of bereavement divined among the jetsam of lives once lived.

In 'Father And Son' Loudon turns to Rufus and attempts to impart some wisdom, or at least advice, on father/son relationships. 'Everything changes but nothing is new,' he sings, likening his own arguments with his father to those that he now has with Rufus. At Rufus' age he hated his own dad and he suggests that now, looking back, hate and love could be interchangeable.

It's as if with the death of his father, he has decided that he needs to try to step into the role of father to Rufus, something that up to this point he perhaps felt he'd neglected to do. The writer Donald Barthelme, who had his own father/son problems, suggested that a son can never truly become a father, that he might with some 'amateur effort' produce children but that he remains a son in 'the fullest sense'.[15] This apparently contrary assertion makes more sense when we consider Barthelme's exposition in his 'Manual For Sons'[16] that the memory of a dead father is often 'more potent than the living presence of a father' and provides the inner voice that guides the son's every thought and action. In 'Father And Son' Loudon speaks to himself as much as to Rufus and speaks as Loudon Wainwright Jnr as much as he does Loudon Wainwright III.

If these songs address Loudon's often struggling relationships with his father and son, then 'Hitting You' is a jaw-droppingly frank account of his difficulties with his eldest daughter. It recalls an occasion many years earlier when Loudon had hit Martha when she had been playing up in the back of the car. He talks about her fear, anger and defiance and makes it clear that he knows she retains a lot of those feelings towards him even now. Coming so soon after their disastrous year together in New York, it's almost as if Loudon is dredging up the very worst thing he can remember doing to her so as to explain away her anger at him. By admitting to this, he is excusing himself by acknowledging he can never make it right. It is as if he hopes his penance will be served in the writing and performing of such a personal song. Martha later admitted that she

---

15. Barthelme, Donald, *The Dead Father*, Farrar, Strauss and Giroux, 1975, US.
16. ibid.

was happy to hear the song because at least it let her know that he felt bad about the incident.

History is a tremendous album, devastatingly frank and auto-biographical yet carefully constructed and multi-layered. If John Cheever, that other chronicler of Westchester County's lives and times, hadn't already been called the 'Chekhov of Suburbia'[17] then with this album alone Loudon could have claimed that title for himself.

That same year Loudon had a new girlfriend, the actress Ritamarie Kelly, and soon he had another baby daughter, Alexandra. He decided that he wouldn't live with Ritamarie and Alexandra imme-diately. He needed more time alone. It was a decision he would later document in the song 'A Year'. Martha recalls this incident as the one that finally inspired her to start writing songs. 'I got my first real burst of inspiration after my father had a child with someone and I found out they weren't going to stay together,' she recalled in a 2006 *Observer* feature on initial artistic inspirations. 'Suddenly life had become larger and more complicated, but in a positive way because now there was something to talk about.'

'The Lexie Song' became Martha's first composition and, of course, it was about her family. Initially she didn't play it to anybody, keeping the whole thing secret until she had written a few more songs.

Rufus had a lot of songs. He had put together a set of originals and a few choice cover versions and had started playing the local clubs in Montreal. Gradually he built up his confidence and devel-oped a set that incorporated piano songs, guitar songs and ad-libbing, rambling introductions which he soon discovered went down well with his audience. Sometimes he would get Martha up to sing backing vocals or to duet. Sometimes he would let her play one of her own songs.

After Loudon had seen him perform, he suggested he might like to come and open for him. He had a short tour booked and was happy to give his son a taste of life on the road. It took a while for Rufus to settle in front of his dad's crowd but after a few days

---

17. 'Evil Comes To Suburbia', John Cheever – review, John Leonard, *New York Times*, 29 April 1969.

Loudon was regretting asking him along. 'The first night I didn't go over too well,' remembers Rufus. 'His audience was a little rowdy, and the angry middle-aged men were there. But by the third night, I developed a thick skin and really did a great show. After that, my father came to me and said, "We're never doing a show together again." He felt threatened.'

In 1993, a Dutch television crew, led by acclaimed rock documentary film-maker Bram Van Splunteren, set out to make a one-hour show about Loudon that followed him on and off stage and even visited Kate and the children in Montreal. *One Man Guy* contains some uncomfortable interviews with Rufus and Martha talking about their father's tendency to write so explicitly about the family, with Rufus made particularly uneasy by some of the songs that Loudon had written about his mother.

'The songs that he writes about the members of the family do cause a little anxiety sometimes,' says Rufus, to which Loudon laughs uproariously and says, 'That's why I do it, folks! Punishment!'

Kate seemed less concerned, admitting that her admiration for Loudon the artist had sometimes got in the way of her anger with him as a person or even about the songs he had written about her. 'It was difficult to separate, "Oh God that's a good song" with "Oh, but it's about me. It's terrible!"'

Kate goes on to say that she thinks Loudon's songs about their time together were his original 'songs of hate' and that after a while she didn't care so much about being the subject of them, stoically admitting that at least they were well written: 'It was probably a good experience for him to spend those five rocky years with me else he wouldn't have gotten those songs.'

Throughout the documentary Loudon obviously relishes the attention of the film crew. At one point he admits that the previous year he had had a slight breakdown brought about by constant lonely touring, eating late at night on his own, always travelling. His difficultly in getting to sleep had resulted in him finding himself at the end of his tether, in tears in a London park. He had had to cancel part of a tour. Hinting that he remained somewhat disillusioned by the state of his career, that he wasn't as successful or as famous as he had hoped to be, towards the end of the film he admits: 'If I could have a camera crew come around with me every day, life would be great.'

If he couldn't be on camera every day at least he had a regular radio slot. Through much of the early 1990s, Loudon was writing and performing satirical songs on the *Morning Edition* show on National Public Radio. It was something he was particularly good at and showed how he could craft memorable songs from the slightest of items. Subjects he ribbed included ice-skater Tonya Harding, Newt Gingrich (to the tune of 'Santa Claus Is Coming To Town'), the 'Fat Gene' ('I'm not talking 501s') and the not-really-dead Elvis. As ever, some of his best material was written about himself including 'Wish List For Christmas' broadcast on Christmas Day 1992 in which Loudon pleads: 'What do I want for Christmas/How about a major break'. Some of these songs were recorded for later albums, and many of them were collected on 1999's *Social Studies* album, but, like most topical satire, they worked best when considered as ephemeral social comment.

Despite being nowhere near as driven as Loudon, Kate and Anna's career continued to garner praise from all quarters. In 1993 they were awarded the Order of Canada, the country's highest listed civilian honour, with the investiture taking place in April 1994. Their official commendation cites: 'Their harmonious voices, whimsical lyrics and instrumental versatility are complemented by the influences of folk, Celtic, gospel and bluegrass music. With their timeless songs, the McGarrigle sisters have touched the hearts and souls of all Canadians.' A decade later they would also receive the Governor General Performing Arts Award.

And it wasn't just Loudon who had attracted the attention of European television. The sisters would soon appear in a show themselves. BBC Scotland commissioned a series called *Transatlantic Sessions*, which was to be filmed at the Montgreenan Mansion House Hotel in Ayrshire and co-hosted by the Scottish fiddle player Aly Bain and the American Jay Ungar, who had composed the theme music to Ken Burns' *The Civil War* series that the McGarrigles had also worked on. The idea of the series was to bring together folk and country musicians from the US and the UK to play songs in an intimate setting. There would be no live audience and no staged performances as such, the musicians casually singing and playing and, on occasion, even reading the words from a page in front of them as though they were joining in with a song for the first time. Kate and Anna recorded their contributions over two days in late April 1995, playing with Emmylou Harris and Mary Black. Rufus appeared singing backing vocals on two songs: Stephen Foster's 'Hard Times Come Again No More' and the traditional 'Wild Mountain Thyme'. When it was eventually broadcast the following year, the series was widely praised for its honest simplicity.

Back in Canada Rufus fell in love for the first time with someone he saw walking down the street towards him in Montreal. Danny was straight and a drug-addict, which made things problematic, but Rufus was obsessed with him for years. In an interview with gay magazine the *Advocate* in 1998, Rufus explained their unusual relationship. 'We would sleep together and kiss for hours, and I was completely satisfied with it for some reason. He was so beautiful. He always had 10 or 12 girls surrounding him. He would come to me when he wanted to escape the constant fight over him. He needed not to have sex with someone and that would have to be a man. It was a kind of brotherly thing. It was beautiful actually.'

Inspired by Danny and with a batch of new songs written, Rufus decided to go into a studio and record some of them. After working on the well-received *Heartbeats Accelerating*, Pierre Marchand had gone on to produce a series of records for Sarah McLachlan, all of which had gone multi-platinum in Canada. Laid-back, easy to work with and well known to Rufus and family, he was the obvious candidate to approach to help make the first demos. The fact that Rufus could call on the help of an established, world-renowned record producer with his own custom studio rather than a local musician with an eight-track in his garage was one of the benefits of coming from a family of professional musicians. Not for the last time Rufus would discover that it's not always who you know, but who you know always helps.

Musicians can use demo recordings like visual artists use sketchbooks: a demo can be a diagram, an outline, skeletons of songs waiting for some colour, more layers, the skin of sophisticated instrumentation. Without a record deal or any imminent prospect of working with other musicians, Rufus just needed a tape to demonstrate that he could play so that prospective club owners and booking agents got some idea of his act.

To this end, the material that Rufus recorded with Marchand in Morin Heights were simple vocal and piano tunes recorded live. Marchand sought only to document the nascent songs, he didn't change anything and he didn't interfere other than to position the microphones and press the record button. Beneath their apparent simplicity the songs on this first cassette[18] showed a maturity in composition, with obvious roots in the classic show tunes and cabaret songs that Rufus adored, that would eventually allow many of them to be more sophisticatedly orchestrated and reimagined on his first album.

But as evidenced on the demo tape Rufus' songs were already quite at odds with his contemporaries. With bands like the Red Hot Chili Peppers, REM and the Smashing Pumpkins all over alternative and college radio, Rufus would have to compete for gigs and record deals with those bands' ever-hopeful, undiscovered, generally never-to-be-discovered soundalikes. He certainly didn't fit in with the alternative rock scene and, contrary to the expectations of those aware of Rufus' family history, his music did not sit any more comfortably with those on the traditional folk circuit.

'I love my mom's stuff and my dad's stuff,' he told the *Montreal Mirror*. 'I was always around folk obviously as a kid and I used to go on tour with them so I saw a lot of folk shows. I am happy for the influence but I've always tried to stay a bit apart from that whole scene. And tried to develop my own persona and aim in a different direction.'

That Rufus' take on singer-songwriting harked back to an earlier

---

18. The comments in the text refer to *Rufus Wainwright/Songs*, a privately produced demo tape recorded in 1995 by Pierre Marchand. This cassette demo is often referred to as 'The DreamWorks Demos', although of course they were recorded before a deal with that label had been made. It is possible that there were different versions of this demo tape which would have featured a selection of the songs in various combinations. The copy referred to here is an original cassette which came with hand-drawn titling and a cover featuring two small black and white photos. The running order is as follows Side A: Foolish Love/ Heart Like A Highway/ Money Song/ Danny Boy Side B: Beauty Mark/ Damned Ladies/ Liberty Cabbage/ Ashes/ Matinee Idol. This is the full set of songs recorded as demos. As evidenced in the documentary film *All I Want* it is likely that one version of the demo existed which featured just six songs on a single side, although Rufus also refers to a demo of only three songs. None of these versions has been commercially released.

age becomes apparent within the first moment of the opening track on the demo tape. 'Foolish Love' is a sepia-toned anti-love song aching with the quiet desperation of somebody besotted but ultimately ignored.

The song's hook (and with this hook the seeds are really sown for his whole career) comes at two and three-quarter minutes in, when the second chorus ends with a drawled 'yeah, yeah' and moves on into a part-vamped honky-tonk piano bridge which meanders and stumbles like Buster Keaton carrying an ice-cream cone across a crowded room before somehow wandering back triumphantly 45 seconds later, cone dripping but intact, into the verse.

And it is this 'yeah, yeah' that really makes the song. Nonchalant but authentic, the opening 'I don't want to hold you and feel so helpless' instantly grabs the attention and sends notions of Cole Porter and George Gershwin waltzing out of the speakers, but it's that 'yeah, yeah' that hits the exact spot, that nails it, that flashes up every cool idea of the dapper pianist in that half-remembered Hollywood film that's spooling by. And it shows that Rufus Wainwright knows that a song, no matter how cleverly structured, has to live and breathe. And has to be human. And it's that simple something that he has carried through his whole career.

From here the whole demo plays out like a bijou, one-man cabaret act – you can almost see the red velvet curtain behind the piano, the gold brocade coming loose, dust in the details, the percussive chink of ice in glasses.

'Heart Like A Highway' features Martha on backing vocals. It's another doomed affair but this time it's Rufus who loses interest and the love in his fickle heart fades away. Lyrically mannered (how many songs include the word 'fandangle') and with the title echoing Anna McGarrigle's breakthrough song, it subsequently became known as 'That Night', yet remains otherwise unrecorded.

More fun is the 'Money Song' in which Rufus imagines himself, like Cole Porter, in a room at the top of the Waldorf-Astoria. It includes a simply comic Canadian take on English monarchy and Commonwealth, resentment and aspiration. Queen Elizabeth tosses off her tiara and finds that not only has her Rubens been stolen but somebody has replaced her corgis with mongrels. Like something from *The Queen is Dead*, you half expect a mooning Morrissey to come in with his sponge and his rusty spanner.

'Danny Boy' is a companion piece to 'Foolish Love'; together they are the beginning and the end of a relationship between a gay and a straight man. The song showed that Rufus was prepared to deal openly with his sexuality and it showed that he was unafraid of using aspects of his private life in his songs in the same way that his father had. While Rufus had prophesised Noah's Ark was floating down Montreal's Avenue Du Parc in 'Foolish Love', here 'Seerauber Jenny's' vengeful 'ship with eight sails' is threatening to come around the bend straight out of Brecht and Weill's *Threepenny Opera*, all 50 guns ablazing. But he wouldn't see it, so blinded was he by love.

Danny was the subject of both songs and would subsequently even have his photo collaged into the artwork for the first album. 'You broke my heart,' sings Rufus before immediately forgiving him.

The Kate-approved 'Beauty Mark' benefits from having been played so often that the demo recording is casually tossed off like a familiar standard and even the piano mistake in the middle endears just because it has been left intact like he knows that he'll nail it the next time and, most importantly, he knows that he is going to be playing a song this strong for many years to come.

If pop songs referencing opera are few, then 'Damned Ladies' must be the only one that references nine of them – a love song to tragic heroines who are doomed to repeat their deaths night after night or revolution after revolution the moment the curtain rises, the needle touches or the laser hits. Heroines trapped for ever in a cyclical tragedy: loved and mourned like family, generation after generation, the venerated dead and sacrificial lambs of opera's relentless theatre of cruelty. 'In the song, I lament how these women are constantly dying brutal deaths, which I can see coming but cannot stop. It gets me every time,' said Rufus.

A politically expedient neologism like the second Gulf War era 'Freedom' fries, Liberty Cabbage was a euphemism for sauerkraut during the first World War. Rufus uses this archaic terminology to question an America that's as likely to strangle him as hug him in its 'strong arms' and where the people he loves can be metaphorically stoned, presumably for their sexual orientation. It's one of his very earliest songs, certainly predating 'Beauty Mark' (and surely too overwrought and lyrically clumsy to have been Kate-approved). Although never properly released, 'Liberty Cabbage', an unusually overt political song, remained an occasional part of the live set for many years. Another otherwise unavailable song languishing on the tape is 'Ashes', which suffers from some ponderous lyrics linking Rapunzel and Rasputin, despite featuring at least half of a quite beautiful chorus.

On Halloween 1993, the actor River Phoenix died of a drug over-dose in the street outside the Viper Room, the Sunset Strip club co-owned at the time by Johnny Depp. While 'Matinee Idol', the closing song on the demo tape, 'a Weimar Republic kind of thing,' said Rufus, is ostensibly about the death of Phoenix, it's the actor in his signature role as the narcoleptic hipster Mike Waters in *My Own Private Idaho* (1991) who is ascending with angels as much as River himself. In the Gus Van Sant movie Mike's unreciprocated love for Scott Favor (Keanu Reeves) must have resonated with Rufus. Mike obsesses over Scott who is merely waiting on his ticket out of there – biding his time for his inheritance – and eventually moving on in the same way that the straight men that Rufus fixed on inevitably would. Rufus spoke about seeing Danny in the street and instantly falling in love: 'It was like meeting a god, the light from him almost burning me.' In the movie Mike remembers seeing Scott for the first time and thinking that he was a comic book hero. 'I'd make a bet with anybody right now,' he says. 'Scott is a saint or a hero, or some higher placed person.' Scott is Danny. Both Mike and Rufus are ultimately let down.

'I remember the day he died. It was such a shock because I was so obsessed with him. I identified with his character in *Stand By Me* (1986) and then from there on, it was a big love affair,' said Rufus, interviewed after the track had been included on his debut album. 'It was shocking, but also a very glamorous, Hollywood kind of demise. Very Valentino-esque.'

The music on the tape was timeless, or hopelessly out of time, depending on your propensity for pathos and passion with your romantic piano. It was easy to understand why some people didn't get past the first song and why others would play the nine songs through, fall in love with them, rewind them and play them again. And again.

Happy to have finally got some rudimentary recordings of his own songs down on tape, Rufus went to stay with Loudon in New York, the idea being to try and get some shows and to somehow work his way into the scene. He hung out at places like the Crow Bar in the East Village, sitting drinking in the corner making eyes at drag-superhero Justin Bond and his fabulous coterie of friends who rejoiced in names like Lily of the Valley or Mistress Formica. If Rufus ever needed a drag name he'd decided he'd probably call himself Lady Cadaver, though nobody ever asked him. The people he saw as the Alphabet City jet-set just ignored him and he'd end up going home alone or else he'd find some other lonely soul and slope away with them convinced that the real fun was going on without him.

He got a casual job working in a movie theatre and between shifts he tried touting his demo around town. There was one place that he had set his heart on playing. Jeff Buckley had built his reputation, while at the same time redefining his whole artistic approach, by playing at a small coffee bar at St Mark's Place in the East Village. After Buckley had signed a major label deal with Columbia it was decided that the label would initially release an EP of these solo performances from New York to act as an introduction to the artist. The *Live From Sin- é* EP was released in November 1993 and it put the venue on the map. Now everybody wanted to play there and Rufus was no exception. If he could just play one gig at *Sin- é* then he was certain that it would be a huge step forward.

He remembers taking his tape to *Sin- é* three times and being turned down each time. As is sometimes the way with setbacks like this, Rufus illogically decided to hold it against Jeff Buckley personally and vowed that he would never listen to him from that point on. Perhaps Rufus thought Buckley was encroaching on territory he had marked out for himself. Buckley was a solo performer with a similarly striking tenor voice and one who wasn't afraid to throw in covers from the likes of Edith Piaf or Billie Holiday.

The truth was that the demo tape was probably never even listened to. At the time Buckley had submitted his first demo back in early 1991, the owners had been receiving more than 80 tapes a week and they rarely had time to listen to those. Since Buckley had made it, the flood of hopeful demo tapes had became a deluge. Nevertheless Rufus took it to heart and without trying any of the other clubs that were putting on gigs he went back to Montreal. 'It was a real failure the first time I came to New York. I felt as if Jeff Buckley had defeated me in this weird way, without him even knowing it.'

2.5

Martha had been studying acting but found that she was more interested in finding out about herself through writing songs than she was in creating characters on a stage or on the page. Almost reluctantly she found that she soon had her own set and was playing solo shows. 'I tried to stay away from it to an extent,' she told the *Guardian* in 2006. 'I always liked to sing but I certainly wasn't as focused as my brother was.' In the same interview she says how it was the pile up of things – falling in and out of love, an abortion and her father's new baby – that had inspired her first song, that got her writing and out singing in bars.

She guested with Loudon on a track on his new record, *Grown Man*. He had followed up *History* with *Career Moves*, another live record which showcased some sprightly performances of his favourite 1980s tracks along with a handful of new songs. It was a shame that he didn't hold over the new songs for *Grown Man* as it was one of the weakest records he had ever released, padded out with corny joke songs, pastiche country and western, misfiring pop and maudlin self-pity.

'Father Daughter Dialogue', however, is an extraordinary song in which Martha sings the charges against Loudon as a bad parent who prefers writing songs than facing reality, to which he replies that the person who sings those songs is only an idealised version of who he wants to be, it's not him at all. He sings that he expiates himself with songs then admits that it's actually not him anyway. As Loudon had scripted both parts of the song, it is a kind of fiction that exists in a strange duality, a contradiction, a double bluff of a double bluff. He is making it clear that in a lot of his songs what appears to be a documentary narrative is an elaborate alternative fiction where the truth is still visible but is hidden between the lines. As the novelist Jeanette Winterson once said: 'Truth is a shape-shifting thing that is not solid. Truth is not to be found in the facts.'

Still smarting from his earlier experience, Rufus was determined to get himself ready for another attempt at making it in New York. To that end he was desperate to play and would perform anywhere for virtually nothing just for the experience. He started to appear regularly at Café Sarajevo on Clark Street, Montreal, a small restaurant and bar that had live music in the evenings.

The bar's owner Osman Koulenovitch remembers Rufus first coming in and asking to be allowed to play a gig. 'He introduced himself and he spoke with me and I found him nice and charming. I've never listened to a demo tape to decide if somebody could play at the club. I look at the person. If the person seems sincere, original, refined I give them a place. If even an established musician was insincere I wouldn't support them. Rufus was completely unknown and didn't play the sort of music I like but I found him original and elegant and dedicated to his art. And he was a good person.'

Café Sarajevo usually hosted nights of blues and jazz. With his Bosnian roots, Koulenovitch was particularly keen on gypsy music[19] but he wasn't afraid to offer shows to young performers who made a good impression on him and even though he was startled by how Rufus looked he was happy to give him a regular weekly slot. 'He was made up like a girl,' remembers Koulenovitch. 'Dyed red-yellow hair, make-up on his eyes and his lips.'

The bar had an established clientele of Montreal bohemians, journalists, poets and artists but Rufus brought in a crowd that Koulenovitch remembers as being punky, and very badly dressed. 'At the time Café Sarajevo was a chic place, but when I first saw the people that came to see him, I wasn't sure whether I should throw them out!' he laughs.

---

19. Café Sarajevo has now moved to a new location on St Laurent in Montreal. It remains an important live music venue.

Within a few weeks the word about Rufus' shows had spread and the small bar would become packed. 'We had about 50 seats but for his shows he managed to cram in 80 or 100 people. They sat on the floor all squeezed together. Far more people than I could really cope with.'

Rufus was paid very little, around $50 per night by the end of his time there, but then his fans weren't making the owner rich by any means. They would stay for hours and spend very little. 'Or nothing at all,' says Koulenovitch. 'But even if I didn't make anything it didn't matter. I'm an artist too, not a businessman and Rufus needed a place where he could develop. It was a good atmosphere to build a rapport with the audience and he had total freedom because there wasn't a boss throwing him dirty looks because his fans weren't ordering anything. If he'd started singing in another bar where the owner thought only about profit, about how many beers he would sell, he would never have had a chance to continue playing.

'He didn't ask for any money in the beginning either, he just got the experience of being supported. I have a philosophical side. I was once a teacher and an educator so I have a tendency to take young people under my wing as if they were my sons. Rufus appreciated that.'

Rufus' hard work was paying off. Within a few months he had developed his basic set into a full evening's show with new original songs, cover versions, an occasional cameo from Martha on backing vocals and even a few witty anecdotes with which he introduced the songs.

The piano at the club was an upright that stood against the wall at one end of the room. Koulenovitch remembers Rufus asking for a mirror to be cut and glued on to the front so that he could look back at the audience as he played. Rufus was intent on becoming an old-fashioned entertainer and he worked on his stagecraft in the same methodical way that he worked on the composition of his songs. He said he liked to be able to see who he was playing to, though Koulenovitch suspected he liked admiring himself too.

Rufus recorded one of his Café Sarajevo shows and started using that as a demo tape, feeling that it was more representative of how he was maturing as an artist than his earlier studio recordings. But by the end of 1995 it was the first demo tape that would finally get him noticed outside of his home town.

Back in 1968, Van Dyke Parks, a maverick record producer/composer, had released the bizarre but brilliant *Song Cycle* album. Previously a child actor in TV shows and in the 1956 movie *The Swan* with Grace Kelly and Alec Guinness, Parks was best known as a session man for the likes of the Byrds and Tim Buckley before he hooked up with Brian Wilson to work on the legendary *SMiLE* album. Parks contributed lyrics to many of the classic Beach Boys songs recorded during the sessions but the project was ultimately shelved due, in the main, to Brian Wilson's deteriorating mental health (they would eventually complete the album together nearly 40 years later). Parks' work with Wilson on songs like 'Surf's Up' and 'Heroes and Villains' was impressive enough for Lenny Waronker to offer him the chance to record his own album for Warner Brothers.

Song Cycle, the resulting record, was an intense mix of styles from film soundtrack, to ragtime, to vaudeville, to musique-concrete, to baroque, often all at once on the same track so at times it sounded like a symphonic pop version of Ornette Coleman's *Free Jazz* album (1961) where two separate bands play simultaneously from the left and right channels. When it was released, Warners' press sheet called it 'the most important, creative and advanced pop recording since *Sgt Pepper*'. Undoubtedly it was an impressive work and contemporary reviewers raved about it. *Rolling Stone* called Parks a creative genius – 'the Gertrude Stein of the new pop music'. There was only one problem. Nobody bought it.

Later Parks would admit that the album hadn't turned out exactly as he had planned: 'It wasn't until after I was finished that I realised there were no songs on there. An album with no songs was entirely unintentional.' Regardless of whether it sold or not, Parks looked upon the record as a learning experience made with a 'mindset about the importance of studio exploration'. It might have cost more than $30,000 to make (the usual budget in 1967 was no more than $10,000) but Parks says 'every cent was spent on the purpose of learning'.

By the mid-1990s Parks had continued to produce his own

records, branching out into film soundtracks, and also regularly worked as an arranger for other musicians. He'd even turned up as an actor again in an episode of *Twin Peaks*. His *Song Cycle* album was rightly regarded as a classic and its influence could be heard on artists like Beck, Flaming Lips, Mercury Rev and Jim O'Rourke.

A couple of people had told Rufus that his music sounded a little bit like Van Dyke Parks. And maybe a little bit like Randy Newman, who himself had been produced by Waronker and Parks. There was the same mix of old-fashioned styles with more modern pop arrangements. When he found out that Loudon knew Parks and was due to have dinner with him he asked his father to pass on his studio demo tape.

Parks loved the songs and sent them on to Lenny Waronker, who had just started creating the DreamWorks record label. Said Parks: 'The tape was a cut above anything I'd heard [at that time], in its individual nature, its intimate interpretations of small, personal events. I got a sense of place in his work, Montreal, the French, European underwear mixed with American defiance and some good, no-nonsense Canadian intellectualism, all thrown into these great, slightly post-adolescence reminiscences. I thought he should be given an opportunity, so I decided to try to effect a contract for Loudon's son.'

Waronker remembers the tape arriving with a note. 'Van Dyke wrote something like "I usually don't try to encourage these young kids, but in this case, this one's irresistible."'

'I was leery,' Waronker told the *New York Times* in 1998. 'Rufus' stuff was rock, it was folk, and it was also full of cabaret and show-tune influence. Part of my job is to think, "Where is this going to fit into the marketplace? Is there a place for Rufus on the radio?" But then two of my children, who are also musicians, told me how much they loved the tape. And then, completely by coincidence I was talking to Michael Stipe and he said, out of nowhere, "Have you heard this guy Rufus Wainwright?" I was sold.'[20]

Parks called Rufus in Montreal and told him that Waronker had

---

20. In an interview in Q Magazine in October 2007, Stipe says that it was actually Waronker who had first played the tape to him after he had visited the DreamWorks offices: 'I went to visit them and Mo is like, "You got to hear this!" They put on Rufus' demo and left the room. Talk about confidence in what they had. I was shocked at how good it was.'

liked his tape and suggested he sent some more songs with a letter of introduction. The night Rufus sat down to compose the letter, the phone rang. It was Waronker and he asked Rufus to go and see him in Los Angeles.

When they met Waronker remembers the first question that Rufus put to him was, '"I'm gay; is that a problem?" I realised that here was a guy so comfortable with himself, yet so aware of what the music world – and the world – is like, that he could be direct and realistic. I knew I could work with a kid like that.'

Although much would be made about Rufus becoming the first openly gay artist to sign to a major label, this isn't strictly true. Back in the early 1970s Steven Grossman, a now almost totally forgotten singer-songwriter, was signed to Mercury records and released his solo LP *Caravan Tonight* in 1974. This undeservedly obscure album sounds a little like Cat Stevens and deals unambiguously with gay issues like coming out to the family (the song 'Out' deals with a mother's disappointment and a father's homophobia) and the perils of cruising. (The explicit 'Christopher's Blues' punchline is 'You're a fool to give candy to a stranger.')

As a more documentary account of a queer life lived, his record was at odds with the then just about acceptable gay-glam half-life propagated by David Bowie. At the time of Bowie's 'coming out' to the press he was, according to one biographer, ensuring his mother knew that he wasn't really gay and that it was just part of his act. For Bowie and the glitter crowd, a man could wear feather boas, make-up and tin-foil gowns and nobody would bat a false eyelash as long as their supposed gayness stayed on the right side of camp showmanship and didn't dwell on the nitty-gritty, sometimes mundane, aspects of homosexual life.

Jobriath, a genuinely out major label act of the time, found there was little public interest in his music, not because he was gay but because he was unfairly seen as being an overhyped Bowie copyist after Elektra squandered so many thousands of dollars on giant billboards and elaborate stage shows that the critics had turned on him before he had even really been given a chance.

Grossman, however, was no glam rocker, nor did he disguise his sexuality with sci-fi similes and euphemistic spacemen. His simple songs spoke freely of the hopes, joys and fears of living life as a gay man in contemporary America. Perhaps because of this frankness, his album received positive coverage in the gay press but barely registered anywhere else and soon disappeared. Proto-supermodel Twiggy covered the LP's title track on her self-titled album in 1976 but a disillusioned Steven Grossman never released another album.[21]

Rufus has always said that even if he'd wanted to, he could not have pretended to be anything other than what he was. He was too poor a liar to try and pretend he was straight. For their part Waronker and DreamWorks couldn't foresee any real problems for an out pop star in the late 1990s. After all, Rufus' sexuality was woven into the fabric of his performance and composition. You couldn't have one without the other. Within days of their meeting, DreamWorks had prepared a contract and forwarded it to Montreal.

---

21. Grossman did record another album's worth of material in a California studio in 1991 but this remains unissued. He died of AIDS in September 1991. *Caravan Tonight* has never been reissued.

ACT 3

'What the world needs is more geniuses with humility, there are so few of us left.'

Oscar Levant

'Ah, But a man's reach should exceed his grasp/Or what's a heaven for?'

Robert Browning from *Andrea Del Sarto*, 1855

3.1

DreamWorks SKG was a media empire founded in 1994 by enter-tainment moguls Steven Spielberg, Jeffrey Katzenberg and David Geffen. With Spielberg and former Disney chairman Katzenberg focusing on the film productions, Geffen, already long established in the record industry, headed up the music department with a remit to produce film soundtracks and to discover and nurture new music.

The idea was to create a company that put the artists and creatives in more control of their work and by building a centralised studio complex provide state-of-the-art facilities for use by both their music and film companies.[1] With plans like these and initial invest-ment capital of around £2 billion, it was obvious that DreamWorks had visions of empire-building on an epic, old-Hollywood scale. In order to run DreamWorks records in a manner befitting these high ideals, Geffen hired two proven old-school record company greats – Mo Ostin and Lenny Waronker.

---

1. As it turned out, the plans for a 1,100 acre project in west Los Angeles, which would have been the first major new studio development in the city since First National Studios bulldozed Burbank in 1926, were ultimately scuppered by environmental protests as the targeted building area was an important wetlands site.

In the late 1950s Frank Sinatra had been increasingly frustrated by his dealings with his record label Capitol and, as one of the first artists to both understand the power a performer actually had and have the clout to act on that knowledge, was looking to move on. He tried to buy the Verve label but was ultimately unsuccessful so instead decided to just take Verve's accountant, Mo Ostin, and set up a new artist-friendly label of his own.

In 1960, Ostin helped create Reprise Records and Sinatra had a new home. Although the label did well, as the 1960s progressed Sinatra's decision to not sign any rock'n'roll bands was proving restrictive and financially costly. Reprise was ultimately sold on to Warner Brothers. Free from the restraints imposed by Sinatra's musical prejudices, Ostin proved to have an uncanny ability to sign talented musicians and would soon bring Jimi Hendrix, Neil Young and The Kinks to the label.

Ostin also retained a reputation for always putting the artist at the forefront of the company, something he put down to Sinatra's founding ethos at Reprise. 'Frank's whole idea was to create an environment which both artistically and economically would be more attractive for the artist than anybody else had to offer. That wasn't how it was anywhere else. You had financial guys, lawyers, marketing guys. Their priorities may not have been the music. One of the great things about Warners, I always felt, was our emphasis and priority was always about the music.' And that Reprise/Warner Brothers philosophy was exactly what Geffen was looking for at DreamWorks.

Ostin's protégé at Warners had been Lenny Waronker, who had been snapped up from Liberty Records after proving himself as a producer of impressive demo recordings with a variety of acts on almost no budget. Waronker was another man with a reputation for understanding the importance of the artist within the company set-up. He'd worked closely with strong-willed musicians like Randy Newman and Van Dyke Parks and had, of course, signed the McGar-rigles to their first record deal. Waronker was a forward-thinking yet experienced executive and together with Ostin formed a dream team to push DreamWorks forward.

The first thing the pair did was to create an A&R department because they knew it was the most important part of any record company. Waronker explained his thoughts about the importance of A&R in an industry training video in 2006: 'You're always looking for somebody who has vision and somebody who's original and who's not afraid to take chances. They scare you a bit because they're always a bit ahead of you which is what you want, so you have to at times just keep your mouth shut, and other times if you have the right dialogue and you have the right words, throw it out there. Smart artists will listen. If you don't have an artist roster that is one step ahead of the record company, the record company is going to be in trouble somewhere along the line.'

Among the first artists to be signed to DreamWorks were George Michael; the innovative, yet doomed, noirish 'low rock' three-piece Morphine; Mark Oliver Everett's Eels and Rufus Wainwright.

DreamWorks signed Rufus in January 1996. However, Waronker had no plans to hurry him into recording and releasing an album; his idea was to take it slowly and allow Rufus time to develop as a performer and give him time to hone his songs on stage. Initially he was to stay put in Montreal and continue to play the circuit there.

Waronker had hired Jim Merlis as a publicist for DreamWorks. Merlis had headed Geffen's publicity department for many years and overseen major artists including Nirvana and Mary J. Blige. Without providing him with anything much in the way of information so as not to give him any preconceptions, Waronker sent Merlis up to Canada to see Rufus play a showcase set at a club in Montreal.

The showcase arranged for Rufus was at Club Soda, on Avenue du Parc, a more formal cabaret-style club than the intimate Café Sarajevo and was set for 24 January, only a week or two after he had inked his contract. It was his biggest solo concert to date. Invigorated by the confidence of knowing that all of his family would be in attendance, Rufus had prepared a longer than usual two-part set. With the knowledge that a recording contract was already in the bag, this would not be the often slightly needy, slightly pleading performance that so many artists end up giving when prospective record company figures are in the crowd.

His charismatic performing style was as much a part of the entertainment as the marked progression in his songwriting since the time of the demos and he carried the two-hour show like an old pro, mixing classic standards with his own numbers and demonstrating how accomplished a performer he had become before ever having made a record. Everything he had learned from his parents, from Loudon's humour and honesty to Kate's musicality and dark romanticism, had prepared him for this and he was more than ready.

After feigning surprise at the number of people at the show ('This is crazy. You're all here to see David Geffen. Well, he's not here!'), Rufus began proceedings with 'Matinee Idol', then vamped a little harmony in the instrumental break on 'Foolish Love', then moved into the parlour with a Schubert song and the wish that those who had seen him at his intimate café shows would now follow him to his inevitable stadium rock performances.

Martha (introduced as 'Pounie', her family nickname) joined him to sing back-up on a song and then sang her own number. 'Question of Etiquette' was a retitling of 'The Lexie Song', the first thing she had ever written and one that looked at the confusing state of her sibling relations, brother and two half-sisters, with the pledge that 'we can pretend that we're a family'. She had played the song as a guest of Loudon at his Bottom Line show in New York just a few days earlier and here, with her father in the audience and out of control of proceedings, she relished spotlighting his implied laissez-faire attitude to child-rearing. In her early performances, Martha often looked a little nervous when she took to the stage alone, unsure of her place, of what was expected of her and of how she would be perceived by what was, usually, either her father's or her big brother's crowd. But the moment she started singing the anxiety seemed to vanish. It would only return when the last note of her performance faded away and 'Martha the singer' disappeared and was replaced by Martha the daughter and little sister.

Demonstrating he had higher aspirations than mere pop success, Rufus resurrected a French aria from Lalo's *Le Roi d'Ys*, although, as he had learned the song from repeatedly listening to a vintage Beniamino Gigli recording, his lyrics were sung in what he called 'Fretalian', turning the aubade into an often meaningless melange of not quite French words buried under Gigli's Italian pronunciation. Nevertheless it was a bold experiment that showed off the legato phrasing that he would carry from opera and turn into a signature style of his pop work. The elongated lines sometimes left him gasping for breath like a new swimmer struggling to get the last few feet across the pool to reach the safety of the side but it was a technical breathing problem, evident also on some of his own songs in his early shows, and one on which he worked as his career progressed.

If an aria wasn't enough to show that he was unafraid to move beyond pop, the pair of show tunes that closed the first set amply revealed both his versatility and his unabashed relish in embracing unfashionable musical genres and making them his own. Cole Porter's 'Get Out Of Town' was quickly followed by a sprightly run through the standard 'Keep Cool Fool' for which he had primed various friends and family members to sing along on the chorus and which ended with him bellowing 'Vegas . . . Here . . . I . . . Come . . .!' like a pastiche of an old showman, head back and jazz hands thrust forward to grab the spotlight. He left the stage to riotous applause.

The second set opened with a strident run through John Cale's 'Dying On The Vine' (Cale had been invited to the show but failed to attend) before floundering with a pair of songs that Rufus announced as coming from an opera which he was writing about 'Bela', his childhood alter ego who lives with his mother in South America, as deposed, ruined aristocracy. Although both showed meagre promise, the lyrics to 'The Bela Song', to put it kindly, sounded as if they had been badly translated from another language and 'Red Thread', played for the first time ever, at five minutes becomes a turgid indulgence far too long before it ends, and more or less invited the audience to start talking among themselves.

It was left to Martha to grab the crowd's attention again while Rufus took a breather. She sounded uncannily like Lucinda Williams on her own 'Country Song' but her standout performance was on the stunning solo 'Gone To Sea' in which she addressed Rufus' new success, admitted to her jealousy, and warned him that his new-found life has got a price. It's an intricate song, compositionally close to some of Loudon's complicated line structures but borrowing from the McGarrigle sisters' vocabulary of water symbolism, and she performed it quite beautifully. No wonder she had asked Rufus to leave the stage before she began to sing. It was almost as if she was stating her own case to be taken seriously as a solo artist now that her brother was on his way, from right in the middle of Rufus' set.

There was something of a public rapprochement as Rufus thanked Loudon for helping him and said: 'We've had a hard time relating in the past, in certain ways, but I know that with music we'll always be great souls together,' before singing a song he had written about his father called 'Two Gold Rings'.

By the end of the show, the whole family were up on stage performing a version of the traditional cowboy song, 'Old Paint', which Loudon had sung with Kate on his second album. 'The generational thing, it's great,' says Loudon before they traded verses, harmonies and wisecracks. As Loudon sang the line, 'His wife she died in a pool-room fight', Kate quipped, 'You wish!' to great cheers, only for Loudon to bat back, 'The night is young!' to an even louder response. Right at the end, the parents almost upstaged the children.

After the show Jim Merlis was suitably impressed with Rufus. He recalls telling his wife: 'This is the most talented musician I've ever seen. This is not about pop culture, it's about centuries of great music.'

At the suggestion of Waronker, and after a teary farewell show at Café Sarajevo, by March Rufus had moved to New York and started playing a residency at Fez, a tiny, 130-capacity, basement club on the corner of Great Jones and Lafayette Street, just seven blocks west of where his father had first found success at the old Gaslight Café almost 20 years earlier. With its gold lamé curtains and banquette seating, Fez was the perfect spot for Rufus to introduce his cabaret-style show to New York. Regulars liked to think of it as the kind of club you might see in an old Dean Martin movie. It was the closest you could get to an old-fashioned variety club in Manhattan at the time. At Fez it was possible to sit and eat a meal while whatever entertainment was unfolding remained just a pleasant distraction, a secondary part of your night out. If you didn't feel like eating you could just as easily concentrate on drinking and digging the music. There was no set policy for booking acts, no particular prevalent house style. One night it could be jazz, the next night soul, the following night a singing impressionist. Everybody from Alex Chilton to Xaviera Hollander had performed there. With his eclectic repertoire, Rufus fitted right in.

The shows were arranged by Merlis. It was still standard practice for a label to support an act through an early series of shows;

Warners had done the same with the McGarrigles' ill-fated Boston jaunt back in 1976, and it meant that Rufus could work on his material without necessarily worrying about bringing in his own crowd. 'He was playing for audiences that were talking through his shows,' remembers Merlis. 'He really had to tough it out and work hard. It made him a better performer, a bit like the Beatles going to Hamburg.' But it wasn't only disinterested spectators that Rufus had to win over – he also had to compete with the no. 6 train that periodically ran along the wall right behind the bar causing the room to vibrate and the punters to shake in their seats.

Penny Arcade went out of her way to bring Rufus to the attention of many of her friends and associates from New York's art and underground scene, urging people to go and see him. Danny Fields, city hipster extraordinaire who had roomed with Edie Sedgwick, hung out with The Velvet Underground and who, as a scout for Elektra Records, had brought Iggy and the Stooges to the attention of the record-buying public (only for that public to largely ignore them), was impressed by what he saw: 'His father was a person of whom I'd always been very fond, and in whose signing to Atlantic I had had an offbeat little part. Naturally, Rufus was talented; think of who his parents are. Because of his pedigree, he would have been taken seriously just by walking in the door, and then of course he demonstrated the strong songwriting talent one would expect. And then some.'

Rufus worked hard, picking up a following by word of mouth alone. If he hadn't already been signed, it's probable that a steady stream of executives would have been seeking him out, caught up in the buzz that his shows were creating. As it was, many of New York's industry insiders were becoming aware of him. By chance Merlis ran into Ann Powers, a connected freelancer for *Spin*, *Rolling Stone* and the *New York Times*. She happened to mention to him that she had heard that Rufus Wainwright was the hot new act. For Merlis this was exciting as he had barely begun pushing Rufus to any kind of media outlet. He was thrilled that his slow-play strategy was paying dividends.

Having passed the New York trial and sown the seeds for later success, by the autumn Rufus found himself in Los Angeles getting ready to make his first album. 'I thought of being in LA as like going to Versailles,' he said. 'You're going to the seat of power. I arrived with fabulous credentials because of my DreamWorks connection.'

Although they had originally considered letting Rufus produce himself, DreamWorks had hired Jon Brion to oversee the record. A talented multi-instrumentalist who had played in his own bands The Bats and then power-pop The Grays, he had achieved more success as a producer for his one-time girlfriend Aimee Mann on whose albums he combined influences ranging from Todd Rundgren to Stevie Wonder. Brion knew his way around a studio and was a perfect guide to getting Rufus' particular vision on tape.

Money was, comparatively, no problem. This, after all, was a label that had thought nothing of getting pop artist Roy Lichtenstein to design the company logo, a characteristic faux comic strip panel of a musical note in a thought bubble over hatched blue and white lines.[2] As the first undiscovered artist on the label, as opposed to the established artists that they had taken on for new projects, DreamWorks were prepared to allow Rufus all the time he needed to come up with his debut. As Rufus would later announce: 'My goal was for someone of my generation to make a record that sounds expensive and is big and over the top and luscious and not trying to sound street at all.' He said he wanted to hark back to the days of Frank Sinatra and Sarah Vaughan when labels spent big and 'records really sounded like records'.

The early recordings were started at Ocean Way Studios in Hollywood, where music business heavyweights like Eric Clapton and Barbra Streisand had recorded and where Quincy Jones had produced Michael Jackson's Bad. Over the coming months, they would drift through many other studios, trying out songs in different ways, generally starting with Rufus laying down the piano and then Brion playing most of the other instruments, adding things, taking things away, paring down Rufus' repertoire of songs until they had settled on a track-list that he could build the album around.

---

2. Roy Lichtenstein claims that the design took him three minutes and it was done as a favour to his friend Mo Ostin (interview, *Entertainment Weekly*, 23 August 1996). Dream-Works historians often suggest that the logo was the artist's final work but this would seem to be company myth-making and quite improbable as he exhibited a series of new landscapes in New York in late 1996 and was working on design proposals for sculptural work through to his death in 1997.

These weren't necessarily sessions in which the final tracks would be recorded, or even, in fact, properly begun; these were elaborate, some may suggest profligate, demo sessions using some of the most expensive studios in the world as other musicians might have used a home eight-track.

3.2

While Rufus embarked on his career as a full-time musician, Kate and Anna were continuing their infrequent visits to a far more modest recording studio to complete a new record. *Matapedia*, named after a town on the border of Quebec and New Brunswick where the Restigouche and Matapedia rivers meet, would be their first new album for six years and see them return to their classic folk styles after the electronic experimentation of *Heartbeats Accelerating*. Indeed, in places, and particularly at certain points of quavering sisterly harmony, the record sounds positively antiquated it is so far removed from how contemporary recordings sounded.

Fittingly, much of *Matapedia* is concerned with getting old and time passing: death, decay or change. It's a theme that is taken right through to the album sleeve with its brown tones and verdigris, its lichen and rust. On the cover the sisters are photographed back to back on chairs on a railway track. It's an image perhaps too reminiscent of a Mack Sennett silent comedy cliffhanger to be taken seriously and, in typical McGarrigles' style, though probably unintentionally, succeeds in puncturing at least a tiny hole in the album's sombre mood.

The title track begins with a story where Martha is mistaken for Kate by one of Kate's old boyfriends who holds her and looks into her eyes like a teenage boy would do. This was an actual event that Kate says 'freaked Martha out'. Kate explained the background to the track on a radio show later in the year: '[Martha] came home and she said, "Mom, this guy kind of grabbed me and he looked as if he had seen a ghost." . . . What had never occurred to me was the fact that I never thought that she looked like me. I mean she kind of has fair hair and blue eyes and she's taller than I am and I started watching and I said, "Oh, yeah, her hairline is the same. And she often likes to wear my old clothes . . ." Half of her is made up of me and you start to understand that.'

When Kate brought this part of the song to Anna, her sister suggested that she incorporate the story of a road trip that the man had taken with Kate many years earlier. This becomes an urgent race alongside the river in order to catch a boat before it leaves. Singing down the distance and the time they have left – 20 minutes/20 miles – the vocal line taking on the rhythm of the road and the sound of the river. It makes for a dramatic opening to the album and is a counterpoint to Anna's 'Song For Gaby' about their mother who had sadly passed away. Both songs in particular, and the rest of the record more generally, are about reconciling one's place in the world as a child, as a parent and as somebody whose own parent has died. As Loudon had found new pathos with the death of his father on his *History* album, here the McGarrigles react to the death of their mother with a record of profound beauty and sorrowful realisation.

'Song For Gaby' is a moving, personal song. To listen to it almost feels as though you are intruding on private grief, rather like a visit to a beautiful country churchyard only to find when you step inside to admire the church, a family funeral is in progress. Anna admitted that the song was a difficult one for them to perform live. 'It's not really a song about our mother because our mother is more complicated than to write just a three-minute song about. But it is about all of the things that you normally love, like a certain kind of bird, or a flower that kind of revolts you because it only reminds you of your mother's death. I find it hard to sing on stage. I don't like to bring people down. But at the time I wrote it, it meant a heck of a lot to me.'

The secondary theme of failed or abandoned or even unobtained love is explored in Kate's 'I Don't Know', a brutal exposition of the devastation that love can wreak, whether that love be familial or erotic. In the beginning she sings that love is like a bullet that can tear your heart apart but by the end of the song it is the grief of a love achieved but cut short that rends. Even on the collaboration with Philippe Tatartcheff, 'Arbre', the tree that welcomes the autumn still fears betrayal: an axe before springtime.

Other songs include Anna's 'Going Back To Harlan', which had recently been covered by Emmylou Harris and ruefully references traditional songs and mythic folk archetypes like Barbara Allen and Willie More, celebrating their 'pure passion and romance' and Kate's clever 'Jacques and Gilles', which plays with elements of the nursery rhyme 'Jack and Jill', to tell the story of poor Québécois emigrants to the factory mill towns of New England, and in so doing places the sisters within the tradition of folk history and ballad singing that 'Going Back To Harlan' celebrates.

The album was released in September 1996 by Hannibal Records and it was widely praised, particularly by the folk press. The sisters played a short tour to promote the record and *Matapedia* would be awarded with a Juno as 'Best Roots and Traditional Album' at the annual Canadian music industry awards ceremony.

If Kate and Anna were coming to terms with growing older, then Loudon was having to accept that he would soon be 50. To celebrate, he played a special show at the Stephen Talkhouse, Amagansett, Long Island, on 6 September, the day after his birthday.

Alongside friends and collaborators, including Chaim Tannenbaum, David Nichtern, George Gerdes and the Irish poet Peter Fallon, were many of his extended family. Kate was there, as were Rufus and Martha, and Suzzy Roche was there with Loudon's daughter Lucy.

Loudon played a solo set, including a selection of the songs that featured the close family who were in attendance. If that made people uncomfortable, that was too bad. As if he had chosen the set to address each of his family personally, he played 'That Hospital', 'Your Mother and I', 'I'm Alright' and 'A Father and a Son'.

Martha joined him for 'Father/Daughter Dialogue' and then showed that she too could mine family history by playing a song of her own, 'Door', which was about clambering around in her grandparent's attic among badminton racquets and old clothes and imagining the places her mother had played as a child.

The rest of the family got up on stage too. Suzzy and her sister Terre joined in with 'Screaming Issue' and Kate, without rancour, chose to fight fire with fire and give Loudon a taste of his own medicine by performing a solo 'Go Leave', one of the bitterest songs she had written about her ex-husband. As if to demonstrate how

far he had come, Rufus, dressed in bright red canvas trousers and a
white T-shirt, and with Martha backing him, played an impeccable
'April Fools', every bit the new star.

Loudon closed the main set with the apposite 'Unhappy Anniversary' and then a version of Marty Robbins' country sob story
'At the End of a Long Lonely Day'. If he was tired and emotional
like any birthday boy could be, Loudon held it together to play one
last, almost inevitable, song.

Hugh Brown, who had worked on the art for Loudon's *Grown
Man* album had prepared dozens of life-size Loudon face masks,
attached them to wooden sticks and left them on the tables so that
when the band returned for the encore, a riotous full cast run-
through of 'Dead Skunk', Loudon was met by an appreciative sea
of bobbing cardboard lookalikes.[3]

In his first months in Los Angeles, Rufus was staying at the Chateau
Marmont. It was the perfect place for him to absorb the mythology
of old Hollywood. Built in 1929, it had been home at one time or
another to stars like Marilyn Monroe, Jim Morrison and Jean
Harlow. Judy Garland had sung in the same lobby that Led Zeppelin
had once driven motorcycles through. Although in recent years the
hotel had carried a reputation for excess best encapsulated by John
Belushi's dismal death in 1982 from a heroin and cocaine overdose in
a poolside bungalow, by the mid-1990s, and under new ownership, it
was intent on reclaiming its position as the hotel of choice for
the young, creative and talented. After all, it had once been the
birthplace of numerous more positive endeavours: *Sunset Boulevard*
was conceived at the hotel; both *Butch Cassidy and the Sundance Kid*
and *The Day of the Locust* were written there; the casting for *Rebel*

---

3. It's entertaining to consider for a moment the implications of the fantastic scenario
the cardboard masks conjure. Although multitudinous doppelgängers would be an ideal
audience for many narcissistic pop singers, Loudon, for all his declared self-interest, in
actuality has forever sought the approbation of others. Confronted by a grimace of Loudons
(surely the correct collective noun), playing to, and in effect with himself, would constitute
a nightmare crowd. Maybe, as in Poe's story 'William Wilson', he'd be driven to kill the
doubles lest they had come to pass judgement on his moral failings (for Wilson there is no
escape as his double returns to haunt his mirror). But perhaps, in these post-Freudian days,
this kind of psycho-analytical theorising is best kept to the bar-room (or the footnote).
(Ref: Edgar Allen Poe – 'William Wilson', 1839, reprinted in *The Complete Stories and
Poems of Edgar Allen Poe*, Doubleday, 1984, US.)

Without a Cause took place there, with James Dean supposedly having to climb in through a window to make his appointment; even Rufus' parents had used the place as their base while Kate and Anna had worked on their first album. With the possibility that fellow guest Helmut Newton[4] might set up an elaborate, risqué photo-shoot by the pool or that passing rock stars would touch down for a post-show party after having played a big California concert, for Rufus the Chateau Marmont was indeed his Chateau Versailles. It was steeped in decadent glamour and what, in Hollywood at least, passed for historic importance and, finally, he was right in the heart of it.

Within a few weeks of arriving in LA, DreamWorks had set him up with occasional solo slots at Largo, a club on Fairfax Avenue. Like New York's Fez, this was an intimate, table-seated venue and it was popular with a hip crowd of LA musicians. One of the people to whom Rufus had been introduced was Kristian Hoffman, who would help him put together a band to play live shows. Hoffman claims he only agreed to meet him because he had been such a fan of Kate McGarrigle's songs and hoped to meet her but he was soon suitably impressed by Rufus' own songwriting abilities.

Hoffman himself was an interesting character who had had a varied career on the peripheries of the music industry. He was perhaps best known for having written for and performed with the astonishing quasi-operatic singer Klaus Nomi, whose vocal range stretched from baritone to countertenor and was perhaps the only artist ever to have attempted to mix Purcell with the sounds of gay disco. Nomi's most famous song, 'Total Eclipse', was one of Hoffman's proudest achievements. Before Nomi, Hoffman had co-founded the New York new wave band the Mumps with his old schoolfriend Lance Loud.

Loud is generally considered to be the first reality TV star after his family appeared in the fly-on-the-wall documentary series *An American Family* in 1973. He also had the honour of being one of the first openly gay people to appear on American television. By the late

---

4. In 2004, Newton, at the time one of the most famous fashion photographers in the world, became another decadent spook of the old hotel, when he lost control of his Cadillac leaving the Chateau Marmont, and crashed into a wall. He had used the place as his winter base since the 1980s and had created numerous photo-shoots on the premises.

1990s, Loud had become an LA-based journalist writing for *Details*, *Interview*, *American Film* and *Vanity Fair*, among other magazines. Through Hoffman, Loud was introduced to Rufus and they became good friends, with the former TV star offering Rufus advice on how to deal with the media and how to take his career further.

When he wasn't working on his demos, Rufus hung out with his new crowd of friends: aspiring actors, musicians and record company employees. Los Angeles was different from New York; in many respects there was no 'show', it was all business. There was the general feeling that even the most creative artists were just a part of a larger entertainment machine; they played their part and served their purpose to provide for that machine. Art was product. On the East Coast, the impression was that artistry was seen as the ultimate accomplishment regardless of how many units were shifted. Rufus had entered into a deal with one of the largest, most corporate, entertainment factories and, regardless of how many times Waronker and Ostin would say that they were returning to the artist-friendly 1970s, he knew he had to deliver.

To demonstrate that it was time to start work, Rufus was moved out of the faded glory of the Chateau Marmont and into the functional Oakwood Apartments, furnished and serviced short-term corporate housing, where you were more likely to bump into a child actor and their family or a temporarily contracted movie industry employee than a drunken superstar. Rufus didn't particularly enjoy his time there, as he later bitched to *Rolling Stone*: 'It's outrageous rent for like a Holiday Inn room. I mean you get a Jacuzzi but of course there are twelve screaming kids in the Jacuzzi as well.'

In November 1996, Penny Arcade asked Rufus to play a special solo show in New York. Travel wasn't a problem as DreamWorks were happy to fly him first class wherever he needed to go. 'Quentin Crisp had asked me for dispensation from his promise to live to be 100 years old,' recalls Arcade. 'I created a live funeral for Quentin called *The Last Will and Testament of Quentin Crisp*.[5] It was held at

---

5. Penny Arcade and Quentin Crisp would later revive the concept of the *Last Will and Testament of Quentin Crisp* for further performances (without Rufus or, of course, Buckley). Close friends since the late 1980s (in 1993 Arcade and Crisp had been photographed together as 'soul-mates' for a *Sunday Telegraph Magazine* feature), they continued to perform together in a variety of different shows right up to Crisp's death in 1999.

KGB Theatre, where we wired three floors with sound and video.'

Arcade had asked Rufus to perform alongside the comedian Steve Ben Israel, poet and playwright Edgar Oliver and her friend Jeff Buckley, who by this point was showing all the signs of becoming a global super star.

'When I announced to Quentin that Rufus was going to sing, he was faux annoyed, saying "I hate music. Music is the most amount of noise conveying the least amount of information."' Arcade remembers the audience taking great delight in Crisp's comment, jeering at Rufus and leaving him somewhat nonplussed. 'Rufus stepped up to Quentin and told him that he was a hero to him and that he was honoured to sing for him. But Quentin sort of turned away.

'The audience were there for Quentin but were mostly new to the actual experience of his personality and they read this as a need to defend him and some started shouting that they were there to hear Quentin speak.'

Arcade had to step in to quieten down the crowd and explain that it was a tribute night to Crisp. 'I told them, as I told several audiences when I had introduced him, that after you hear Rufus sing you will be telling everyone for the rest of your life that you heard him first.'

With the audience hubbub temporarily quelled, Rufus began singing and the crowd started listening. Suddenly the entire PA system broke down and Rufus was left without a working amp or microphone. More jeers. Jeff Buckley crawled from the back of the stage with a guitar amp into which he'd plugged a microphone and he held the mike up for Rufus to sing while he cradled the amp in his arms. By the end of the song the audience erupted, partly for Rufus and partly for the impromptu appearance from Buckley. Buckley declined to perform at the event himself but afterwards Arcade introduced the two singers.

'As they were both song repositories they started asking each other if they knew this song or that song and they started singing together,' recalls Arcade. 'At the end of the night I came downstairs to Rufus, Jeff and the violinist and songwriter Stephan Smith, who'd sat in with Rufus on a song, and they serenaded me. Looking down on Rufus, and Jeff, who I was close to then, I had an overwhelming out-of-body experience. In this perfect moment was this dark moment and I thought to myself, "One of these boys won't be here again." Then the three of us went down to my neighbourhood to Sin-é which had just opened up and was empty and we sat there drinking and talking and we ended the night sitting on the kerb of Clinton Street talking until dawn.'

Within six months Buckley would be dead. In a later interview with salon.com, Rufus remembered the meeting at KGB and regretted the opinion he had held of Buckley before he'd even met him after he had held the singer personally responsible for not getting to play at Sin-é himself: 'It was my first lesson about measuring your ambition against other people, because he was just so weak. He was the antithesis of what I thought he would be. I really felt bad for having had that attitude. [When] he died I still didn't get totally into his music. I think because of trepidation.' It wouldn't be until Rufus heard Buckley's version of 'Hallelujah' that he came to appreciate his work. 'It dawned on me at that moment the incredible loss, and the incredible talent that he was.'[6]

---

6. Up until he wrote a tribute song to him ('Memphis Skyline' on *Want Two*), Rufus remained, in public at least, ambivalent about Buckley's talents. It's hard to believe that he hadn't heard anything by Buckley until after he had recorded his own version of 'Hallelujah' in 2001 but such was Rufus' self-belief and general disinterest in most contemporary music it is entirely possible that he had not bothered to explore any of Buckley's records. It's also just as likely that Rufus' long-held resentment of Buckley dating back to his failure to get a gig at Sin-é extended to jealously at Buckley's growing success. Perhaps he felt that the similarities between them would somehow lead to unfavourable comparisons or perhaps he simply didn't care. By his own admittance, Rufus' level of self-absorption could be astonishing.

In a later interview (Simon Hattenstone, the *Guardian*, 14 April 2007), Rufus spoke about the time Danny Fields reminded him what had happened when he'd called to tell him that Jeff Buckley had died: 'He told me this story which I had no memory of, but kind of illustrates how I can be mean without wanting to be. He was very good friends with Jeff Buckley and I was living in LA and had just finished my first album and Jeff died and Danny Fields called me and he was in tears, devastated, and he was saying, I can't believe this has happened to Jeff and it's so awful and so sad and he was so great and it's so terrible, and I was listening and I said, "Oh, that's terrible but, you know, my new album's really great."'

Perhaps Rufus could only have been more self-serving if, like W.B. Yeats to his sister on hearing Swinburne had died, he had said to Fields, 'Now I am king of the cats.'

3.3

In Montreal, Martha was becoming increasingly frustrated at being left behind. Although Rufus was thousands of miles away, his big record contract was the only thing that people ever wanted to talk to her about. 'I left Montreal for that reason,' she explained, 'because there was too much talk about Rufus.'

Martha moved to New York and started finding gigs for herself. She remained fiercely independent, sometimes difficult, perhaps a little hard to handle with her intensely performed songs, shouting and hammering at her acoustic guitar. But she was intent on making it her own way and her approach to live performance was inventive enough for her find places that would let her play. 'I never really fitted in,' she remembers. 'There were a lot of singer-songwriters but their stuff might be a little less subversive and more la-la-la-la, and I was screaming and yelling.'

Part of her anger stemmed from an underlying resentment at her treatment by her father, a subject she would repeatedly return to in song, but there was also the fear of somehow being pushed to the side, known only as the daughter of . . . or the sister of . . . At best people would praise her for her backing vocals on her parents' records or at their concerts. Indeed many of Loudon's long-term fans were more than happy to praise her, some going as far as to say that the earlier songs in the set when played with Martha were, for the first time, sounding as good as they had when they were originally recorded with Kate. Even when Rufus had let her play a solo slot in his set and she was well received, she knew that she could offer more.

Her time in New York was spent hanging out with 'strange people', drinking, doing drugs, writing songs. She lived in a tiny Brooklyn apartment with an aspiring actress and an aspiring artist and no air-conditioning. It was so hot in the summer that they would all just walk around naked and take cold baths. As she would later proudly boast: 'I've frolicked with the bohemians at the bottom of the barrel.'

Initially she had complained that she felt intimidated by the successes of her parents as they had 'set the bar too high'. Now that her brother was on the verge of making it, it only compounded her unease in pushing herself forward. Years later she would admit to having always had a chip on her shoulder. 'I felt less than other people, inadequate – it's actually indulgent and self-obsessed. What keeps me up at night is not whether I will sell more records than Rufus, but will I be able to write more great songs?'

In many respects this is the key to the professional rivalry, sometimes manifesting as petty jealousies, that has always run through the family. Loudon, brutally frank, egocentric and pledged to 'the song' to the detriment of all else around him; Kate, the existentialist songwriter bound by family and committed to the narratives of place and emotion; and Rufus, the driven, charismatic, major-label sanctified narcissist. And then there is Martha sitting, emotionally and artistically, almost exactly between the three of them. All were committed to music, song and performance to such an extent that it could almost seem to be a family curse as much as a blessing.

It's easy to imagine Martha with the fear of ending up like Branwell Brontë, burdened and defined by a famous name, yet unable to find his own place in the world except as a reference to his celebrated siblings. She didn't want to be only known as a backing singer to famous family members or as the subject matter of snide comedic songs by her father any more than Branwell can have wanted to be best known for being the ghostly absence at the centre of his only famous work – his portrait of Charlotte, Emily and Anne – unremarkable as portraiture except that it is the Brontë sisters and that there is a strange blurred yellow column of light at its centre where Branwell once stood, now vanished as though he had been posthumously teleported out of the painting by ignominious failure.[7]

---

7. Branwell Brontë (1817–1848) aspired to be a great writer like his sisters, although he seemed to have lacked both their ability and application. He then attempted to become an artist but was rejected by the Royal Academy and was unable even to establish himself as a local portrait painter. Eventually he succumbed to depression and an addiction to laudanum and alcohol. His one famous painting, as referenced, is the only known portrait of his sisters together. He had originally included himself in the picture but, for unknown reasons, decided to paint a pillar over his image. Over time the paint he used, apparently improperly mixed by the unfortunate artist, has become translucent and his ghostly, tragic image haunts the portrait like a reminder for all those siblings who have tried, and then failed, to keep up with their more successful family members. (Ref: Daphne Du Maurier, *The Infernal World of Branwell Brontë*, Victor Gollancz, London, 1960.)

Failure was never really an option for Martha, she was too single-minded. She would prove that she was as talented as the rest of her family. While Rufus recorded in high-end studios in California, she started taping some of her own songs on a cheap eight-track. While he partied at lavish record company receptions, Martha was playing live five nights a week, at Nightingales in the East Village or any-where else that would take her. 'It was a necessary period,' she says. 'I wanted to define my own relationship with music. And I also wanted to know for sure whether I was really going to do music. Because it was incredibly daunting.'

Her resulting home-recordings were put on to a cassette and titled *Ground Floor*.[8] Nominally a debut album but in reality an extended demo tape, *Ground Floor* contained almost all of the original songs she had written up to that point. Some of the songs would be remade for later albums or appear as bonus tracks on singles but most of them, eventually replaced in her set by new and better material, were never rerecorded.

These early songs showcase Martha as a competent, yet basic, guitarist, and a careful, yet over-cautious, singer. The vocal sweeps, the flutter and wow that distinguish her later recordings are almost wholly absent. The demos sketch out her abilities but never really convince the listener that she fully believes in what she is doing.

Songs such as 'Laurel and Hardy' (a song about Rufus that praises his taste in furniture and his photogenic looks while hinting at an antagonistic brother/sister relationship) and 'Wandering Eyes' feature simplistic rhyme schemes – elixir/mixer/pitcher descending into doggerel – that render the words childish and rein in any potential for expressive singing. 'The Car Song' is worse, like a simplistic singalong for kindergarten but one that would probably have the kids fidgeting before the second verse comes along. The standout songs are 'Door', which she had played at Loudon's birth-day show, and the chilly 'Don't Forget', which would appear on her debut album and remain part of her live set for the next ten years. It's no coincidence that these two are lyrically superior, and are

---

8. *Ground Floor* was a self-produced cassette-only album. The full track-listing is as follows: Don't Forget / Hate You Too / The Car Song / Door / Precious Smiles / Laurel and Hardy / Gone To Sea / Wandering Eyes / Question of Etiquette / Wanna Wanna. None of these recordings have ever been commercially issued.

rhythmically structured to allow Martha's voice enough space in which to move mellifluously around the words.

When some early Tom Waits demos were released against his wishes in the early 1990s, he is supposed to have said: 'Demo tapes are like baby pictures, everybody's got them, you just don't want them passed around.' And it's true that it's unfair to judge too harshly material that is mere juvenilia, albeit Martha was in her twenties when she recorded the tracks, especially as it's material that is no longer available, in effect withdrawn from circulation by the artist.

However, it's worth pointing out that while Rufus' first demo tapes clearly demonstrated his talent, and in some instances his demo versions are arguably superior to the finished tracks, *Ground Floor* failed to showcase Martha's proper potential and it would have taken an incredibly clairvoyant A+R executive to have put a case forward for signing her on the basis of these tracks. As it was, Martha used her cassette album as a promotional tool to get gigs and as a means to earn a little extra pin-money selling the tapes for a few dollars after her shows. She sent out copies to a few labels but didn't hear back from any of them.

Although the reaction to *Ground Floor* might have disappointed her, Martha received a huge confidence boost when the critic Ann Powers went to see her perform as part of the 'Required Listening Series' at the Bottom Line in early December and filed a glowing report for the *New York Times*. The review identified Martha's links to her mother and aunt and compared her to Jane Siberry and, more tellingly, the great New York singer-songwriter Laura Nyro: 'Ms Wainwright imbued her vignettes with the sonic ranginess common to her generation of musicians. The folk tradition she mined is a feminine one. [She] expanded the song form to bring the listener inside her experience of the everyday world.' Powers, who would also become an early supporter of Rufus over the coming months, concluded that '[Martha's] skills were evident in the supple draw of her vocals and her knack for exuding emotion while simultaneously standing back and examining it. Hers was an auspicious debut.'

While Martha had been struggling to get her career started, across town Loudon was at work on his sixteenth album. The recordings were taking place in the East Village apartment of his new producer

John Leventhal, who had recently finished working with Rosanne Cash on her *10 Song Demo* album.[9] Although the home recording set-up offered a casual, relaxed environment that allowed Loudon some welcome spontaneity, it did have its own drawbacks as Loudon explained in an interview he did for the Rosebud Agency, his management company: 'We would have to wait for the guys in the apartment overhead to stop walking around and making noise. They became known as the "Clump Brothers". Between them, car alarms, and buses roaring outside the apartment, there was a lot of noise to contend with. John had to duct-tape sound-baffling to his bathroom door because the toilet kept gurgling.'

Loudon called the album *Little Ship* and the cover shows him frantically paddling a rubber dinghy out of the path of an oncoming cruise liner. Having recently split up with his most recent girlfriend, the journalist Tracey MacLeod, with whom he'd been living in St John's Wood, London, he claimed that the album was coming direct from the People's Republic of Splitsville where 'everybody has had their passport stamped at least once'. Their love had been like a little ship tossed around on the ocean.

If Loudon was upset by the break-up, he wasn't going to let it show. The track 'So Damn Happy' is driven by a cheap-sounding drum machine and a steel drum. Loudon sings that he feels 'sheer relief' at the end of his relationship, although he is aware that this admission is potentially so annoying to his ex that he invites her, and then the listener, to slap him.[10]

---

9. In 1996, Rosanne Cash's career was beginning to fade and she had been dropped by her label. In response she made an album of simple demo recordings. Of course her father Johnny had done much the same thing with his *American Recordings* album (1994). Loudon had been incredibly proud that Johnny Cash had chosen to include one of his songs ('The Man Who Couldn't Cry' from *Attempted Mustache*) on *American Recordings* and on more than one occasion said that this was the best thing that had happened to him in the 1990s. Rosanne herself would later ask Loudon to contribute to a book she was editing, *Songs Without Rhyme: Prose by Celebrated Songwriters* (Hyperion 2001), where his short story 'Schooldays', an extension of his song of the same name, appeared alongside work by David Byrne, Lucinda Williams and Lyle Lovett among others.

10. A few years later, Tracey MacLeod offered Loudon a symbolic kind of slap when she sold off various items that he had left behind in London to members of his internet fan message board. The items included Loudon's old motorcycle helmet, the one that he'd worn on the cover to *Therapy*. MacLeod light-heartedly suggested that no fan could resist 'something that's been on Loudon's actual head'. She was right, the helmet soon found a new home.

'OGM' is more considered. It's one of Loudon's classic micro-dramas based around the leaving and receiving of answering machine messages. OGM stands for outgoing message, noting how a pause can mean more than anything that is said, and highlighting the emotional impact of whether it's a red '1' or '0' that's flashing back at you from your machine when you get in the house. It's perfectly paced, poignant and witty, and played out in under three minutes.

The album is evenly split between songs about himself and his situation and more general songs about the world. 'What are Families for' is a sour look at the traditional family unit, but this time it's Loudon looking at other people's lives rather than his own. Even 'Bein' a Dad', something of a stomp that flirts around the tune of 'Messing about on the Water', could only be vaguely considered autobiographical – did Loudon really enforce curfews and confiscate weapons and pagers? Doubtful, don't you think? It plays more like a theme song to a family sit-com.

For perhaps the most ridiculous song on the album, Loudon, the deliberate, provocatively comic contrarian, set out to create the world's most pessimistic banjo song, claiming that people always thought banjos were so positive-sounding, and written in order 'to piss Pete Seeger off'. With 'The World' he succeeds. It's a maledictory rant against the planet and all who find themselves on her and it reaches such peaks of irritant bile that it's hard not to laugh. If the neo-con, anti-ecology lobby ever want an anthem, then this song could be it.

As usual, Loudon toured the album extensively but sales-wise, while by no means washed-up, he was treading water. *Little Ship* was his final album for Virgin Records. Any disappointment he had about leaving another label was completely overshadowed by the death of his mother Martha, aged 74.

Her death hit him hard and by the end of the year Loudon found himself back in northern Westchester, upstate New York, having decided to move in to his mother's old cottage, the Mouse House. He rattled around among her old things, remembered old times, revisited places he had been to as a child and hung out with his sisters who ran a coffee shop nearby. Every now and then he would visit a psychiatrist in New York. Much as his father's death had focused his mind and helped him to create the magnificent *History* album, then his grief at his mother's death would eventually be the catalyst for some of his best-ever songs.

In March 1998 Rufus received a rapturous live review from Ann Powers at the *New York Times*. As a precursor for his imminent album, it couldn't have been bettered. Powers described how the Fez crowd 'embraced his sometimes campy, often rhapsodic estheti-cism'. And, though admitting he needed to learn to pace his set better, stated that 'as someone tapping esoteric reservoirs to nourish a singular voice, Rufus Wainwright is one to watch. What he finally becomes will add to the possibilities of pop.'

That same month Loudon and Rufus had both appeared, sep-arately, at the music industry conference/festival South by South-west. It was a place where new bands were discovered by critics, where deals were brokered, where careers could be made. Almost 800 bands played and Rufus vied for attention among showcase gigs by the likes of Royal Trux, Dwarves and Jimmy Eat World. He had managed to charm critics, including, crucially, *Rolling Stone*'s music editor Joe Levy, into staying for his whole set – this was almost unheard of; the traditional practice for jaded music business insiders was to take in just a couple of numbers at as many shows as they could bear in a night just in case they missed out on a hot act. While Rufus' show had the aura of something happening that was new and exciting, Loudon had played to his regular, small but dedicated group of fans, plugging his latest record to any journalists who might have wandered in either by mistake or for old times' sake. For Loudon it was just another night on the road. Rufus denied that there was any great rivalry, blaming his father's reading of Freud for creating competition where there wasn't any. He knew he would find his own audience his own way and it would be a different one from his father's.

Loudon had suggested to Rufus that his debut album should be just piano and voice. A stark, basic recording that let the quality of the songs come to the fore. Rather like the approach he had taken on his own debut LP. Instead Rufus chose to go in the opposite direction: 'Since I was doing it with Lenny Waronker, and it was DreamWorks and they had a lot of money, I figured why not go all the way? I didn't want it to be lukewarm and tepid, like "Oh, we'll just put a little band or a little drum on here." I wanted it to be big.'

The album sessions had run from the end of 1996 and right through 1997. Rufus had recorded in more than a dozen studios and filled 62 reels of tape with almost as many different takes of songs. 'It basically drained my life's blood,' he said. 'It took a lot of time and resources. But Lenny didn't care how long it took, as long as we were doing good work.'

Some of the sessions were recorded at Pierre Marchand's studio in Morin Heights, Canada, but the bulk of them were in Los Angeles under the control of Jon Brion. The producer and artist did not always see eye to eye. Although Brion had a reputation for rococo arrangements, he also had an ear for the pop purity of bands like the Beatles. He found some of Rufus' more elaborate ideas exasperating as he later admitted to the *New York Times*: 'Rufus had all these beautiful songs but every time the vocals would kick in, he'd write some complicated keyboard part so you couldn't hear them. He wasn't interested in listening to ideas about simplifying arrangements.'

At least Van Dyke Parks was somebody who never let a tune get in the way of a complicated arrangement and Rufus was thrilled to be working with him. 'I went to [Van Dyke Park's] house and he played some of [his arrangements] on piano, and I was actually a little worried,' he told *College Music Journal*. 'Let's just say he's not very good at getting it across. He's a total mad genius. If you can imagine him playing all of this stuff – like 30 strings – on the piano. It's a little scary. But then we went in and did the session and it was amazing. It all came together. He really knows that language so well, the string language.'

Parks conducted his orchestrations in sessions at Studio B in the Capitol Studios complex housed underneath the famous circular stack-of-discs Capitol Tower on North Vine Street. A Los Angeles landmark since 1956, the building had been used by legendary artists like Louis Armstrong, Ella Fitzgerald and Nat King Cole. Rufus could look over and watch Parks standing on his podium conducting the orchestra and imagine Nelson Riddle working with Frank Sinatra in the same spot. As if he needed any further reminding that he was now fully immersed in the *That's Entertainment* fantasies of his childhood, 13 floors above his head the light on top of the needlepoint tower incessantly flashed H-O-L-L-Y-W-O-O-D in blinking red Morse code.

In addition to Parks, Rufus had the luxury of being able to call on some of the most accomplished session musicians that money could buy. Drummer Jim Keltner had a résumé as long as a 2B drumstick: he'd played on albums by John Lennon, George Harrison, Elvis Costello and Steely Dan and immediately prior to joining Rufus' sessions, he'd been hired by Bob Dylan to play on his career-reviving *Time Out of Mind* album. Benmont Tench, a piano player and another Dylan alumnus, had helped found Tom Petty's Heartbreakers, played with The Rolling Stones and had more recently played on Alanis Morissette's multi-million selling *Jagged Little Pill*.

Rufus had more than enough self-belief not to be overawed by such illustrious players. Using his own basic piano and vocal sketches as the starting point, and with his particular, and at the time peculiar, cast of classical maestros and silver screen crooners hovering above his head as ever present influences and guides, the musicians helped create a debut album that set him apart from his contemporaries.

'I really tried to create a style that was a mix of a lot of older styles. And I worked at trying to camouflage those styles but still have them present because it's very important to me that [the songs] sound contemporary – or at least new,' Rufus declared.

Waronker was pleased with how the recordings came out. 'From a musical and lyrical standpoint, he's clearly on the edge, which to me is always exciting. He's doing something that his peers haven't done. It's very sophisticated in a time when true musical sophistication doesn't often emerge.'

From the hours of sessions, Rufus and Waronker agreed on 12 tracks for the *Rufus Wainwright* album,[11] of which five of the songs

---

11. Two songs from the album sessions were in fact released prior to the debut album. Recorded at sessions with Ethan Johns, who had been asked to engineer by Brion, 'Le Roi d'Ys' and 'Banks of the Wabash', a version of the Indiana state song, appeared on the soundtrack album for the film *The Myth of Fingerprints* (dir. Bart Freundlich, 1997). The film did little business and Rufus' contribution went equally unnoticed. Johns, who would also work on *Poses*, remembers recording 'Le Roi d'Ys' with particular fondness. 'It's one of my favourite Rufus tracks actually. We had fun cutting that track. I reckon it was completed in about six hours.'

had been on the demo tape. How far Rufus had come in the two years it had taken to get from a tiny Montreal studio to a giant Californian recording complex gradually becomes apparent as the album's opening number builds.

'Foolish Love' had been the first track on the demo and it fulfilled the same function on the album, basically . . . Heeeere's Rufus!

He sings the opening lines with just piano accompaniment, his voice coming in at almost the very second that the track begins; the tempo is slightly faster than the demo, the playing more assured, the vocal has more controlled sustain at the end of the line. Little by little the track builds, there's a snare, upright bass, vibes and marimba, drums, accordion – Rufus adds another layer of piano, a chamberlin – Van Dyke Parks' strings build and all of a sudden you reach the instrumental break and it sounds for all the world like Fred and Ginger should be dancing across it, not the slapstick stumble, however endearing that was, that the demo actually evoked. Rufus said the song was supposed to be happy-sounding but still sad. 'It's about the type of person you fall in love with who, when you take a look at him, you know it will end tragically . . . I remember writing it almost like a mantra saying to myself, "Lighten up and trudge on."' But it's better than that, it doesn't trudge, it glides.

Likewise, 'Danny Boy' benefits from being given a big production – it still rolls and swaggers like a sea shanty – but with the advantage of some ululant horns and a modicum of weirdness courtesy of Jon Brion's optigan, a novelty 1970s organ that came into vogue after Tom Waits had used one on *Frank's Wild Years*.

Waits must have also been a touchstone for the album version of 'Matinee Idol' as it channels the same old-time Weimar cabaret spooks that he had done on *Rain Dogs*. Brion drives the song with marimba and Rufus' voice is treated like he's singing through a megaphone (*Rolling Stone* called it 'orchestral noir' with 'lurid carny stylings'). Paradoxically, it's the most contemporary-sounding track on the record as the decadent syncopation of Kurt Weill had always been a favourite for any rock act with a penchant for the theatrical, from The Doors through David Bowie to Nick Cave.

Elsewhere, the musical references are more out of step with the majority of artists releasing albums in 1998. Although many critics would cite Randy Newman as a ready reference, Rufus always maintained that he hadn't listened to him at all until Van Dyke Parks had suggested he might like him. The same went for Nilsson, another comparison. The similarities occurred because these writers had come from the same place, had admired the same source material – writers like Cole Porter, Irving Berlin, Herman Hupfeld. Rufus would acknowledge John Cale and Laura Nyro as possible influences but otherwise he said he listened mostly to classical music 'because you can steal so much and no one will notice it'.[12]

'In My Arms', a story of doomed junkie romance, is the only song that made the record that was recorded by Marchand at his Montreal studio. It has a markedly different feel that sets it apart from the other tracks on the album. There's an authenticity to its brush drums, slurred vocals and Martha's weary harmonies that make it sound like it's the last song of the night from a worn-out cabaret singer waiting for that too-drunk couple to stop grappling with each other on the dance-floor so he can finally close the lid on his piano and go home.

Compared to it, the Parks' orchestrated 'Baby', covering the same subject (Rufus has said it's about the same person), is a masterpiece of artifice. Whereas 'In My Arms' sounds as though it's written about a real person, 'Baby' would appear to be about a character, a fiction. There is a sublime instrumental middle section that seems made to accompany a montage of louche indulgence on the frayed bedspread of a worn-out motel room, but one on a theatre stage or

---

12. It would be wrong to suggest that Rufus was the only artist referencing classic singer-songwriters or having lush orchestration on his records at this time. There had been a vogue for string-laden songs, especially in the UK, since the mid-1990s. Although albums by Tindersticks or Divine Comedy may only sound superficially similar to *Rufus Wainwright*, their grandiose aspirations render them philosophically united (in looking for comparisons I am discounting the myriad bands that had gone down the Scott Walker/ Jacques Brel hip-cabaret route). Closest to Rufus perhaps is the undeservedly obscure Epic Soundtracks, formerly a member of punk/new wave band Swell Maps, who released a series of piano-based albums, beginning with 1992's *Rise Above* (Rough Trade), that came straight from the Nilsson/Nyro/Newman school. This is not to suggest that Rufus heard the Epic Soundtracks records, almost nobody did, merely to point out that there is always somebody somewhere rebuilding and reworking what has gone before. By the late twentieth century, as far as music-making was concerned and to paraphrase an old saying: 'Nothing is new, everything is permitted.' Rufus had the good fortune to be backed by a sympathetic and supportive major record label allowing him the space and time to develop his talents and which had the infrastructure in place to get those talents noticed.

a movie set, not in reality. Rufus praised Parks' accompaniment, saying it had turned his sad little song into a 'gorgeous, sweeping Tennessee Williams screenplay'. It's not quite *The Fugitive Kind* but it does include a wonderfully visual lyrical vignette: 'If you bring along your needles/Then I'll bring my sharpened pencils/And draw one more comic tragedy.'

Indeed, Rufus' lyrics are uniformly excellent. From the snapshot of school life in 'Millbrook' to the oblique Verdi referencing 'Barcelona' where Rufus takes Macbeth's cry of 'Fuggi Regal Fantasima' at the sight of the ghosts of Banquo's unborn sons as a device to articulate his sheer terror of AIDS, to the nonchalant simplicity of the red face against green seat juxtaposition in the album's closing track, the yearning 'Imaginary Love'.

Perhaps the most instantly accessible of the new songs on the album was 'April Fools', a genuinely catchy song with upbeat lyrics. Superficially at least, the song was actually about Rufus having failed to have scored in a 'kissing booth' (and this was an actual occurrence; it's not meant as an effete variation of the old put-down for the inept, e.g. 'pulling in a brothel'). With 'You will believe in love' as its radio-friendly chorus, the song would be the one that the label hoped would help push Rufus on to the radio and on to music TV channels worldwide.

DreamWorks had hired veteran photographer David Gahr to shoot Rufus for some publicity photos. Gahr was an old hand at music photography, having taken pictures of Miles Davis, John Lennon and Janis Joplin among many others. Twenty-five years earlier, he'd even taken photographs of Loudon, Kate and Anna when they were performing on the festival circuit. In fact, he was most associated with folk music having published *The Face of Folk* with Robert Shelton in 1968 (Citadel Press, US), an encyclopaedic book featuring hundreds of photographs of characters from the mid-Sixties folk scene.

For the album's front cover, Rufus chose a portrait by Gahr. A head and shoulders shot that pitches him – doe-eyed, slightly unshaven, wearing a bead choker – somewhere between boy band dreamboat and hustler from the cast of Andy Warhol's *Lonesome Cowboys*. Among the lyrics in the album booklet, Rufus collaged some photographs of his family, including him and Martha larking about as children. He also included a photograph, uncaptioned, of Danny, the one-time object of his obsession and the unwitting inspiration for many of the tracks.

The album was released in May 1998 and the early responses were good. Even when you have something as slick as the DreamWorks marketing machine in full effect, it can be difficult to bring new artists to the attention of the media but Rufus' lineage had the added advantage of a ready-made peg to hang a story or a review on. The *New York Times* previewed the record by interviewing Rufus and Loudon together. It came at an interesting point where, perhaps for the last time, Loudon remained the most famous of the Wainwrights.

In the interview, Rufus implied that he had felt betrayed by Loudon writing songs about him and Martha when he hadn't been around much. Loudon countered by saying, 'But the songs are not therapeutic; they weren't written to heal rifts, or to open any up. A writer has to find things that interest people and it's been my experience that my listeners are extremely interested in hearing about how I've screwed things up with women and children.'

The writer Ken Tucker suggests that Rufus had shied away from writing similarly autobiographical songs because his sexuality may have alienated some of his target audience. It's true that, except for the opening lines of 'Sally Ann' and the actual track 'Danny Boy', the subject of the songs are not gender-specific. We could even legitimately discount 'Danny Boy' as hundreds of singers, both male and female, had never had much difficulty in singing 'Oh Danny Boy I love you so' in the traditional Irish ballad that shares the song's name, so why wouldn't Rufus admit that a Danny Boy broke his heart. But in reality, Rufus was not deliberately obscuring anything. The songs were largely autobiographical, tempered with the kind of classical references and folkloric similes more often used by his mother rather than the more direct Loudon. Rufus admits to couching gay romance with euphemism and metaphor but likened it to Cole Porter's style of writing, not as an attempt to hide his true feelings.

'I can't spend my life writing answer-songs to my father,' said Rufus. 'Anyway, as far as I am concerned, all of my material is love songs about boys, mostly romantic music about failed love. My father demonises and satirises love. I just pursue it.'

Loudon, perhaps remembering his own experiences of being touted as the 'new Bob Dylan', had some words of caution for his son: 'Rufus is brash and talented and he knows it. And, I should add, that's not a bad thing to be in this business, because it's brutal. It's great that he'll have some initial buzz, but he'll also pay for it. His gifts and his self-awareness are going to serve him well.'

Impressing Joe Levy at South by Southwest had paid dividends as *Rolling Stone* got behind Rufus from the start. While acknowledging that Rufus was lucky in having connected parents, the *Rolling Stone* review said that he had the talent to match his good fortune, noting that: 'If the songs on Rufus Wainwright remind you of old pop standards, it's because they're so damn classy.' The magazine would eventually hail Rufus as its 'Best New Artist of the Year'.

The *Advocate* called the album 'stunning', praising it for its 'unmistakably gay slant'. Although Rufus would eventually become critical of some of the gay press for its perceived lack of support, in his first major review in a national gay magazine, he couldn't have asked for more: 'The music's utter lack of machismo or commercial competitiveness speaks of a freedom that comes to outsiders disinterested in meeting the requirements of the dreary status quo. Like all good pop musicians, Wainwright is all about escapism. The difference is he takes you further.'

In order to facilitate a concerted strategy to get himself and his album noticed, Rufus hired a manager. Nick Terzo had been a successful A&R executive for Madonna's Maverick Records and had just co-founded an artist management group. He'd been introduced via Rufus' attorney at the time, Peter Paterno. Terzo says: 'Rufus used to tell others, jokingly I assume, that I had left Madonna to manage his career and that was why he'd hired me.'

Working closely with publicist Jim Merlis, Terzo formulated a plan that would capitalise on Rufus' charisma and performing talent to try to build a fan base and to avoid him becoming an 'obscure critic's darling'. This entailed getting Rufus to play as many places as possible as often as he could. Terzo arranged support slots with Lisa Loeb, Barenaked Ladies (a mystifyingly successful Canadian comedy frat-rock band sometimes cruelly dubbed 'The Fat Housemartins') and a media-friendly famous-father/famous-son double-header with Sean Lennon for which Rufus was the opener until the Canadian dates where Lennon insisted he headlined. It was an extremely provident tactic for which Terzo can rightly remain proud: '[In 1998] I believed that the internet would ultimately hurt record sales for artists, thereby making touring more important both as a financial resource and for building a fan base. In my humble opinion every artist should build their touring business and brand. And, if by the strike of lightning you have a hit single, that's just icing and luck. I think my strategy is borne out today by most young artists and the fact that the touring business has ultimately been much more important to Rufus' career.'

Despite many radio stations finding Rufus' material a little too baroque to easily schedule among their regular contemporary pop play-lists, his constant touring brought him spikes of popularity in certain places, especially metropolitan areas like San Francisco, New York and Chicago. When he played solo headline sets in major cities he would generally fill the clubs.

Initial sales of the album were disappointing. Rufus was creating a buzz, and the general feedback from both the critics and the public, those that got to hear him of course, was good, but it wasn't translating into people actually buying the record. Terzo remembers DreamWorks not being particularly concerned. 'Lenny Waronker and Mo Ostin were two of the last great label executives that believed that talent trumped overall commercial considerations. They signed artists and Rufus was an artist. I think I probably exerted more pressure on the label than vice-versa. DreamWorks were incredibly patient, sometimes to a fault. Never were onerous requests made upon us by the label.'

In order to kick-start the album sales, DreamWorks commissioned a video for the lead track 'April Fools'. Sophie Muller, who had made videos for Blur, Jeff Buckley and No Doubt, was a huge fan of Kate and Anna McGarrigle and jumped at the chance of working with Rufus. 'I really wanted to do this because it wasn't like anything else,' Muller said. 'It's always interesting to move beyond the rock genre, and Rufus' fascination with opera presented some intriguing possibilities. Most videos are just formula, but I knew this one wouldn't be.'

Rufus proposed using the lyrical theme of his song 'Damned Ladies' as the basis for the video. Muller planned a way that she could link Rufus' performance of the song with the five female characters that featured in it. The plot device was that each of the opera heroines would have to die in the way that they do in their respective operas and Rufus would have to try to save them. That meant six concurrent plot lines that had to be co-ordinated so that they ran along with Rufus singing the song, rather than having to cut away to a separate performance.

The video was filmed over two days around Silver Lake and East Hollywood. Muller's friend Gwen Stefani let them use her house for the internal scenes and appeared in the video as a waitress. Martha played Cio-Cio San from *Madam Butterfly* and was forced to spend the full two-day shoot trapped in her kimono as the Japanese consultant they had hired to enfold her in the traditional robe couldn't make the second day, meaning she couldn't change out of it after day one as there would be no way of getting back into it for the following day (no wonder she looks so relieved when she gets to stab herself with a butter knife).

Melissa Auf Der Mar, who at the time was playing bass for Courtney Love in Hole, appears as Gilda from *Rigoletto*. She was a close friend of Rufus and he had been staying with her in Los Angeles for a few months. 'I grew up with Melissa in Montreal,' he explained in an MTV interview. 'We went to high school together. We were actually in love when we were young but we never consummated. We were always too shy to get together. But I thought she was fascinating when I was a kid and I still think she's fascinating.'

The conceit of killing off a series of glamorous divas on the dusty streets of East LA and then reviving them at the last minute may have been confusing to those unaware of the subtext. Muller considered captioning the video in order to explain who the characters were and why they were doing such bizarre things but in the end they left it as it was. 'That's another way "April Fools" is unusual,' said Muller. 'Like most videos, it's a series of beautiful images, but if you want to look into it further, you can learn something. I believe the people who see it and don't know what's going on but want to know will take it upon themselves to find out.'

Whether the appearance of the video prompted confused MTV viewers to investigate the lives, times and tragic demises of operatic heroines is debatable but in a crowded marketplace it was certainly enigmatic enough to stand apart from the parade of straight performance videos. That said, although it raised Rufus' profile, it didn't result in the hoped for boost in record sales.

3.4

When not on the road Rufus was splitting his time between Los Angeles and Montreal, where he lived in a top-floor apartment above his mother's house. Kate and Anna had called the family together to make a new album that was the logical extension of their homespun attitude to music and creativity.

The McGarrigle Hour plays like a radio broadcast from the past, an hour-long programme of traditional folk and newer family songs on which the McGarrigle sisters recreate the parlour-singing sessions of their childhood. You can imagine the music coming out of an old valve radio that is somehow picking up a signal that has been lost for 60 years (an idea reinforced by the placing of old radios among the audience in the strangely lifeless filmed version of the album that would subsequently appear in 1999).

Alongside Kate and Anna, the record featured both Rufus and Martha and Anna's children Lily and Silvan Lanken. Sister Jane McGarrigle made an appearance, as did many of their more regular collaborators including Chaim Tannenbaum and Anna's husband Dane. More surprising perhaps was the contribution of Loudon. If the album was to be a true representation of their past 30 years of music-making and the integral part it had played in all of their lives as both career opportunity and, more importantly, emotional crutch and artistic outlet, then the inclusion of Loudon was vital. It moved the project beyond mere nostalgia and embraced the family's belief in the overriding importance of song and its reconciliatory powers while tacitly acknowledging that family life is complicated and difficult and all the more powerful for that. When he was later asked what it was like singing with his ex-wife and the kids, he replied, 'Singing together is always easier than being together. It's a pure unadulterated way of being together. If you happen to be a singer.'

Loudon's 'Schooldays' kicks off the album, as it had his debut record in 1970, setting the tone as one that is as much an exploration of the past as it is a celebration. Traditional songs like 'Alice Blue Gown' and 'Dig My Grave' demonstrate the sisters' curatorial approach to folk music but it's the songs which connect more personally with the family that really resonate. The Stephen Foster number 'Gentle Annie' was one that the sisters had sung with their father as children, and the breathtaking cover of Irving Berlin's 'What'll I Do' is all the more heartbreaking when you know the sisters had sung it at their mother's funeral in 1994.

All of this is not to say it's a depressing record. As usual there are moments of levity: the incongruous cover of the Tab Hunter/Sonny James song 'Young Love' with almost all of its rock'n'roll stripped away and the version of Kate's 'NaCl' are light relief from the brittle brilliance of 'Cool River' and 'Talk to Me of Mendocino'.

Rufus' solo contribution 'Heartburn' plays like a song from a musical, but not a very good one. Notionally a comedy number, the lyrics juxtapose the symptoms of heartbreak and heartburn referencing Rolaid and rhyming 'I love ya' with Ebola. It's fine in theory but it misfires – Noël Coward it ain't. Better though is Martha's 'Year of the Dragon', which is lyrically superior to anything from her *Ground Floor* tape and is performed with a confidence buoyed by her ongoing stint as back-up singer for Rufus on his recent tours. The closing stanza – 'They say that I'm too free/But one day soon I'll be just like them/And hate people just like me/So let me be' – hints at the themes of her later songs where belligerence battles vulnerability.

In lieu of any new songs by Kate and Anna, it's the original material by Rufus and Martha, however successful the songs are individually, which raise the album above being a mere ersatz parlour session. The reviewer for *Salon* described the album as though it were the aural equivalent of a photo album, something to preserve their legacy. By including the new material from the next generation, the sisters ensured that it went beyond that; it showed that there were always more pages to fill, more songs to sing.

The album received exceptionally positive reviews heralded as 'a poignant meditation on the meaning of family and the power of shared history' by *Entertainment Weekly*, 'gutwrenchingly beautiful' by *Crawdaddy*, while the *New York Times* said 'the folksy purity of the music along with a sense of these intertwining creative lives offers a realism rarely found in pop'. Interestingly, Stephen Holden's *New York Times* review placed the record at number two in his survey of the year's best 'music for the middle-aged', an article he began with the words: 'Attention fellow dinosaurs', indicating that the sisters, like many of his other choices, were not exactly new kids on the block. Further down the list was the *Rufus Wainwright* album, closely followed by Loudon's *Little Ship*.[13]

Rufus' album had been out for six months by the time *The McGarrigle Hour* was released and it's interesting to note how rarely his record got mentioned in the reviews. It's almost as though he was getting his wish and was appealing to a totally different audience to his parents so that he would not be compared to them. Reviewers perhaps felt that his 'pop' album would be of little consequence to the people reading about his mother's folk album.

Rufus' sexuality was, of course, no secret but whether it had impacted on his initial success is a moot point. Elton John, a perfect example of how commercial success and homosexuality need never be mutually exclusive, would later say that he believed that Rufus' sexuality hadn't harmed his sales; it was more the fact that his music was 'much more complex than what you hear on the radio' that had limited his appeal.

Aside from his shows with Barenaked Ladies, Rufus claimed to have not experienced overt homophobia from any audience. When the BNL fans started yelling insults at him at a stadium show, he temporarily froze but then thought, 'You're right. I am really gay. It's kind of like stating the obvious' and shrugged it off. Martha recalls how Rufus had stood up for himself, and then for her in the face of the braying fans: 'These jocks are calling him a faggot or something, and then I came up to sing and they started laughing at me because I was singing in French and I remember him stopping

---

13. When Rufus was asked to compile his own Top 10 of 1998 for the Canadian website jam.canoe.ca he placed the *McGarrigle Hour* album in second place behind Imani Coppola's *Chupacabra* (which had actually come out in 1997). In a rare moment of modesty he managed to keep his own album down at number ten. The full listing is as follows: 1) Imani Coppola – *Chupacabra* 2) *The McGarrigle Hour* 3) Sloan – *Navy Blues* 4) Burt Bacharach and Elvis Costello – *Painted From Memory* 5) Gillian Welch – *Hell Among the Yearlings* 6) Beck – *Mutations* 7) Fatboy Slim – *You've Come a Long Way, Baby* 8) Barenaked Ladies – *Stunt* 9) Elliott Smith – *XO* 10) Rufus Wainwright – *Rufus Wainwright*.

and saying, "This is my sister Martha and she has more balls than all of you combined."'

Although Rufus' own notes explaining the songs that formed part of the original DreamWorks press pack made it clear that he was singing from a gay perspective, the actual press release for the album didn't make any mention of his sexuality. Rufus didn't want to be seen as some kind of homosexual evangelist and it was left to individual writers to make as much or as little about Rufus being gay as they felt was necessary. 'I'm a huge pioneer, I'm like Columbus,' Rufus sarcastically commented to one interviewer who quizzed him about his stance before admitting that he was out because he would have found it impossible to lie about his sexuality. 'I don't know if I'm a pioneer . . . I'm definitely a soldier in the little army of people who are fighting for [liberation] but I'm not the only one.'

Once Rufus' press interviews started being published, clearly demonstrating that he was unafraid to discuss his sexuality with interviewers, he sensed that employees within the record company wished that he wasn't so frank. As he told an interviewer on the radio show *Fresh Air* on NPR (National Public Radio) with regard to him being gay: 'Certain people in the company itself [were] very put off by it sometimes . . . Once the press started coming out and they saw that I was actually as honest about [it] and as forthright, there were some people who said, "You know you just shouldn't talk about it" or "Just say that you like girls too."' In the same interview, Rufus mentions that Kate had once warned him that certain people who had come out later in their careers had been 'ruined'. Rufus laughingly said he was happy to start ruined and then work his way up from there.

The artist and film director Derek Jarman, who particularly in his later years wrote so negatively about the domination of queer-culture by 'heterosoc', his term for the oppressive heterosexual majority, once complained that, 'It is still quite common to read that the uncovering of a Queer life has diminished it',[14] by which he meant that although society was occasionally prepared to allow a gay artist to have a career and exist without censure, the second

---

14. Derek Jarman, *At Your Own Risk* (Hutchinson 1992, UK).

that artist speaks the truth about his lifestyle is the second that 'heterosoc' will at best stick its fingers in its ears and stop listening, or at worst actively attempt to suppress the artist. 'No-one could be Queer and celebrated,'[15] wrote Jarman, referring to the revisionist film biographies of Leonardo, Michelangelo and Shakespeare but touching on the difficulties that an 'out' artist had in dealing with the straight press and, indeed, the fears that kept other artists from coming out in the first place.

But times had moved on post-Jarman. Rufus' attitude to his sexuality and the casual way in which he spoke about his life went some way to demonstrating how for somebody of his generation it would be perfectly possible to be queer and celebrated. Rufus saw no reason to hide anything from anybody. He would just be outspoken and honest from the very beginning, even if the idea of that seemed too risky a strategy for some of his advisers. If Rufus' proclamations in the straight press concerned his label, then they would be even more worried when he spoke to the gay press. There, at least initially, he would talk even more openly about his ideas on sexuality and how they impacted on his life and career.

His first major solo cover feature was for the *Advocate*, in which he introduced himself as coming from 'a typical gay family: single mother, three sisters, heavy duty matriarchy'. In the interview with Barry Walters, Rufus is loath to align himself too strongly with any particularly gay ideals. Although he admits to admiring dead gay artists like Cole Porter or Tchaikovsky, he refuses to acknowledge any living gay peers: 'I don't know any. I have very high standards. I'm not gonna like somebody just because they're gay.'

In fact, he took this further by pointing out that in the past, the more oppressed a gay person was, the more intelligent and stylish they had to be to escape that oppression, the more they had to take off into fantasyland. And he implied that increases in freedom and equality have resulted in many gay people becoming more boring.

Towards the end of the article, Rufus touches on a subject that would prove alarmingly prescient. When Walters asks him if there are any gay issues that he feels particularly strongly about, Rufus replies: 'Drug abuse. I've done a lot of drugs and I'm not sober or

15. ibid.

AA. But I've always had a strong family network, I've always had something to come back to. Drugs can create a dangerous environment for people emotionally, especially crystal meth. I've done it twice, and it was crazy sexually but also horrifying and compromising, and I wanted it again immediately. Being in LA for two years I've seen lots of it. So many of the great clubs are gay. We open up these establishments and leave people hanging, and I find that irresponsible. There should be somewhere to go afterward, some support group.'

In light of this admission, an interview feature in early 1999 for the Canadian press became more alarming. In *Saturday Night*, David Hayes wrote that he had noticed fans making comments about the amount that Rufus was drinking on stage and how sometimes he was relying on his charms to carry the show, something which he had experienced himself at a club date in Toronto. When he had mentioned this to Van Dyke Parks he had responded: 'It's not good. Charm will not work. We've seen the act. You can't do it better than Judy Garland or Oscar Levant.'

Hayes himself questioned Rufus about his drinking, to which he received the frank reply: 'Yeah, I worry about it sometimes. I've tried to cut down. I really can't do my stage show if I'm too screwed up. I don't see it as being a problem but it's true I do like to drink.' Rufus also mentioned that during his time staying with Auf Der Mar in Los Angeles, he had seen a lot of drugs and he was still seeing them around him now. 'Horrible,' he says, then adds, 'but sometimes fun.'

If Rufus' sexuality was going to help get him noticed in any particular place then the wise money would have gone for San Francisco. As it happened, a San Francisco-based company would provide the vital breakthrough that Rufus and DreamWorks had been hoping for. Somebody at the advertising agency working for SF-based clothing company Gap had seen Rufus play and thought he would be perfect for their upcoming Christmas ad campaign. It wasn't the first time Rufus had agreed to take part in an advertising deal: he had already appeared as a poster boy for hip spectacle company LA Eyeworks, but this would be far more wide-reaching.

Gap had a special Christmas campaign planned, consisting of a series of 30-second musical TV spots with selected musicians playing seasonal songs. Everclear did a frantic version of 'Rudolph the Red-Nosed Reindeer' and Johnny Mathis crooned 'Winter Wonderland'. Rufus performed a solo piano version of the classic Frank Loesser song 'What are you doing New Year's Eve?' wearing, presumably, Gap-supplied, casual clothes on an all-white art deco set decked with streamers. The adverts were produced by A Band Apart Commercials, a company set up by Quentin Tarantino, Lawrence Bender and Michael Bodnarcheck. Although Gap traditionally spent heavily on advertising, their budget was mostly set aside for placing the adverts within the expensive commercial breaks of hit shows at the time, shows like *Ally McBeal* or *Dawson's Creek*. The musicians themselves were all paid the same set fee. It was not a huge amount (Everclear claimed they made as much by just doing one show), but it was the exposure that they were looking for – the recognition that came from the repetition of seeing the artist in a popular advert. Earlier in the year, the Verve had experienced a huge leap in their popularity in the US after reluctantly allowing 'Bittersweet Symphony' to be used by Nike in a series of adverts that were placed among NFL play-off games reaching audiences of 20 million. Their album had subsequently shot into the Top 40 in the Billboard charts for the first time.

Though Rufus' Gap advert appearances would not propel his album up the charts, it did provide a marked boost for his profile. The DreamWorks marketing department saw his sales increase by hundreds of percentage points and noticed that most people who were filling in the mailing list request cards inserted into all of their CDs were saying that they had first heard of Rufus via his TV commercial. With the advert in heavy rotation (in the US only), and with his selection as *Rolling Stone*'s Best New Artist of the Year, Rufus' publicist Jim Merlis found that the doors to getting Rufus on to TV shows like *Late Night With Letterman* and *The Today Show* were slowly starting to open. 'It was the synergy of these two things that sealed the deals with these TV bookers. Because of the television bookings we saw a spike in sales, but those bookings came from the commercials.'

For the grand finale of his debut solo tour, Rufus played a pre-Christmas show at the Bowery Ballroom on Delancey Street in New York. The recently opened venue had been given a $1 million retro-fit to convert it back from a shoe shop into its original state as a traditional 1920s theatre-style venue. Before the refit, the ballroom hadn't been used as an entertainment centre at all. Its original completion coincided with the stock market crash of 1929 when nobody was in the mood for dancing and it remained empty for decades until it had been turned into retail premises. With a capacity of 575, it was a perfect size for artists that were on the verge of making it big and as Rufus' first year as solo artist drew to a close, the signs were looking good for him to break through in 1999.

Having spent the preceding months touring, Rufus' performance was constantly improving, now it was more than just songs – Rufus was the all-round entertainer that his early Montreal shows had always promised he could be. Buoyed by the Gap advert exposure, publicist Jim Merlis had ensured that there were plenty of press in the house for the show and Rufus made sure that he delivered.

Won over by his quips and his easy manner, *Rolling Stone* likened Rufus to a 'gay, singing Woody Allen' and said that he 'cupped the New York audience in the palm of his hand and charmed the very wits out of them'; the *New York Daily News* talked of 'piano chords elegant enough to sweep Cole Porter off his feet, swelling through melodies as grand as a Manhattan skyline'; the *New York Times*, not for the first time, was even more effusive, 'Time takes a sabbatical when Rufus Wainwright sings. Most of his songs float above languidly strummed guitar chords or homey piano shuffles, circling until they alight on a yearning chorus. And his voice, with an apparently infinite breath supply, sustains phrases in pure legato, a moan that pays no attention to gravity.'

In addition to the material from his debut album, Rufus had introduced a couple of new songs into the set. 'California' turned the ennui of his months of monotonous sun-filled days watching *The Golden Girls* on television and waiting to go to the studios of Los Angeles into a catchy, top-down and driving radio-friendly bounce, and 'Greek Song', which he introduced at the Bowery Ballroom by explaining how it was about his unfulfilled lust for Greek men while on vacation. Both of these songs would feature on his next record.

Another song, introduced as 'These Four Walls' but later called 'The Cowboy Song' (and also sometimes 'Shut Down The World (I'm

Leaving You)') was written in response to Gus Van Sant's request for music for the *Brokeback Mountain* film project he was then working on.[16] Thrilled to have been asked to contribute to a project by the director of *My Own Private Idaho*, Rufus provided a song with an intense lyric on the power of forbidden love and of having to hide a secret even from God himself. It was flippantly introduced at the Bowery, stating that it was 'about a forbidden affair in the West . . . Doesn't have to be about boys or girls. Could be anyone: boys, girls, cowboys . . . cows. Or about Bill Clinton and what's his name? I mean what's her name? That drag queen, Monica Lewinsky.'

Kate, Anna and Loudon went to the concert to show their support. With Martha still part of the touring band, it was no great surprise when everybody came together for an emotive encore of 'What'll I Do', creating an oxymoronic picture of a happily dysfunctional family for the audience to take with them into the festive streets of New York.

Through his touring and exposure on TV and video, Rufus found himself the unexpected focus of a strong fan base of teenage girls. It was something that took everybody by surprise. 'I wasn't sure exactly who his audience would turn out to be,' said Lenny Waronker, 'but I certainly never expected young teens.'

It was more the fact that the fans were young, the expectation having been that Rufus would slot into the 'Adult Contemporary' market, than that they seemed oblivious to his sexuality, that surprised the label. Heterosexual female fans of gay musicians were not an uncommon occurrence; after all, a lustful relationship between fan and artist exists only in the fan's imagination where actual sexual preferences, or indeed any genuine sexual attraction at all,

---

16. Gus Van Sant's *Brokeback Mountain* project eventually collapsed with rumours that studios and the mainstream actors that were needed to get the funding in place were wary of committing to such an overtly gay film. Eventually Ang Lee resurrected the project to great acclaim in 2005 with Jake Gyllenhal, who would become a friend to Rufus and guest with him in concert, and the late Heath Ledger taking on the roles of the 'gay cowboys'. In mind of the difficulties that Van Sant had in casting the movie, it's interesting to note that when Ledger was asked at a press conference whether he thought it was a daring and brave decision to play a gay role he shrugged and said: 'Firefighters are daring and brave. I'm just acting.' Although Rufus contributed a song to the film soundtrack, it was a new song 'The Maker Makes' and not 'The Cowboy Song' which remains only available as a bonus track with certain formats of the *Release the Stars* album.

remain irrelevant because reality will almost never impinge on the fantasy. The most obvious, glitzy, outré example is the grinning, satisfied, blow-dried army of female fans that surrounded Liberace throughout his career – it wasn't that they didn't know, it was just that they didn't care.

In a *Newsweek* story, Rufus said the girls who had started to flock around him made him feel like Luke Skywalker surrounded by Ewoks. 'A lot of them were young, like 14, 15,' he said. 'They know I'm gay but it doesn't really factor. I don't think they are thinking of sex. They just want to know about guys, just hang out and flirt and be open.' He'd later say that his success with teenage girls came from the fact that he smiled a lot and wasn't afraid to comment on what they were wearing. Either that or the fact that 'A Dreamboat is a dreamboat is a dreamboat.'

Even if Rufus had been mobbed by Ewoks at every single show, there weren't enough of them putting their furry paws in their pockets and buying his album. The debut had sold less than 55,000 copies in the US almost a year after being released so it was a tribute to Jim Merlis' genius at publicity that mainstream media outlets like *Newsweek* would still cover a somewhat marginal artist. Even accounting for modelling assignments for Anna Sui and Perry Ellis and the Gap advert increasing his profile, Rufus was getting an awful lot of media mileage from comparatively tiny sales as Nick Terzo concurred when talking about his time as manager through to 2000. 'The hardest part of guiding his career was that his profile was so much larger than record sales.'

In fact, the media profile versus record sales conundrum remains the 'elephant in the room' when discussing Rufus within business rather than artistic terms. Countless other artists have suffered a discrepancy between their actual sales and their critical profile. Ryan Adams, Elliott Smith and Steve Earle are just three examples close enough to the Rufus 'model' to make the point. A sympathetic record label would stick by them in the hope that they would gradually build commercial success from their positive critical acclaim. That said, most artists would have had their budget capped at a realistic level based on their expected success. Rufus had been given a luxuriant budget and recouped almost none of it.

By anybody's standards, Rufus' first record had been incredibly expensive and time-consuming. According to Terzo, the original deal had been based around a total budget of a little under $1 million to cover advances and all expenditure on two albums with options to be negotiated along the way. The actual recording costs for the first record alone were reported to be in excess of $700,000 – approximately three times that of an album for an established, successful band in the late 1990s – leaving little in the pot for the follow-up.

Rufus would later partially blame Jon Brion for the huge recording expenses of the record by saying that it had been the producer's responsibility to look out for costs as he was too inexperienced to know any better. He would also suggest to Mim Udovitch of *Rolling Stone*, in an interview published while he was touring to promote the record, that part of the problem was that Brion had had difficulty in dealing with his lifestyle. 'I just don't think he knew how to handle that,' said Rufus. 'With some people I've found that because they are not aware of what you are attracted to or of the world you live in, they feel a little powerless over you.' The disagreements have obviously rankled. In a radio interview with Nic Harcourt on the Los Angeles station KCRW in 2003, many years after they had finished working together, Rufus suggested that Brion was just 'a failed songwriter'. A reunion is very unlikely.

Although he was obviously aware of the costs he was generating, it would be many years before Rufus started to publicly express concern at the huge debts to his label that he had been accruing, his ornate palatial albums in effect mortgaged to the hilt. In 1999 he was more concerned with building a career and getting famous, screw the costs.

The failure of *Rufus Wainwright* in the marketplace would test, and indeed prove, DreamWorks' commitment to Rufus as a long-term artist, but even with the full backing of Waronker and Ostin, a lot would be riding on the second album. Rufus planned to quickly start recording his next album in the autumn so it would be ready for a swift winter release. However, it would turn out to be another extended project.

When Martha wasn't playing shows with Rufus, she would often play with Loudon. She'd guest on a few songs in his set, often after having played her own songs as the evening's opening act. By now she was intent on continuing as an artist in her own right and though the familial gigs were a useful proving ground for her new songs, she couldn't help but feel somewhat resentful at always being both literally and metaphorically bottom of the bill. The nadir came during a tour of Europe playing with Loudon where Martha grew increasingly uncomfortable at sitting backstage and hearing Loudon's fans laughing and cheering at songs she knew were about her.

When she got to play her own solo shows, the response was generally positive. Her songwriting was improving and, most noticeably, her vocal stylings were becoming more powerful and more original until she had reached the point where she could switch between soft, tender whisper and concupiscent wail within a single line. After seeing a solo gig in 1999, *Crawdaddy* journalist Peter Jesperson would describe her as 'the riskiest (and sexiest) music' he had heard all year and added that 'the most staggering thing might be her potential'.

Martha had recorded a few new songs since releasing *Ground Floor* and put together a new CD EP. *Martha Wainwright* consists of six songs and Martha sold it at shows but, although it was carried by Amazon, it otherwise had no distribution.

The best two songs from the original cassette album ('Laurel and Hardy' and 'Don't Forget') were included alongside the superb 'G.P.T', a wanton drink-soaked country rocker, and the clinging, lachrymose 'You've Got a Way'. On 'Jimi (takes so much time)', the most autobiographical of the new songs, Martha addresses her insecurity at her place in the world and her existence as defined by her relationship to others. When she moved out of her home and left her mother alone, was that the same as Loudon abandoning the family? The song is full of questions and, like a true McGarrigle lyric rather than a Wainwright song, it is haunted by ghosts.

Despite being a huge improvement on the debut tape, Martha still seemed to lack confidence in her material. She was happy to continue playing at small clubs and to gradually creep into the consciousness of the public by positive word-of-mouth, but she was less happy to force herself on to the music business. It was as if she was waiting for somebody to come to her and ask her to make a record, rather than go out and hunt down a contract herself. In an interview for the womanrock website not long after the CD had come out, Martha admits to not having total self-belief in her abilities and in still being apprehensive about being judged in relation to her family. 'I think if I was really shitty, people would have picked up on it early on. So I am just going to keep doing what I am doing. We all have to prove ourselves at the end of the day. People either like it or don't like it. I mean there definitely is a pressure. Sometimes you feel like maybe there are people in the wings waiting for a fall. Like, "Oh, the youngest one just sucks!" And are ready to pounce on that story, you know? . . . "There couldn't be another great Wainwright."'

Other people were more than pleased to work with her: she guested on Boo Hewerdine's *Thanksgiving* album and at the end of the year she was asked to perform in a group show at St Ann's Church, Brooklyn. The *Songs of the Century* show featured various musicians singing 29 of the best songs of the century as informally selected by the organisers and through the 20,000-strong mailing list of the church's arts/performance department. Although the performers – Marshall Crenshaw and Jimmie Dale Gilmore were among the best known and other musicians included ex-Bangle Vicki Peterson – were not anything like as high profile as some of the more celebrated participants of similar themed nights, it was a great opportunity for Martha to appear in an event that was sure to attract publicity. She ended up singing what she described as a 'children's set', which included 'Over the Rainbow' and 'When You Wish upon a Star' (in the second half she was allowed to rock out a little with a version of 'That's All Right Mama'). However, the high point of the night for Martha was getting to meet fellow performer Beth Orton.

Orton, who was set to play songs including 'Summertime' and Robert Johnson's 'Love in Vain' arrived late. She had been buying a snack on the way to the venue when somebody had a heart attack right in front of her and she had had to wait inside the shop until the ambulance came for him. Shocked and disturbed by her experience, she arrived after the show had begun and the first thing she saw was Martha in a short skirt with football socks rolled up to her knees, singing on stage. Orton says that she was so stunned by Martha's voice that she burst into tears. Backstage the pair hit it off straight away and, although it would take another year or so before they got together again, they would become close friends.

3.5

If Martha was unsure of her position in the Wainwright/ McGarrigle musical hierarchy, then Rufus was using his increased profile to try to establish himself as the most important male member of the family. As he toured through 1999, he would often boast that he was playing in places that his father had never been able to play. He'd later regret some of the ungracious things he said about Loudon in the press at the time, especially after learning that Loudon would often have to fend away prying questions about his parenting skills after a journalist had read something that Rufus had said about him.

Rufus was interviewed for *Rolling Stone* in June. The interview covered a 24-hour period when Rufus played a show in Columbus, Ohio, and then travelled to play another show in Louisville, Kentucky. It's a fairly standard interview feature in which life on the road is described: the shabby tour bus with the Andy Warhol DVDs playing; the post-gig trip to one bar, then another bar, then another bar; the larking around at the sound-check.

Rufus explained how he was still looking for a lifestyle. He said that he wanted to be Tammy Wynette to somebody's George Jones, or Gertrude Stein to somebody's Alice B. Toklas. He was looking for either total devotion or violent possession. 'I'm a great prize,' he trilled, 'I'm like the singing bird. You can put me in a cage.'

When asked how his success was affecting his relationships, Rufus replied, 'I'm still in a weird way looking for interesting gay people. I'm still wondering where that blissful wonderful kind of gay lifestyle is that I will lead one day and part of my music is about that. So I figure that now I'll advertise it. But of course the more you advertise it the more elusive it becomes. I mean the reason I am doing this is essentially to get laid . . .'

Eventually the talk got around to his parents and Rufus spoke about Loudon: 'Now that I'm actually making it and doing quite well, I think it's a little harder for him because he's still making records and he's still touring and he's still doing his thing. I just think it's hard and there's still a side of me that wants to conquer him in a certain way.'

It wasn't so much what Rufus said about Loudon in interviews that riled his father but more what he said to him in private that would prove so divisive and bring to a head the deep-seated resentments that Rufus had held and failed to address. After a photo session for the *Rolling Stone* feature, Rufus and Loudon were having dinner when Rufus bullishly suggested that the only way his father would get into *Rolling Stone* now was off the back of his son's career. It was a cheap shot, especially considering that his father had tried to make amends for part of his long absences from Rufus' life by trying to help him get his music career started in the first place. Loudon was incensed and literally chased him out of the house. They didn't speak again for months.

After the incident Rufus wrote one of his most poignant songs, and one that he felt was so personal and raw that he avoided recording it or playing it publicly for many years. With 'Dinner at Eight',[17] Rufus intended to write a song that was filled with anger. Rufus casts himself as the biblical David to Loudon's Goliath, promising to strike down his father 'with one little stone' and he invites him to 'put up his fists' and take him on. Later in the song, forcing the confrontation, he's looking for Loudon to shed a tear in recognition of the hurt he had caused the infant Rufus by abandoning him. By the end of the song, there has been some resolution, or at least Rufus sees the possibility of a resolution. It's almost as if in writing the final couplet ('Long ago, actually in the drifting white snow/You loved me'), Rufus has received an epiphany and understands that divorce can be as difficult for the parent as it is for the child. The writer and actor Mark Gatiss has called the song 'an eloquent hymn to the oddness of all families and relations'.[18] What had been intended as a song of hate becomes a cathartic song of love. After he had recorded it (during the *Want* sessions), Rufus played the song for his father and promised him that he would not release it if Loudon felt it was too personal. As it happened Loudon loved it, but before he'd even heard it, he acknowledged that it would be

---

17. The song took its title from George Cukor's 1933 film of the same name about a chaotic society dinner party that teeters between tragedy and farce as everything goes wrong for the hostess Billie Burke (six years away from playing Glinda in *The Wizard of Oz*), who at the peak of her botheration famously squawks: 'I've had the most ghastly day anybody ever had. No aspic for dinner!'
18. Jeremy Dyson, Mark Gatiss, Steve Pemberton, Reece Shearsmith, *The League of Gentlemen's Book of Precious Things*, Prion, 2007, UK.

somewhat hypocritical if he was to object to songs written about him after everything he had written himself.

Perhaps Rufus could have compared parental notes with his friend Teddy Thompson, another son of famous folk-singing parents who had also been through a difficult divorce when he was a young child.

Richard and Linda Thompson had made a series of superb folk-rock albums together, including their sublime 1974 debut *I Want to See the Bright Lights Tonight*[19] before an acrimonious split just after their final album *Shoot Out the Lights* (1982). Richard, in a Loudonesque way, had dissected their relationship quite clinically in the songs on the record (although, contrary to popular belief, it can't truly be considered as a virtual soundtrack to the divorce as many of the songs had been written before the marriage had floundered). On some songs, notably 'Walking on a Wire', Richard provides lyrics that prove uncomfortably close to the bone when his soon to be ex-wife sings them – it's not unlike Loudon getting Martha to sing 'Father Daughter Dialogue'.

Teddy and Rufus had been aware of each other since they were children as their parents had been friends – and Richard, of course, had worked with Loudon on numerous projects in the 1980s – but they didn't become close until Teddy found himself in Los Angeles looking after his father's apartment while Pa Thompson was on tour. Teddy had played in his father's touring band for a while and was now striving to get his own record deal as a singer-songwriter while Rufus, riding high on the DreamWorks coin, was doing his best to devour as much of the Californian party scene as he could.

In fact, it had been Kate who had called up Linda Thompson and suggested that their boys hook up. Like caring parents at a coffee morning, both mothers thought it would be a way for their children to look out for each other in a city a long way from home.

Their rendezvous was arranged for Gladstones, a seafood restaurant that hangs over the beach on the Pacific Coast Highway just outside Santa Monica. It's a popular hang-out for families and

19. Not long after they had hooked up with each other, Rufus and Teddy played the album's title song together as an encore at one of his shows at Largo just before Thompson's first album was released.

homesick Brits looking for fish and chips for whom the possibility that an occasional celebrity might call in on their way back up the coast road to their Malibu mansions was an added attraction.

At the time Rufus had entered full rock-star mode and would be driven around from appointment to appointment, lounging in the back of the DreamWorks-appointed car, resplendent in colourful and flamboyant outfits, draped in scarves and perma-sunglasses. Teddy remembers him pulling up at the restaurant in a huge blacked-out limo and stepping out in purple trousers, yellow top, ridiculous hat and outsize women's sunglasses. 'He looked like Dame Edna Everage,' he would later recall.

They bonded over their somewhat turbulent relationships with their fathers. 'My constant need for and not getting my father's approval was very similar to Teddy's own experiences,' said Rufus. 'And then of course there was another bond, one that revolved around partying.'

Rufus remembers Thompson as being a little 'dorky' and 'foppish' when he first met him. Although he was convinced that Thompson was shocked to be in the presence of a 'raving homosexual', it didn't take long for Rufus to lead the reserved, shy Englishman astray. Thompson thought Rufus was very cool and bohemian, he remembers him as being 'a fun guy to be around, the kind of person who would down a bottle of wine at lunch. Which I thought was very daring. I was quite sheltered back then.'

Before long it was more than bottles of wine for lunch as Rufus and Teddy set about tearing up the town. Thompson had already been introduced to the kind of casual debauchery that was available in La La Land when he'd taken a part-time job at a Santa Monica hairdressers while he tried to establish his music career. 'It was like stepping into the film *Shampoo*,' he remembers. 'The people there were nuts. They would lock the door in the middle of the day and chop out lines of cocaine. My eyes were open very quickly, and if I hadn't been a serious party person before, I was then.'

The pair hit party after party with Rufus introducing Teddy to the circuit of industry events, launches and openings, where the drinks were free and the drugs formed an orderly line right in front of them. Eventually they gravitated to the bohemian scene to be found on the Eastside of town towards Silver Lake and Echo Park and centred around the Silverlake Lounge on Sunset Boulevard. This was a grungy low-key venue where acts like Elliott Smith and Black Rebel Motorcycle Club would develop their material on the club's tiny stage while local hipsters rubbed shoulders with off-duty celebrities and aspiring pop stars like Rufus and Teddy and everybody just coolly ignored each other. It was also the kind of place where Rufus learned how to surreptitiously ask for and buy his own drugs without drawing undue attention to himself.

Teddy owned a battered old Volvo but as if to emphasise their different positions on the ladder of success, Rufus would drive them around town in a series of extravagant cars that had been loaned to him by his record label. He maintained a rather lax attitude to drink-driving laws. One of their acquaintances at the time remembers Rufus trying to follow directions he had been given to a house party in the Silver Lake area. He was too drunk to remember the route he had been told: 'There used to be a chiropodist on Sunset near the Silverlake Lounge with a sign that had a smiling foot on one side and a sad foot on the other and it was lit up at night and the foot slowly revolved. We were looking for this party, everybody else had already gone ahead and we were driving up and down the street and Rufus kept insisting he knew what he was doing but we kept driving past this foot, over and over. Smiley foot. Sad foot. Smiley foot. It was like one of those films where the hero thinks he's escaped but ends up exactly back where he started. Eventually I asked him to stop the car and I just got out.'

Thompson recalls one occasion when Rufus was so drunk that he got in the car to drive home but ended up sitting in the passenger seat unable to find the steering wheel. Like many artists before him, or, as some might counter, like many apologists for misbehaving artists, in Thompson's opinion their hedonistic nights were driven by a need to push themselves into difficult areas in order to make them better musicians. 'Music is the biggest motivation in my life, and you can't make really good art if you are happy,' he later said. 'I think both Rufus and I strived for a certain kind of pain to make us better at what we do.' Interestingly, Thompson identified Rufus' continual infatuation with straight, and therefore unobtainable, men as a deliberate, though perhaps subconscious, means to increase his levels of, if not exactly unhappiness, then at least emotional conflict in order to provoke his muse.

As two musicians trying to make it, there was understandably a certain amount of rivalry. Thompson, perhaps unsurprisingly, was an accomplished guitarist. Before he'd reached his teens his father had paid for guitar lessons, having weaned him off his initial desire to play the drums by only letting him have one drum at a time. '[He] bought me a snare-drum and said, "When you get really good at that you can have the next drum,"' remembers Teddy. Of course he was bored before he even got to the tom-toms and cymbals.

Thompson had developed an engaging but slightly stiff and awkward-looking performance style (when he plays guitar and sings he sometimes moves as though he's left the coat hanger in his jacket) and was playing a weekly show at Largo. A few record labels had begun sniffing around and he eventually signed to Virgin and released his self-titled debut album in 2000. The record was not a commercial success, due in part to a lack of promotion by the label and to the fact that, contrary to the successful strategy employed by Rufus' management, he didn't have an established fan base other than at a few local clubs in Los Angeles and New York.

Whereas Thompson considered Rufus had arrived fully formed and ready to take on the world, he felt it was always going to take him a little longer to find his feet. Unfortunately his label decided that they weren't prepared to wait for that and almost instantly dropped him, withdrawing all tour support and promotion when the album failed to take off immediately.

The album itself is an unconvincing mix of bland soft-rock and easy-listening country. One of the best tracks, the opening 'Wake Up' sounds like Oasis and is all but ruined by Father Thompson crashing in halfway through with a trademark guitar solo overshadowing the rest of the track – it isn't because it's a particularly good solo (it isn't), but because it acts as a somewhat crude reminder of the family tree when it would probably have been wiser, at least on the first track of his first record, to have let Teddy step out from under the branches.

Rufus guests on the vapid 'So Easy' but it's 'Missing Children', almost a cowboy lament for broken families, that is the track that pointed the way forward for Thompson's songwriting and is most representative of the direction he would take. He wouldn't make another solo record until 2005 when he returned with the more developed country-rock sound of *Separate Ways*, having been reinvigorated by the success of coaxing his mother back into the studio for her *Fashionably Late* album in 2002, on which he enlisted the help of both Rufus and Martha.

Even though he was already signed and had achieved such acclaim for his first record, Rufus admitted to feeling nervous that Thompson might somehow surpass him artistically and commercially. He can even remember when he first heard a song of Thompson's that really impressed him and he knew that if he ended up being eclipsed in any way, he would have to hate his guts for ever. As if to prove the point, and to illuminate the often repeated, rarely refuted claim, that Rufus is self-obsessed to the point of narcissism, when Teddy played Rufus the finished album he was dismissive of it, which hurt Thompson enough for him to vow that he would never again look for Rufus' approval.

3.6

Rufus' intention to start work on his own second record in the autumn of 1999 hadn't panned out. Aside from recording a few songs for film soundtracks and compilation albums and a couple of guest appearances on other people's records, he had hardly entered the recording studio since the marathon sessions for his debut. By the summer of 1999 he had relocated to New York and got a room at the Chelsea Hotel where his partying continued and he gradually began to step towards ever darker areas.

'I had a few songs that I liked going into the second record. But I was a little worried, since the first record had taken 17 years to make, theoretically,' Rufus explained to *Nylon* magazine. 'So I moved to New York and I lived in the Chelsea for a few months. I met a whole cast of characters who are quite well known in downtown New York social circles, fun people. I started hanging out with these guys and had a bit of a rebirth. This sounds really funny but it was my time to be gay in New York. That's when I started writing *Poses*. It was very much about a time, being a young person in the city.'

Hotel Chelsea on 23rd Street had long been a place for artists, musicians, actors and writers to both live and congregate. It had inspired numerous songs since the 1960s, including work by Lou Reed, Bob Dylan and Leonard Cohen, who famously described Janis Joplin giving him head in one of the hotel's rooms. Aside from its legend as a kind of cultural lodestone, the Chelsea had a parallel reputation for sleazy disreputability and fatal excess that appealed to its artistic clientele, while giving it enough of an edge to maintain its outlaw status in an otherwise comparatively affluent part of Manhattan. Dylan Thomas drank himself to death while staying there, Sid either did or didn't stab Nancy, and Charles R. Jackson, author of *The Lost Weekend*, committed suicide in his room in 1968 after a lifetime of struggling with both alcohol addiction and his suppressed homosexuality. There could be few hotels anywhere in the world that could harbour a fable about a guest keeping a tiger in their room as pulp novelist Theodora Keogh, the granddaughter of Teddy Roosevelt, was supposed to have done in the 1960s with so few people even questioning the truth of such an outlandish tale.[20]

---

20. The cat in question was a margay (a kind of small ocelot), not exactly a tiger. Legend has it that Keogh had her ear chewed off by the beast when she passed out in her room after a few too many drinks, a story repeated in her obituary in the *Daily Telegraph* (29 January 2008). Others dispute that there was a cat or that she had ever stayed at the Chelsea at all.

It's probably spurious anecdotes like this that best represent the Hotel Chelsea mythology, where the dissolute and the decadent forever float down the corridors in a miasma of half-truths, wishful thinking and urban folklore. The very idea of the 'Tiger Lady of the Chelsea' would have surely fired Rufus' imagination more even than the indisputable fact that Arthur C. Clarke had written his novel *2001: A Space Odyssey* at the hotel. When Rufus spoke of wanting to 'live the Chelsea life', it's not difficult to imagine the fabled Tiger Lady leaning over his shoulder and nodding her approval.

The phantasmagorical nature of the Chelsea Hotel milieu is perhaps best encapsulated by Joe Ambrose's *Chelsea Hotel Manhattan* (Headpress, 2007, UK), a kaleidoscopic mix of reportage, conjecture and fantasy that captures the hotel before its current, and controversial, gentrification kicked in when its legendary manager Stanley Bard was squeezed out. At the time Rufus was staying there, the hotel was moving away from what it had once been.

'Things had changed at the Chelsea by the late 1990s,' explains Ambrose. 'It was no longer the beacon for bohemia that it had been all through the sixties and seventies. The neighbourhood had changed. Chelsea had once been run down and cheap – by the late 1990s it was becoming prosperous. Inside the hotel the Stanley Bard era was coming to an end. Though Stanley was still in charge, he'd been persuaded by his business partners to hike up the rents and you now had to be a pretty successful type of boho to reside at the Chelsea. The principal working artists of serious intent rooming there were signed up music acts with impeccable college radio/indie credentials like Ryan Adams and Wainwright or Hollywood hipsters like Ethan Hawke. The atmosphere was still funky enough – literally funky sometimes in terms of the smelly refuse in the hallways – and you could still do whatever you wanted to do in its rooms, but it was fast becoming a rich kids' hangout.'

No wonder some people read Dee Dee Ramone's punk rock zombie novel *Chelsea Horror Hotel* (Da Capo Press, 2001, US) as though it was the bassist's autobiography.

Rufus had most recently been staying in Los Angeles with Leonard Cohen's daughter Lorca (in an apartment directly underneath her father who Rufus claims he rarely saw but always remained aware of his looming presence) and it was she who suggested that Rufus should move into the Chelsea as he told an interviewer in 2005: 'We both came to New York together and we both stayed in the Chelsea, and she turned to me one day and said, "You know, my dad lived here for a long time," and I said, "Oh really," and she said, "Maybe you should live here, we should go talk to the manager." So I went down with her and said, "This is Leonard's daughter, her dad lived here," and that was sort of an "in" to get in.' In fact, in the end Rufus found out that an associate of his was moving out and he took over their room, situated at the front of the hotel with its window near enough to the E in the buzzing neon *HOTEL* sign that the walls glowed at night.

Much as he had seen his initial stay at the Chateau Marmont as being a signal that he had arrived as a serious musician, then Rufus looked upon making his home at the Chelsea as signifying that he had returned to take his throne and make up for his failure in the city a few years earlier.

'When I was in New York as a younger person, nobody wanted to know who I was,' he explained. 'I didn't have anything to offer – I didn't have a record – but once I had an album, I could walk back into the city and have something to talk about, something to show. So I decided to move into the Chelsea, because you know, it was a good address for them to send their calling cards, and I did that and I really did grasp the whole idea of the Chelsea and live to the fullest.'

With the small amount of money left from his advance but with the more important currency of being a hip young musician with a much-lauded record under his belt, he discovered that many more doors were opened to him than had ever been in his earlier stays in the city. He found himself welcomed at more openings, previews and nightclubs than he could fit into any given night. 'All of a sudden I had a calling card and a bit of a reputation,' he explained to writer Barney Hoskyns. 'And I immediately started to cash in on that. I really did treat it as: This is my dolce vita time, and I'm gonna run this for all it's worth. I went to all these parties and met all these people, and found that basically it's like a big revolving door. People come in and out, and there's a definite hierarchy – especially in the gay world, I have to say – around who you are and what you do. Like, are you a hustler, or are you a designer? Are you cute or are you smart? And I basically found that I was in it, but I couldn't tell which one I was. I couldn't tell if I was the one who was spiralling into self-destruction or if I was causing other people to spiral into self-destruction.'

He even found himself welcomed into what he'd dubbed the 'Alphabet City jet-set' that had formerly ignored him when he ran into his hero Justin Bond of the über-camp duo Kiki and Herb in one of the city's less salubrious gay bars. By this time Bond knew exactly who Rufus was and as they were introduced – Bond in what he called his 'tranny-hooker garb', Rufus in a fake fur coat that made him look like a teddy bear – he told him he was a fan. Rufus would later say that this meant more to him than if Prince or Barbra Streisand had said it. 'I knew at that moment I'd made it. I respect him so much more, as a legendary performer, than countless people who are wealthier or more famous.'

When he wasn't out partying, Rufus worked on songs for his new album on a piano that he had brought into his hotel room. One of the first songs he wrote, 'Poses', which would become the title track, served to create a character, partly fictional, but as he would later realise, also partly autobiographical, around whom Rufus was able to build the rest of the record.

'When I started writing ['Poses'] life was crazy,' he remembered in a later interview. 'I'd step out of the hotel and it was like stepping into a universe where beautiful boys reign supreme and are coveted by everyone who sees them. It fucks with your head and it can ruin you if you let it. By the end of the song, the character is a drunken, drugged-out mess, tripping down the streets in flip-flops, a shadow of his former self.'

At the clubs, bars and parties he frequented, Rufus saw young men arrive in the city, spend their time getting wild and wasted until, at summer's end, they were worn down and worn out. 'By the end they looked ancient,' said Rufus, 'gaunt. It's a real mill. I saw some of that happening to people and I wondered if it was happening to me. I ended up writing that song about that subject. It's sort of a fictional character, but it's based on a lot of people. After I wrote that, I knew I had a record. Everything else spun from that.'

After six months, Rufus was out of the Chelsea, vowing that one day the hotel would mark his stay with a plaque in the lobby among those honouring former guests such as Thomas Wolfe and Dylan Thomas. He moved back into the self-contained apartment in his mother's Montreal home determined to start recording.

There had been talk of Rufus producing the next album on his own, but instead he opted to start the recordings with Pierre Marchand in Canada. Rufus had decided that he wanted to make a more pop-sounding album, partly to get away from being seen, as he put it, as another one of Lenny Waronker's artists – meaning he wanted to avoid the Randy Newman references – but also because he felt that his talents deserved some commercial as well as critical success. Marchand was in the middle of producing a string of hugely successful albums for Sarah McLachlan, whose previous two records had sold 11 million copies in the US alone. Rufus was looking for some of Marchand's 'pixie dust' to fall on him.

Temporarily putting aside his more complicated 'dirge-ish, monster songs' and the songs he likened to American Lieder, Rufus concentrated on editing his material to fit in with his idea of making a more accessible record. He cut out whole verses to shorten songs and generally spent less time laboriously working on his lyrics, preferring to go with what sounded good at the time. Aside from two older numbers, 'Greek Song' and 'California', which had proven themselves in his live shows, his intention was to create a whole new album from scratch.

Rufus was keen to show that he could do more than just sit behind the piano and play; if anything, he wanted the new record be a little more contemporary, both in its sound and in its construction. Although he had loved the first record, he now wanted to move away from the big California studios and the session musicians and work with people who were closer to his own age. To this end, in addition to the tracks completed in

Canada, Rufus recorded material in New York with Alex Gifford of Propellerheads, a British big beat/trip-hop team who were signed to DreamWorks in the US.

Rufus eventually returned to Los Angeles to complete the recording sessions for the album. He rented a plush house in Beverly Hills with its own tennis court and requisite swimming pool. Its former resident had been Puff Daddy. The idea was to bring in recording equipment and make the record in situ. It was a way of keeping a lid on costs while allowing the luxury of relaxed experimentation. Rufus hated it; instead of allowing him time to work through different arrangements of songs, he found that he felt trapped. 'It was a horrible idea,' he admitted. 'I like going to the studio, being in the studio. Getting away from the studio.'

When the recordings were completed and finally mixed, Rufus took the tapes with him to London where he was due to spend Christmas with Teddy Thompson and his mother, Linda. He had imagined that the city would be full of Dickensian Christmas cheer but instead was disappointed to find that, like in most big cities over the Christmas period, nothing much was going on and that most people preferred to stay indoors with their families watching television. He wandered the quiet streets alone, listened to his album sessions over and over on a pair of outsize headphones and decided on a final running order, grouping the songs by style and feeling. When he played his final choice to Kate, she thought it was the worst sequencing job ever.

Kate and Anna had spent September 2000 in London recording backing vocals at Abbey Road studios for Nick Cave and the Bad Seeds' *No More Shall We Part* album. Cave had been a fan of the sisters since they had appeared at the 1999 Meltdown Festival for which he had been guest curator. Kate and Anna had performed the apocalyptic 'John The Revelator' with him as part of the Hal Willner-produced 'Harry Smith Anthology of American Folk Music Night', which had featured an ensemble cast of cult musicians including Beth Orton, Bryan Ferry, Jimmy Smith and, making his London live debut, Van Dyke Parks. (The concert would be repeated with a fluctuating cast at later performances in both Brooklyn and Los Angeles.) 'I was kind of unaware of them till that point,' says

Cave. 'We sang a couple of songs together live and they sang the backing vocals to a version of "Henry Lee" I did and they just sounded incredible – beautiful, haunting backing vocals. They were always in my mind while I was writing the [album], thinking that they'd be good.'

No More Shall We Part is often considered Cave's masterpiece. Coming four years after the sparse and highly personal piano-led The Boatman's Call, the album was a watershed both lyrically and musically as Cave completed his move away from the sardonic bombast of his early songs and introduced more delicate themes and styles that he would explore further on subsequent albums.

The record is a sophisticated amalgam of religious symbolism and gothic romance and the Bad Seeds use the sisters' voices as though they were another instrument, often interwoven with Warren Ellis' spectral violin. Their voices form an integral part of what is, in places, an ominous-sounding record which, according to one critic, was capable of darkening the listener's mood like 'poison seeping slowly into a well'. Indeed, when the sisters' answer to Cave's plaintive 'Where is Mona?' comes eerily out of just one speaker at the beginning of the song 'Fifteen Feet of Pure White Snow' it's a genuinely creepy moment.

Kate and Anna were considered to have played such a vital role in the recording that they became virtual Bad Seeds, photographed in the hazy band portrait on the CD booklet, in which Kate is the only one with anything approaching a smile, and given equal billing with the other band members in the credits rather than being listed as session players.

Their voices lent themselves well to Cave's writing style with its debt to classic blues and folk forms but which still manages to sound utterly unique. It was the first time that they had been involved with making music that was created by contemporary rock rather than folk musicians. Later they would add new dimensions to work by Rufus and Martha but it's interesting to imagine how artistically successful they could be if they were to work on an album of wholly contemporary music with somebody like Nick Cave as musical director. Although they would work with Cave again on Hal Willner's Leonard Cohen tribute project, they did not feature on any subsequent Bad Seeds recordings.

Before his new album was released, Rufus had cut some songs for use in big-budget movies that could only help increase his profile when they were released later in 2001. Baz Luhrman's *Moulin Rouge!* was a spectacular musical that harked back to the great *That's Entertainment*-style Hollywood films that Rufus had so loved as a child. Although he had originally been asked to write a number of songs for the film, one of which was 'Tower of Learning' that would appear on *Poses*, he was proud to have his version of the song 'Complainte de la Butte' on the soundtrack. The song, with lyrics originally written by Jean Renoir, was something of a French standard and would be one of the few numbers heard in the movie that could be considered, in any way at all, authentically Parisian. The majority of the soundtrack featured reworkings of songs by the likes of The Police, T. Rex and Elton John in stylised productions by sometime Madonna cohort Marius de Vries. De Vries did not produce Rufus' track but he would later come to play an important role in his career.

However, although it was useful for Rufus to be associated with a film that would be as hugely successful as *Moulin Rouge!*, in truth few moviegoers would have been particularly aware of his contribution to the soundtrack as his song was used only very briefly in one early scene. Perversely, his association with the movie *Shrek* would prove to be more effective in getting his name across to the general public, in spite of the fact that he was not actually heard singing in it at all.

In *Shrek*, the Leonard Cohen song 'Hallelujah' appears in a version sung by John Cale (taken from a 1991 Cohen tribute album *I'm Your Fan*). Cohen himself had recorded the song in 1984 but, like most of Laughing Lenny's work, and despite being covered many times already,[21] it hadn't crossed over into the general public's

---

21. Cohen had written dozens of verses for 'Hallelujah' and it had taken him almost two years to complete it. In the 1980s the song had often been played live by Bob Dylan to whom Cohen provided further stanzas from those which had appeared on his own recorded version on *Various Positions* (1984). The difference between the versions being that Dylan had chosen to include some more upbeat, positive verses while Cohen's take had been typically acidic and generally lacking in hope. When John Cale asked Cohen about the song before he recorded his version, he was also given even more unrecorded verses. Subsequent performers would pick and choose which lyrics to use depending on their inclination so that the song's very nature enabled various interpretations.

Rufus claimed not to have heard Jeff Buckley's singular version when he recorded his

consciousness. Its association with the lovable, lovelorn green monster in the film soon changed that.

Cale's version is superior to Cohen's. It's a clinical, cold-eyed rendition that is part menacing and part melancholic. It was a trick for which Cale already had form after his vicious reimagining of 'Heartbreak Hotel' back in 1975 became the definitive example of how to gut an instantly recognisable song and show that there had always been something else lurking inside it. Quite how his 'Hallelujah' attracted such affection in what is ostensibly a children's movie remains a mystery but it became a phenomenon, introducing the song to millions of people around the world who took it to their hearts, no doubt helped in part by the fact that a whole slew of TV shows subsequently began to use versions of the song as a soundtrack signifier whenever there was death or tragedy on the screen.

Those that chose to bring the *Shrek* experience home to their hi-fis would discover that the version of 'Hallelujah' on the soundtrack album was not by Cale at all but by Rufus Wainwright, who had been asked to record a new version especially for the CD.

In one radio interview, Rufus mischievously suggested that the reason his version was not featured in the film was because of the 'glass ceiling' he was hitting because of his sexuality. The reality of the matter would seem to be rather more mundane. The movie was created by DreamWorks: Rufus was a DreamWorks artist and John Cale was not. Licensing issues had precluded Cale's version from appearing on the soundtrack album but the film-makers' original

---

for the *Shrek* album. It's true that the similarities between them seem to be coincidental as Rufus' recorded version is much closer to Cale's subdued interpretation. Later, in live performances, and perhaps in posthumous tribute to somebody who he by then acknowledged to be a great artist, Rufus' intonation and delivery would veer closer to the more histrionic and theatrical Buckley version.

Alongside the versions discussed above, the song would be covered by Bono, Kathryn Williams, Sheryl Crow and, in a truly beautiful version by k.d. lang, among many, many others. In fact, even the moderately successful, bombastic live version by Bon Jovi (more bombastic than Bono's if you can believe that) was convincing evidence that the song is bomb-proof, an idea dispelled by the recent mauling the song received by the contestants in the reality TV show *The X Factor*.

As a brief but enlightening aside, when Cohen was asked in a radio interview about why he came to structure the song in such a way as that there are rhymes and half-rhymes at the ends of each line, he said: 'Sometimes I'll just read the rhyming dictionary as if it were fiction and just allow the rhymes to associate with one another and produce possibilities in the mind.' (Leonard Cohen in conversation with Mark Lawson, *Front Row*, BBC Radio 4, 9 July 2007.)

intention had always been to use the Cale version in the actual film.

After the movie came out, 'Hallelujah' would become a hugely popular live number for Rufus and, though not technically a single (except as an iTunes special some time later), it was, thanks to the *Shrek* factor, an instantly recognisable song which served to hook in even the most casual observers when he played to a general audience at festivals or large outdoor concerts.

Poses was released in June 2001. It saw Rufus make a conscious decision to package his sound into what he hoped would be a commercially successful record. Across 12 songs he encompassed the swooning lyricism of his debut, the cabaret-style show tune and the out and out pop song (one of the poppiest numbers even appearing twice in case the listener missed it the first time). But although the album has many high points, it is still a deeply flawed collection. It's not that the songs are necessarily of lower quality than his debut, just that many of them appear to have been worked over until almost all of their personality has disappeared. If *Rufus Wainwright* announced the arrival of an exciting, innovative new musical force, then *Poses* was *Rufus Wainwright* made by committee. With five different production teams on the record, there is a lack of cohesion from one track to the next as if nobody had any real conviction about the way the album should sound.

It wasn't as though his label had been exerting any undue pressure on him. When Lenny Waronker was asked if Rufus should be looking to smooth out his eccentricities in order to achieve success, he replied: 'I don't think he has it in him. I do think he has it in him to write a passionate song that will ultimately reach out to a bunch of people. That will happen now or it will happen later.'

Rufus may have had nagging doubts about his music and the commercial failure of the debut album may have smarted, but if there was a restraining order to rein in his musical excesses then he had placed it on himself. It's almost as if he was playing a role as a pop singer and had chosen to compromise his music in order to aim for commercial success. This was something which he all but admitted to in an interview with Jay Babcock for *LA Weekly*. Babcock wondered if Rufus was merely posing as a conventional pop singer in order to pave the way for his more flamboyant projects further down the line. 'Well, I look at it in a pragmatic kind of way,' said Rufus. 'At the moment, I'm 27. I have a good face for this stuff, I'm thin and healthy — with a certain healthy dose of unhealthy. I feel like when I signed up with a major label that there was a certain obligation, let's say, to spread the wealth in my success, and that that counted on me having a traditional kind of success in that field. So this is more of a way to allow me in the future to really be heard, when I make the decision to go in that direction. And, I'm sure that that's a very dangerous road to walk — one can sort of forget why they started on this.'

The title track was the semi-autobiographical/semi-fictitious story of a young man cast adrift in New York, which came from Rufus' voyeuristic forays from his Hotel Chelsea base into the gay club scene of Manhattan. In the song Rufus uses 'poses' as a synonym for 'roles', as if the song's protagonist was playing a part — striking a pose — that he thinks he can step away from if it becomes difficult or hazardous. By the end of the song, Rufus, or the imagined lead character, finds himself 'drunk and wearing flip-flops on 5th Avenue', the currency of his youth and beauty all spent with a final grim self-realisation coming in the despairing kiss-off couplet, 'Singing all these poses, now no longer boyish/Made me a man, ah but who cares what that is'.

Who cares what that is? By looking to create an out-and-out pop record, Rufus was striking another pose that could leave him floundering if he failed to pick up the new fans that he was so evidently courting. Worse still perhaps was the possibility that if commercial success did come along, he might feel that he had in some way sold himself out to get it and would end up having to begrudgingly play songs that he didn't really believe in when his 'real' songs were all but ignored. It could turn into a Loudon dead skunk scenario.

Rufus likened it to a 'blood sacrifice' in that he was prepared to go all out for the glamorous, limousine lifestyle of superstardom because it was his duty. As he said, 'It's something that should be available to young people who are constantly bombarded by the most inane, meaningless shit. I feel if I missed out on that I'd be letting a lot of people down.' (By contrast he also admitted that real life could get in the way and he could imagine himself blowing out a headlining show at Madison Square Garden because he'd fallen in love with a bricklayer.)

There is a dichotomy of ideals and aspirations that runs throughout Rufus' recorded work. On the one hand, he admits to wanting nothing but to create high art like the classical composers he reveres; on the other, he admits to wanting to sell thousands and thousands of albums in order to facilitate a luxurious lifestyle. Like many before him, he would discover that high art does not often equate with serious money, particularly in a medium like pop music where a certain broad appeal is necessary if success seeks to be judged in base units shifted rather than unquantifiable artistic achievement and cultural resonance.

Back in 1975, in an essay looking specifically at the similarly uncommercial Randy Newman, and more generally at the unsatisfied status of the cult artist, Greil Marcus implied that Newman's most popular songs were parodies of his talent. And, to take it further, that by 'altering his work in order to make it matter' any artist 'loses all sense of what impelled him in the first place'.[22] Marcus suggests that the only conclusion available to Newman, on discovering that his best work doesn't shift many units, is that 'his audience just isn't good enough for him'.[23]

Marcus is echoing Oscar Wilde, who knew a thing or two about artistic purity and aesthetic elitism. 'The public has always, and in every age, been badly brought up,' wrote Wilde. 'They are continually asking Art to be popular, to please their want of taste, to flatter their absurd vanity, to tell them what they have been told before, to show them what they ought to be tired of seeing, to amuse them when they feel heavy after eating too much, and to distract their thoughts when they are wearied of their own stupidity. Now Art should never try to be popular. The public should try to make itself artistic.'[24]

The problem with *Poses* (and it was a problem that would reappear as Rufus 'went for the sound of cash registers' on the *Release the Stars* album) is that rather than waiting for the public to 'make itself

22. Greil Marcus, *Mystery Train*, E.P Dutton, 1975, US.
23. ibid.
24. Oscar Wilde, *The Soul of Man Under Socialism*, 1891 (reprinted 2001, Penguin, UK).

artistic' and to follow him wherever he chose to lead them, he decided to go out looking for an audience, pandering to what he thought was expected of him and letting those expectations lead him. On a few tracks it is successful, but as an album it doesn't work.

Although *Poses* is undoubtedly compromised, its main fault is that whereas the debut record was anachronistic and therefore, with sweet perversity, timeless, then this second album is very much of its time. Almost every track now sounds better when performed live than it does in the fixed-in-2001 recorded state, indicating that the songs are, mostly, strong enough to transcend the studio versions.

The problem is exemplified by 'Greek Song', an operatic narrative that should be read as a duet (each verse is an alternating point of view) that details a brief holiday liaison between an out gay visitor and the object of his affection, a straight or possibly bisexual man. It's a sophisticated lyric and one that touches on sexual freedom and cultural identity in juxtaposing the attitude of the liberated tourist with that of the repressed local community. Here it is over-powered by saccharine strings and some kitsch chinoiserie. What could have been one of Rufus' most accomplished songs ends up sounding like an advert for a Chinese restaurant.

Likewise, the Alex Gifford collaboration 'Shadows' is a disappointment. A lyrically slight, misfiring adventure into electronica on which Rufus never seems comfortable and which now sounds chronically old-fashioned. At the time of recording, Alex Gifford's Propellerheads were at the cutting edge of dance music but after their debut album in 1998 and an illness that struck down co-founder Will White soon afterwards, the band had gone quiet. Rufus had also recorded 'Welcome Home' a duet with k.d. lang for the group's second album but this project was continually post-poned and is still yet to appear some ten years after their debut.

Rufus said that until he had made his first record, he hadn't really listened to pop music but had then become ensconced in a new pop world and found that he wanted to steal ideas from it. 'When I started happening I was completely freaked out about it,' he explained to *CDNow*, who had asked him to explain how he had come to use beats and loops on the record. 'A lot of the time I felt like I was making a huge mistake and that I should completely fire everyone. But in the end it worked out really well. I think.' He goes on to reveal that he was really worried that he would come over as trying too hard to be hip. 'Music is so heavily influenced by hip-hop and black music which is not where I come from as a person. I'm very uptight and white and I feel silly if I'm trying to boogie away. That was part of my worry; that I would come off like I was trying to be "hip with the kids". And I really don't want to be hip with the kids. But it's a whole musical ocean I still wanted to work with.'

The inclusion of a cover of Loudon's 'One Man Guy' had no obvious appeal to the 'kids' and seems to be either a belated nod to his father after all the badmouthing he had received in the press or a matter of just ticking the folk box on the way to making an album with the broadest possible appeal. It's certainly a beautiful rendition, with Martha and Teddy Thompson providing harmony and counterpoint[25] but its positioning on the album somewhat jars. It seems to have been spliced in from a different record altogether.

There are great moments on the record. The lilting 'Grey Gardens', with its multi-tracked vocals, references to Thomas Mann and sample of Little Edie Beale from the Maysles Brothers classic documentary *Grey Gardens* (1975) is sublime, with 10cc-style harmonies in place of the West Coast voices. Rufus claimed that he wrote the song on acid while at home in Montreal. He had originally written it as a slow song but after a night out partying he came home and realised that a faster tempo was, as it were, 'the best costume for the day'.

Rufus had intended 'Grey Gardens' to be a single but that role went instead to 'California', a garage-pop song which was Rufus' response to too long spent in Los Angeles while recording his debut, and one that he had been playing live since the end of 1998. 'The

---

25. In his book *31 Songs* (2003 Penguin, UK), Nick Hornby identifies 'One Man Guy', and more specifically the beginning of the second verse where Martha's harmonising begins, as a visitation from God (and this from an avowed atheist). Hornby suggests that this performance, crucially it is the performance not the song (which he discounts as being 'a little jokey'), allows him to hear and feel things that aren't really there and make him realise that there is such a thing as a 'unifying human consciousness'. In the synthesis of the two Wainwright voices, Hornby discovers something that he doesn't hear in religious music, a kind of secular spirituality.

song itself is kind of tongue in cheek,' he explained to *Nylon* magazine. 'I'd been living in LA making my first record, and working with Van Dyke Parks and Jon Brion. All my players were West Coast and there was this kind of Beach Boys sound we were going for. It occurred to me that I was a West Coast artist all of a sudden and that was a kind of nightmarish experience. "Oh God, am I going to end up like Brian Wilson, beached on the beach? Or be living up in Malibu with my rent boys, licking coke out of some 20-year-old's butt?" Which would be fun. I was becoming very California and I wrote that song to make me aware of that.'

Marchand had called in Ethan Johns to play on some of the *Poses* sessions and Rufus subsequently asked him to help him put a band together to try out some new material. It was this band which played on the track 'California'.

'I called in Richard Causon and Butch,' remembers Johns. 'Martha is singing with him, and his bass player Jeff Hill came in from New York and was great. We rehearsed for a week and the band sounded fantastic. "California" was a song that Rufus brought into those rehearsal sessions. We worked it up and Rufus and Lenny wanted to record it for the album. They asked me to produce and engineer the session, which I was very happy to do. We cut the track live at Ocean Way Studio B on to 24-track tape. It was done very fast by today's standards, I'm pretty sure it was a two-day session. We didn't use any computers either. I think that's why the track has the feel it does. Simply put, it's a recording of a good band playing a good arrangement of a good song.'

An entertaining video was commissioned for the single featuring Rufus as an awkward karaoke singer dressed in a red football shirt with 'Prettyman' printed across the shoulders. Teddy Thompson and Martha make cameo appearances as barman and hard-drinking moll in a black and white insert seen on the karaoke screen.

There had also been talk that 'Cigarettes and Chocolate Milk' should be a single but concern from the label that the fact that it had cigarette in the title could hinder its chances of getting airplay scuppered that. Nevertheless a video was made for it using the remixed, more beat-laden version of the song – billed as 'Cigarettes and Chocolate Milk (Reprise)' on the album – which was presumably thought to make the track sound more contemporary. In the video

Rufus wanders the streets in a red Miu Miu coat, clogs and sun-glasses looking like an alien visitor to the planet, intercut with him performing the song looking goofy and confused in a piano warehouse.

In 'Cigarettes and Chocolate Milk', Rufus explicitly states that he has an addictive personality and though the titular vices are minor, the underlying themes are more harmful – some substances, which he sings can't be mentioned, are 'a little bit stranger, a little bit harder, a little bit deadly'. In his private life he was getting ever more deeply involved with drugs and alcohol. The song acts as both a warning to himself that perhaps he wasn't yet ready to hear, and as an apology to others for him getting relentlessly wrecked, as he sings in the final stanza, if you see him and he's a mess, leaning like the tower of Pisa, 'please be kind'.

If Rufus was being lyrically coy, he was his usual frank self when discussing his ongoing excesses with journalists, many of the questions prompted by his confessions in 'Cigarettes and Chocolate Milk'.

'I've definitely stared into that abyss a few times,' he admitted to *Flaunt* magazine. 'I've done things like walking around and almost getting hit by a car because [I'm] too out of it. I've realised how fragile life is. It's not so much I would kill myself or ever OD or something. I'd probably just fall down a flight of stairs or freeze to death passed out on the street. It's that type of thing, more the Chet Baker type of death, which is more frightening to me.'[26] .

He admitted that he could only stay indoors perhaps one night a week because 'when those lights go down and dusk comes creeping. I simply have no choice' and went on to describe a typical night out: 'I start with wine. Then you say, "Oh maybe I'll have a little aperitif or sambuca." Then you're into a Cosmo or two, and then you think, "Well, I better have some beer" because you can always drink beer. Then you top it off with a few whiskies, and the next

---

26. Jazz trumpeter Chet Baker (b. 1929) died when he fell from his hotel room window in Amsterdam in 1988. Although conspiracy theorists like to suggest he was murdered, the likelihood is that he simply lost his balance while high on drugs (he had a chronic heroin addiction and a fondness for cocaine). The room was locked from the inside and there was no sign of a struggle. The lack of a note and the fact that he was only on the second floor were also considered reasonable grounds to rule out suicide.

thing you know somebody's going, "Hey, wanna tequila shot?"
I kind of do that kind of drinking. I mix it all up, and it's horrible.
I have a pretty strong constitution, even though I look quite frail.'

If Rufus' attitude to alcohol was blasé, he expressed more concern
at the prevalence of drugs in the bars and clubs he was frequenting.
Although he was from a generation who had had the concept of safe
sex drummed into it, he was becoming aware that parts of the gay
community were beginning to slacken in their adherence to safe-
sex practices, a phenomenon exacerbated by heightened drug use.
He admitted that this caused him anxiety. 'I think there's a big drug
problem in the gay community,' he told *LA Weekly*. 'On one hand
it's denial about everything that's going on, but it's also that people
just don't care about each other. You know, I've done drugs, and I'll
probably do drugs again at some point, but I do believe that drugs
connected to sex equals AIDS. I'm talking about crystal [meth] and
Special K and GHB, those club drugs – those kind of wild sexual
drugs. The attitude is, if you're taking pills to have fun, just to get
your dick hard, why not take some extra pills for your virus, you
know? You do meet a lot of people who, I guess after years of being
so sexually repressed, are just like "Gimme the fuckin' virus. They
have these new medications, I don't really care about it any more."
And even I have felt that way in the heat of passion.'

ACT 4

Je suis gai! Je suis gai! Vive le soir de mai!
Je suis follement gai, sans être pourtant ivre! ...
Serait-ce que je suis enfin heureux de vivre;
Enfin mon coeur est-il guéri d'avoir aimé?

Les cloches ont chanté; le vent du soir odore ...
Et pendant que le vin ruiselle à joyeux flots,
Je suis si gai, si gai, dans mon rire sonore,
Oh! Si gai, que j'ai peur d'éclater en sanglots!

Émile Nelligan from *La Romance du Vin*, circa 1899

In order to get as much fame as one's father one has to be much more
able than he

Rameau's Nephew, Deni Diderot, 1762

4.1

When he was a younger, Rufus had adored old-fashioned television
chat shows, classic late night reruns of the *Tonight Show* or the *Jack
Paar Show* with guests like Debbie Reynolds, Judy Garland and
Bette Davis. He watched them and dreamed of being interviewed
himself.

Both Loudon and Kate had shown him how beneficial it could be
to cultivate a good rapport with journalists and they had both
benefited from ongoing support from certain publications, notably
the *New York Times*, where a positive feature or review would lead
to an increase in the turnout for their shows. As a result of this,
Rufus put a lot of effort into his press and publicity duties. He was
an engaging interviewee, no matter how obscure the publication or
how few readers it might expect to reach. When the tape recorder

or the camera clicked on, he could usually be relied on to deliver. 'I've had a lot of practice in front of the mirror,' he explained to the *Phoenix New Times*. 'I've stayed up long enough doing mock interviews with Letterman and Barbara Walters in bed, before masturbating. So, I think I'm ready.'

Since the very beginning of his career, he had been building a strong base of supporters in the media and many of these would continue to stand solidly behind him as his career progressed. *Poses* received almost unanimously positive reviews, with many writers praising the fact that it was more restrained and therefore easier to love than his debut. *Rolling Stone*'s critic was happy that Rufus had reined in his excesses, having decided that *Rufus Wainwright* had been altogether too precious (although the review was less enamoured by the mangled grammar on the title track).

But Rufus' triumphant entrance into the mainstream seemed as elusive as ever. This lack of immediate success and his impatience at their slow-burn approach to getting him noticed had strained his relationship with his first manager to such an extent that Rufus had fired him (by telephone) in 2000 and hired the more corporate Ron Stone and Gold Mountain Entertainment, who also represented mainstream artists like Tracy Chapman, Bonnie Raitt and Baha Men (whose depressing novelty hit 'Who Let The Dogs Out' had been a recent Grammy award winner). Stone's main strategy was to get Rufus heard by the general public by getting him on the radio, but he was discovering that Rufus' self-styled 'popera' was still seen as difficult to categorise, and therefore impossible to schedule into restrictive traditional contemporary rock radio station play-lists. With the exception of college radio and public broadcasting stations like KCRW in Santa Monica, who had long supported him, songs from the album received negligible airplay.

In the summer of 2001, Rufus had been scheduled to take part in Wotapalava, which was being billed as the first gay-friendly music festival. He was booked to play alongside Sinead O'Connor, Soft Cell, Magnetic Fields and event organisers the Pet Shop Boys. Like Perry Farrell's Lollapalooza, the idea was that the event would be a rolling festival, with multiple stages, DJs, films and theatre, and would travel to 17 cities across America, sending out a message of positivity to the gay community and welcoming anybody and everybody who wanted to come along, regardless of their sexuality. Unfortunately, shortly after tickets went on sale O'Connor pulled out and the entire event collapsed and was cancelled, officially because no other suitable headline act was available, but in truth because ticket sales were poor.

To replace the missing tour dates at a time when promotion for the album was crucial, Rufus was hastily booked in to open for Roxy Music on the US leg of their comeback tour. As is the way with support acts at huge stadium concerts, his newly arranged set, performed as just a three-piece to keep costs down, was politely received by a mostly disinterested crowd in half-empty arenas as the Roxy fans mooched around at the concession stalls waiting for the main event. The tour certainly didn't generate the kind of media interest in him that would have been expected had Wotapalava gone ahead and most reviews of the Roxy shows gave Rufus little more than a sentence or two, if they mentioned him at all. Gavin McInnes, *Vice* magazine founder and fellow Montrealer, did take the trouble to call Rufus 'an insufferable bore that, despite selling no records at all, has somehow converted sucking shit into a big ball of vau-devillian piano hype' in his typically misanthropic *NME* review of a Roxy Music concert in New York.

The part about selling no records was almost right. Although Rufus was touring relentlessly, *Poses* had not really taken off in the way that the label had hoped. It had charted, peaking at 117 on the Billboard chart (the debut album had not entered the chart at all), but the sales had not been anything like as good as had been expected. According to an *Entertainment Weekly* story, by late August 2001 *Poses* had sold less than 52,000 copies in the US.

If, for the most part, the general public were still ambivalent about his music, Rufus was at least picking up fans from within the music community who were recognising his rare skills as a songwriter and performer. Elton John invited him to sing backing vocals on a song for his new album, *Songs From the West Coast*.

The album saw Elton return to the more intimate sound of his earlier albums. Perversely, in light of Rufus' decision to embrace technology on *Poses*, it was albums like *Rufus Wainwright* and, particularly Ryan Adams' *Heartbreaker* that had inspired Elton to turn his back on the studio tricks and dance beats that he'd used in the 1990s and return to simplified piano, bass, drums and a little orchestration.

The song that Rufus was to sing on was 'American Triangle' about the despicable murder of gay student Matthew Shepard in Wyoming in 1998. Shepard had been brutally beaten, robbed and left tied to a fence. When he was discovered by a passing cyclist some 18 hours later, he had at first been mistaken for a scarecrow. Shepard's head injuries were so severe that he had lapsed into a coma and had never recovered consciousness.[1]

The aftershocks of Shepard's murder and the subsequent trial of the two men convicted of the crime resulted in a public outcry and demands that the hate crime legislation be amended to allow prosecution for crimes committed against a person because of their sexual orientation. Elton had been both shocked by the murder and moved by the compassionate response of Shepard's family, who had asked the court to spare their son's murderers from the death penalty. He would dedicate the album to Shepard and set up a scholarship in his name.

Rufus recorded his backing vocals without ever meeting Elton personally. He put down his part in New York while Elton stayed in the studio in Los Angeles. After he had recorded his vocal, Elton called him and thanked him for taking part. 'He wanted to let me know he was honoured that I worked on his record,' said Rufus, 'and that years ago he had a terrible, terrible crush on my father. But more incredible than talking to him was when I was in the studio singing the back-ups, trying to meld with that voice.'

According to Rufus, Elton had once been so enamoured of Loudon that he had taken to flying in by helicopter just to see him perform at festivals. Eventually both Loudon and Rufus would get to meet and play with him when he asked them to perform at his 'The Concert – 20 Years with AIDS' benefit show that took place on 12 December in Universal City, California, and featured musicians including Bon Jovi, Sting, Matchbox Twenty and LeAnn Rimes.

---

1 This horrific murder would inspire many musical tributes to Shepard, including songs by Tori Amos, Melissa Etheridge and Cyndi Lauper. Rufus himself would record another song about Shepard in 2002. 'Scarecrow' appeared on an album of duets released by his former band member Kristian Hoffman. The record, *Kristian Hoffman &*, also featured El Vez, Van Dyke Parks and Russell Mael.

On the night, Rufus had the unenviable task of having to follow a set by Alicia Keys, then very much a star on the rise, who had blown the roof off the house with an emotional reading of 'Ave Maria'. Dressed down in a blue denim blouson jacket and patchwork flares he was hampered by problems with his monitors and looked nervous and unable to relax and hit his stride. Relief came when Elton and Loudon joined him to play a version of 'One Man Guy'. Loudon, in his button-down shirt, V-neck sweater and holding acoustic guitar, looked as casual as a supply teacher come to fill in at nursery school rather than someone about to play in front of 6,000 people. Throughout the song, Elton beamed at him like it was the happiest moment of his life. At the end of the song Elton and Loudon kissed. 'I'm their love child,' joked Rufus, gesturing to the two old hands. Backstage, where the artists mingled with guests like Elizabeth Taylor, Antonio Banderas and Jeffrey Katzenberg, Elton had met up with the two Wainwrights for the first time. When he stood between them to pose for photographs, he looked from one to the other smirking and blurted, 'This is *so* fucking weird.'

Elton closed the event with a barnstorming set during which Rufus joined him to sing on 'American Triangle'. The concert had raised more than $1 million for Elton's AIDS charities.

Earlier in the year, Rufus had been asked by his friend Sean Lennon to take part in a tribute concert for John Lennon that was to be recorded at Radio City Music Hall on 20 September. 'Come Together: A Night For John Lennon' was planned to commemorate Lennon's life in his adopted home city and, in the light of his death, to link it with the Million Mom March and the New York Violence Policy Center's work on promoting gun control and youth non-violence. The show was to be co-ordinated by Dave Stewart and feature Beck, Lou Reed, Alanis Morissette and the Stone Temple Pilots among others, and was to be taped and broadcast later in the year.

After the devastating attacks of 11 September had showered the city in grief and sent waves of shock and horror reverberating around the world, the concert was postponed. By the time it had been rescheduled, it had become a musical focus for a city that was coming to terms with the death and destruction brought to it by terrorist violence. The concert, which was eventually staged and broadcast live on 2 October, became a fund-raiser for numerous World Trade Center charities and an event that could cherish what was lost and embrace a more hopeful future. From the stage in New York, the performers sent out messages of peace, with their performances gaining such resonance from the extraordinary context of the show that even host Kevin Spacey's eccentric and tuneless 'Mind Games' became an exhortation for the world to look at what it was becoming and to promote the idea of progressive pacifism.

Although it is perhaps churlish to highlight some of the particularly woeful performances in what had become an emotionally charged charity event, without remarking on the sheer dreadfulness of Dave Stewart and Nelly Furtado's inane 'Instant Karma' or Lou Reed's monotonous 'Jealous Guy', it's impossible to contextualise the impact that the one genuinely interesting performance had on an event that was close to drowning in good intentions and misguided posturing. Rufus, Sean Lennon and Moby's reading of 'Across The Universe' was the highlight because it didn't treat the source song as an 'easy listening' standard and it didn't turn it into over-rehearsed bland funk. With Rufus taking lead vocal, Lennon on acoustic guitar and harmony and Moby playing electric guitar and grounding Rufus' soaring vocal line with a subdued baritone, the performance was electrifying because it was flawed and somewhat ragged and because the chorus of 'nothing's going to change my world' rang out like a hymn of defiance in the face of bitter violence. It was no wonder that the song brought the audience to its feet.

Rufus said that he had never heard 'Across The Universe' until Sean had played it to him when they were discussing what songs to do before the event. He remembers listening to John Lennon records with Sean and noticing Sean had a similar reaction to the music that he felt when listening to Loudon or Kate's albums; that he was almost listening to a part of himself. By coincidence, around the same time as the Lennon tribute show was being put together, Rufus had been asked to contribute a Beatles cover version of his own choice for the soundtrack to the movie *I Am Sam* (dir. Jessie Nelson, 2001). After being almost gifted 'Across The Universe', Rufus wanted to record it properly so on 9 October, which coincidentally was both John and Sean Lennon's birthdays, he went into a studio with Sean and recorded a version for the film.

Like 'Hallelujah' before it, 'Across The Universe' served as an easy introduction to Rufus for many first-time listeners. Although the film version was quite sparse, another more lush mix of the song was created with added orchestration and a new vocal and was included as a bonus track on a hasty repackage of *Poses* (in the US only) in an attempt to boost flagging sales. A music video was shot by Len Wiseman (now best known for the *Underworld* vampire movies), which featured *I Am Sam* star Dakota Fanning running around with a red balloon while Rufus is suspended in the air above her, surrounded by Rene Magritte-inspired 'raining men'.[2]

4.2

After the death of his mother, Loudon had suffered from severe depression. He had continued to play live shows but hadn't released an album of new material since 1997's *Little Ship*. In the days imme-diately after her death, he had even wondered whether he would ever be able to write another song. As he explained to *Entertainment Weekly*: 'This was different from writer's block. I [usually] just write bad songs until some good songs come along. This time, it felt like there was no reason to write any songs; that the exercise was futile – it seemed silly. Maybe because my mother was my purest fan, without her there, it seemed pointless to pick up the guitar.'

Gradually, with the help of his therapist and by absorbing the healing powers of the beautiful countryside around his mother's old home, including swimming in what he considered to be the sacred and medicinal waters of Lake Waccabuc, he gradually began to write again. He worked slowly on a collection of songs that dealt with his feelings after losing his mother, a project that he would refer to in concert as being his 'songs of death and decay'. By the time the album was ready for release, it had become known as *Last Man on*

---

2. In Rene Magritte's original painting *Golconda* (1953) from which the video imagery is taken, the men are wearing bowler hats. Perhaps there was a shortage of bowlers in California as the men (or digitally multiplied singular man) in the video sport fedoras, rather diminishing the effect.

Earth (this title winning out over the alternatives, *Living Alone* or *Missing You*, in an audience vote at a gig at McCabe's Guitar Shop in Santa Monica earlier in the year). One photograph that was almost used as the CD cover showed a photo of a child lost in the supermarket looking for his mother because that, simplistically, was how Loudon had been feeling.

The album would be a triumph. *Last Man on Earth* saw Loudon reach new heights as a lyricist as he elucidated his despair in songs that were both deeply personal and resonantly universal. Although certainly dark, the songs were saved from being morose by Loudon's lyrical wit and by the sophistication of their simple but effective arrangement developed over extended recording sessions.

By working in producer Stewart Lerman's own studio, Loudon had had the luxury of not having to be overly concerned with the financial costs of recording. They worked over the songs for a year, a rare luxury. 'Normally, my records, I cut 'em in two weeks and you take a week's break and you mix 'em in five days and throw 'em out there,' Loudon explained to *Dirty Linen* magazine. 'And then six months later you think, "God, why did I do that?"'

'I'm very happy that we had the time and were able to do the record properly. I've had a kind of chequered career in the recording studio. I've made a lot of different kinds of records, and some certainly more successful than others. And I don't mean just in terms of units sold.'

On 'Homeless', Loudon relates a story about his mother that he credits for getting him started singing songs in the first place. He explained the song when he talked about his mother to Terry Gross on NPR: 'She was my biggest fan. I have this memory of singing this old folk song "Roisin The Bow" for my mother and my aunt Mary, who was her twin sister. This would've been when I was about seven. I was a smash hit in Aunt Mary's kitchen and they clapped and it was "Oh Loudy, you're so great!" It was the reason I got into showbusiness. That's all it took. From then on I knew that I wanted to be some kind of performer.'

Although the album focuses on Loudon's feelings brought about by his mother's death, it is to his father he returns on the album's standout track. 'Surviving Twin' recounts Loudon's difficult relationship with his father and talks about how he had always tried to get the better of him and to hurt him. If Rufus' recent successes had made him acutely aware that he was uncomfortably competitive when it came to fame and talent – witness the *Rolling Stone*-inspired argument that had dragged on for months – then Loudon himself uses the same complaint against his own father. He realised that if he became famous it could wound his father ('If I made it big enough I could kill him off quick').

Loudon identified a masochistic streak in his father, who had been convinced that to be a real writer you had to write books, not journalism. Loudon Jnr, though a very successful and famous journalist, had long harboured a desire to write a proper book and to perhaps accept the acclaim that a Tom Wolfe or Norman Mailer received. For all his trying, he continually failed to get his book projects off the ground, which became a source of huge frustration for him that spilled over into his relationships with his family, as Loudon explained: '"The Book" was a phrase spoken over and over by my parents throughout my childhood. It was a phrase that induced feelings of hope and excitement initially but then it just became two words synonymous with failure and incompletion.'[3]

Although they were composed independently of each and without either writer having heard the other's song, 'Surviving Twin' and Rufus' 'Dinner at Eight' have remarkably similar sensibilities. Both begin by wanting to bring down their father and both end in a realisation that father and son are too alike, or too intertwined, for one to ever overcome the other. In Rufus' case it is the realisation that Loudon had always loved him and in Loudon's it is the fact, encapsulated in the song's conceit, that he has grown a beard that makes him look just like his father, that he and his father are really the same person after all. Indeed, Loudon's attitude to his father could not help but have been tempered over the years since his death by his own difficulties in relating to Rufus.

Perhaps the process of dealing with his own issues had helped Loudon in his familial relationships. Although he had always been happy to admit that he was immensely proud of his children, it was

---

3. Loudon Wainwright Jnr would have one book published in his lifetime. *The Great American Magazine: An Inside History of Life* (Alfred Knopf, 1986, US) detailed the history of the magazine to which he was most famously linked.

rare for him to go so far as to confess that they might have affected his music. Loudon paid a compliment to his son by admitting that his song 'Bed' owed a debt to the younger Wainwright as he explained to *Dirty Linen*. 'When I hear it, I think it's influenced by Rufus! Just melodically. Obviously I listen to his stuff. I don't listen to a lot of contemporary music; I've always made a point of not doing that. But I think I've listened to too much Rufus Wainwright, because the song seems to be very influenced by him.'

With songs as strong as the poignant and witty mother/son middle-class drinking song 'White Winos' and the melancholic and determinate 'Graveyard' allied to Lerman's strong production and sympathetic arrangements from Dick Connette, the album became Loudon's most fully realised recording to date. However, although artistically successful and lauded by the critics, the album didn't become the late breakout hit that it deserved to be, but Loudon had long since stopped worrying about mainstream appeal. As it happened, his second career as a part-time actor would be the thing that would see Loudon attract an influx of younger fans.

On 25 September 2001, the day that the album was released, Loudon was also appearing in the premier of a new television show produced by Judd Apatow. It would be the first of a series of ongoing collaborations with Apatow.

Loudon had continued to act in film and television whenever he got the chance. Most recently he had had a small part in the rehab drama *28 Days* (dir. Betty Thomas, 2000) with Sandra Bullock and Viggo Mortensen, where he got to perform songs as an inpatient at a hospital and was known only as 'Guitar Guy'. But Judd Apatow had remembered seeing him a long time before that. As a teenager in the 1980s he'd loved Loudon on the David Letterman show and had been impressed that somebody had been able to successfully meld humour with good music and, as Apatow's parents were in the process of splitting up, he'd particularly appreciated Loudon's ability to write songs about difficult relationships. Apatow had continued listening to and enjoying Loudon's albums and, as his own career progressed from writer to producer on a series of hit shows with comedians like Ben Stiller and Gary Shandling, he had long hoped to be able to bring Loudon into one of his projects.

After the disappointment of his high-school-based comedy *Freaks and Geeks* getting canned after just one season, Apatow came back with a follow-up show featuring many of the same actors. *Undeclared* was *Freaks and Geeks* goes to college and the forerunner of many of the hugely successful films like *The 40-Year-Old Virgin* and *Knocked Up* that he would produce a few years down the line. It was also the perfect opportunity for him to get Loudon involved. Apatow had been particularly impressed by the song 'A Father and a Son' from *History* and had wanted to write a dysfunctional family comedy loosely based around that. With his new show he saw a way of incorporating some of his father/son ideas into the college format and he tracked down Loudon to see if he'd like to play the father in the show. Loudon was thrilled, especially when Apatow did all he could to ensure that he didn't have to go for a dreaded audition.

Apatow explained his tactics in an interview with Bullz-Eye.com. 'I knew that Loudon hated auditioning, and there's nothing worse than auditioning for the network, where you get thrown into a room full of 30 people who barely crack a smile. It's very easy to get thrown off your game and not get the job, even though you really deserve it. So I told them he was out of town, and I showed them a tape of him . . . so I saved him the trouble, even though he was really only five minutes away at the time!'

Loudon had been recording the series off and on for most of the year. Although he was far from being a professional actor, he was more than capable of holding his own in the ensemble cast. Apatow certainly had no doubts in his ability: 'When you've worked with a lot of 14- or 15-year-old kids who haven't acted much, you quickly realise that a guy who's been performing on stage for 30 years and wanted to be an actor probably can be drawn out to do a great job on the show. I liked him because he has a great personality, and you can write to it. It's a way of having an original character without having to think of it yourself.'

Later Apatow took the cast of the show to see Loudon perform in Los Angeles. Unaware that their 'TV Dad' had a career away from just being the quiet and conscientious actor they had seen on set, the young cast were blown away by his performance.

The success of *Undeclared* saw *Rolling Stone* feature Loudon as 'Hot Dad' in their 'Hot' issue (with nary a mention of Rufus), and Loudon was pleased to see some new fans coming to his shows, as he told *Dirty Linen*: 'There are some new converts. Younger people are coming. That could be anything from the *Undeclared* thing to parental indoctrination to "I'm the dad of Rufus Wainwright." There could be all kinds of reasons for that. All of a sudden, if I'm signing CDs, I'll look up and there's a 22-year-old there. Which is, of course, delightful.'

Loudon was fully committed to promoting his album and was pleasantly surprised by the positive reactions he was getting for his portrayal of the eccentric dad in *Undeclared* but, as a long-time resident of New York, he found that thoughts about the terrorist attacks and the rising uneasiness that was creeping out into American society were playing on his mind.

As a musician who had frequently commented on current affairs, people would ask him if he was going to write a song about 9/11 but he said that he thought it was just too immense a subject to try and tackle. A few days after it had happened and just before leaving for a brief UK tour, he had told a journalist: 'I'm not even thinking about how it relates to my job. I'm just trying to process it as a person who happens, in fact, to live incredibly close to where the World Trade towers were, and have people in New York who essentially are all okay. But I haven't even thought about what it means to me as a songwriter. And it's going to take a while to process it, like everybody else.'

Loudon was as surprised as anyone that by the time he came to play a live Radio 1 John Peel session in the UK on 27 September,[4] he had written the song 'No Sure Way', which illuminates 9/11 in a typically oblique Loudonesque way by describing his regular subway journey from his home in Brooklyn Heights to Manhattan which would have normally passed under the World Trade Center. On his return to America, he incorporated the song into his set alongside a revival of the now prescient song from the 1980s, 'Hard

4. The session took place at Peel's home, Peel Acres, which the DJ had begun using as his base for his shows after growing tired of the commute from Suffolk into London. Eight tracks were performed live during the programme. As would be expected from a seasoned professional like Loudon, the set-up and sound-check was completed so quickly that he was able to join the engineers in Peel's swimming pool to pass the time while he waited for the show to start. As previously noted, Peel was a long-time supporter of Loudon and would get him to play 15 sessions between 1971 and 2003. Twenty tracks were collected together on a superb album released as *The BBC Sessions* (Strange Fruit 1998).

Day on the Planet', with its lyric about hijacked planes blowing up.

To end the year, Rufus appeared as support to Tori Amos on her StrangeLittleTour, which ran from September through to November. The Amos fans were generally far more receptive to his material than the Roxy Music crowd had been, even though his now extended between song anecdotal rambles, which could take in *Dallas*, Marilyn Manson, *The Golden Girls*, body searches at airports and anything else that came into his mind, could often prove somewhat baffling when bounced around a half-empty arena.

Perhaps the most important thing he took away from the tour was that Amos forced him to confront a problem that had been nagging away at him for many years. As a regular part of her set, Tori Amos included the chilling song 'Me and a Gun', which concerned her rape after a concert when she was 21. After her ordeal she helped set up the Rape, Abuse and Incest National Network (RAINN), an organisation offering support to victims of sexual abuse. At her shows there would be a RAINN stand offering information and she would sometimes meet people backstage to talk with them about problems of abuse that they had suffered. In an interview with the website me-me-me.tv in 2007, Rufus said that it was the fact that Tori had spoken so openly about her rape and had faced it and survived it that he realised he needed to deal with his feelings about his assault in London as a teenager. He acknowledged that it had taken him some time before he realised that what Amos was doing was important and totally honest.

'For about two or three weeks I really slagged her off,' he admitted. 'I just thought, "Who is this ridiculous person kind of profiteering from her experiences?" I just had this viscerally bad reaction to it and then, about a month into the tour, I was like, "Hold on a minute. I have never been able to sustain a successful relationship and I was raped at a very young age and it had affected me to this day . . ."'

Rufus declined to speak to Amos personally but he did eventually credit her with opening his eyes to the fact that what had happened to him had been more serious and had had more repercussions than he had ever previously admitted and was actually having an increasingly negative impact on his immediate situation.

Although his songs often implied a longing for love that was classically romantic, almost mythical, his reality was that he had never had a long-term boyfriend. It was almost as if he had written off the possibility of a lasting relationship and that anything beyond a succession of one-night stands must be, as he had sung on his debut album, 'imaginary love'. When he wasn't working or staying at his mother's in Montreal, he would visit New York and check into a hotel or stay with friends. There he would take drugs, anything from cannabis and cocaine, to ecstasy and ketamine, and cruise places like dive-bar *The Cock* taking part in lip-synch karaoke contests and washing down the drugs with copious quantities of alcohol. His scene since the Chelsea Hotel days had got a little more sleazy and a lot more extreme. When he wasn't cruising in bars, he might go online to gay dating sites to find partners and meet up with them. Occasionally he would wind up at an orgy and delight in putting on a CD of *Poses* and miming for the crowd.

In a rather indiscreet interview with *Nerve* from August 2001, Rufus calls himself a 'sicko' and, along with owning up to an extensive collection of pornography, admits that his intrinsic shyness is not something that he lets hold him back. 'I'm basically a slut. But I'm also really really shy,' he explained. 'I'm a real prude, but once the prudishness is gone I'll have sex with 20 guys.' By the end of the interview Rufus is on a couch in a Lower East Side nightclub kissing the interviewer. 'At the end of an evening of intoxications, it is one more drug for us to try, a sweetness to experiment with,' writes the reporter, suggesting that Rufus is 'in love with longing' and that he just happens to be the nearest person.

Just before Christmas 2001, Rufus' friend Lance Loud died in a hospice in Los Angeles. Loud had been HIV-positive and had also contracted hepatitis C. His health had not been helped by his habitual abuse of speed and crystal meth for many years.

In his final weeks he instigated a final documentary about his life, allowing the cameras in to his bedside as he said some of his final goodbyes to family and friends and commented on events in his life. Although he had often been bemused by the amount of attention his family had received by taking part in their early 1970s fly-on-the-wall series, he also appreciated the role that documentary filming could play in educating the public – at one point he expresses a wish that everybody has safe sex and avoids drug use – and in finally demonstrating that his family were genuine and lovingly committed to each other, something which he had thought the original television series had neglected to fully make clear. The resulting documentary, *Lance Loud! A Death in an American Family* was broadcast by PBS in 2003. It includes footage of Rufus at Loud's memorial service singing 'Over The Rainbow' accompanied by Kate on the piano.

Looking somewhat wild-eyed and louche in a huge-lapelled pale suit and cravat, Rufus is interviewed after the service and explains how Loud had championed his music, counselled him and encouraged him not to make the same mistakes he had done as regards drugs. Speaking fondly of Loud he explains how, 'He would always say about me to other people, "Oh, Rufus is like I was but he's a lot smarter and he's a lot more together." I don't know if that's true or not but I just think he really wanted me to succeed so badly, perhaps for some of the things that he didn't succeed in in his life in a way.'

Rufus had kept the extent of his own drug abuse from Loud. Perhaps he had felt guilty or hypocritical when he spoke to the camera about Loud's warnings to him but, more likely, he remained blissfully unaware of how dangerous his behaviour was becoming. He had already begun to habitually use crystal meth, the very drug that had proved so calamitous for Loud.[5]

---

5. Although Rufus had used crystal meth casually in the past, it was not until he became fully ensconced in the New York gay club scene that his use escalated. Crystal meth is the street name for methamphetamine, an artificially manufactured stimulant that is highly addictive. If taken in sufficient quantity, the user can stay awake and euphoric for days at a time. It can also dramatically increase the libido while lowering inhibitions and delaying orgasm so that users can engage in prolonged and multitudinous sex acts, often for many hours at a time. This sense of liberation and abandon has led to the drug being blamed for increasing HIV infection as users often disregard safe-sex practices. Prolonged use can lead to mental health problems, including paranoia, mood swings and physical health problems related to the toxicity of the chemicals used in its manufacture. The drug, added to chocolate bars, was given to soldiers in the German army during the Second World War and it is alleged that Adolf Hitler himself received regular injections from his private doctor during the last few years of the war.

4.3

Through the early part of 2002, Rufus took to the road to continue promoting the *Poses* album. It was his biggest solo tour to date and his band included Martha and Teddy Thompson, with Thompson acting as opener on most of the tour except for twin New York shows that were shared between Martha and Antony and the Johnsons.

Before embarking on the tour, Martha had been working hard on new songs. She had started to record some more tracks, was playing the odd solo club date in New York at small, supportive venues like Tonic, and was building up the confidence to try to make a debut album. In the meantime she released another EP.

The Factory EP included four tracks, one of which ('The Car Song') had featured on her cassette album and another was a sweet version of the standard 'Bye, Bye Blackbird'. Of the two new songs, 'New York, New York, New York' is a languorous lament with a hint of Billie Holiday in the vocal line. It's at least half a good song, but as the title itself hints, by going one New York beyond Liza and two beyond the Sex Pistols, it's overlong and eventually fades away into soporific jazz. The title track, however, is superb and by far the most accomplished track that she had released to date. 'Factory' is reminiscent of Mazzy Star or, more accurately, Melanie singing with Hope Sandoval's first band Opal. Lyrically obtuse with references to transvestites, poor souls and open-sored destitutes, the song manages to remain uplifting among an air of regret and loneliness and becomes almost beatific with the lyric shifts from sun, sun, sun to run, run, run, seemingly embracing every beautiful loser in New York.

Martha had looked upon her earlier tours with Rufus as being great for her experience and to help make her a better musician, but she couldn't help but feel she was being taken advantage of. Before agreeing to take part in the *Poses* tour, she made it clear that there were some rules to be laid down. 'I said that I would do it again if he was nicer to me on stage and he didn't make me feel like a clown,' she revealed to the *Guardian* years later, when her insecurities had been allayed by the warm reception her first record eventually received. At the time of the tour she had felt slightly exploited, the butt of the jokes. 'I became a character, a puppet. Rufus is very funny, it's charming. But I wasn't going to hurt for the benefit of a laugh. He was torturing me like an older brother does – like suffocating your younger sister under a blanket and thinking it's funny . . . I wanted to do my own record when he said, "I need you to put your thing on the backburner." I said, "I'll do it but only because I love you, but you can't make me feel like I only exist because you exist."'

Martha's discomfort at being Rufus' stage stooge went as far back as the early days of the Café Sarajevo shows, according to owner Osman Koulenovitch, who remembers Rufus would often seem dismissive of Martha if she performed with him and only occasionally allowed her to sing solo. 'I encouraged Martha a lot,' he says. 'I convinced the people sitting around me to clap like mad when she sang, because I wanted them to encourage her, too. Now she sings, she's extraordinary. But I remember that Rufus never really did anything to help his sister.' It's a charge that may well have held some merit in those early days before Rufus was actually making records but one that, certainly in recent years after offering Martha show-stopping guest spots at venues like the Hollywood Bowl or the London Palladium, he would seem to have answered. Martha frequently refers to Rufus as her mentor.

The shows were well received, aided by a slowly increasing profile, thanks in part to the songs that were becoming familiar from film soundtracks. Rufus ensured his *Moulin Rouge!* song, 'Complainte de la Butte', as well as 'Hallelujah' and 'Across the Universe' all featured in the set and even found space for the upbeat and bouncing, 'Instant Pleasure', a cover version that had featured in the Adam Sandler comedy *Big Daddy* (1999). With the luxury of a larger band, he also played around with the arrangements of some of his other songs, turning 'Evil Angel' into a goth-rock growl that would end with him stripping off his shirt and baring his chest.

Despite not having had anything like a hit record, Rufus had become something of a celebrity, well known enough to be asked to record a cameo call-in for the hit TV series *Frasier*,[6] in which he became the latest in a series of famous voices that had appeared on the show – others had included Daryl Hannah, Jennifer Jason Leigh,

---

6. *Frasier* – 'Cheerful Goodbyes', Season 9, Episode 21 (2002).

Freddie Prinze Jr and Pat Boone. Rufus voices 'Jeremy', a young
boy who Frasier counsels by telling him about his brother Niles'
childhood bed-wetting. Later in the year he would film another sit-
com cameo, playing himself, for the UK show *Absolutely Fabulous*[7]
and be amused when Joanna Lumley told him she had liked his
website. 'The thought of her on a computer, going to a website was
funny to me,' he said.

A highlight of the summer was being called to contribute to
maverick producer Hal Willner's latest project *Stormy Weather:
The Music of Harold Arlen*. Willner had been asked to create the
soundtrack to a hybrid drama/documentary film on the life of the
1930s and 1940s songwriter Arlen, being directed as a TV movie
by Larry Weinstein. Rufus flew to Los Angeles to record with an
incredible orchestra assembled by Van Dyke Parks that included
legendary musicians like drummer Earl Palmer, whose career went
all the way back to having played on Little Richard's 'Tutti Frutti'
and who had recently appeared on albums by Tom Waits and Elvis
Costello, and session pianist Mike Melvoin who had worked with
everybody from Tim Buckley to Bobby Vee.

Rufus sang 'It's Only a Paper Moon'. It was the first session of
the entire project. 'Rufus arrived about five o'clock,' remembered
Willner. 'By eight o'clock we had recorded an absolutely beautiful
take – Rufus singing live with the orchestra. Finished! It was a
revelation actually. It reminded me of some of the records I had
recorded a few years back with no overdubs, like the Rat Pack – it
had been a while since I had done that. It was really exciting.'

Rufus also contributed another song to the film, 'I Wonder What
Became of Me', which he recorded solo on piano. He can be seen
performing both songs in the film alongside other performers like
Sandra Bernhard and Debbie Harry. The Arlen project was close to
Rufus' heart as all year he had been repeatedly listening to the
Judy at Carnegie Hall album that had recently been remastered and

---

7. *Absolutely Fabulous* – 'Gay', Season 4, Episode 7 (2002). Rufus was asked to take part
by the show's producer Jon Plowman, who was an old friend of Loudon's. The show would
mark the start of various minor collaborations with Jennifer Saunders and her comedy
partner Dawn French. Rufus appeared as a humourless folk singer in the *French and
Saunders Celebrity Christmas Special* (2005) and both French and Saunders took a turn at
the spoken word section of 'Between My Legs' during the series of concerts at the Old Vic,
London, in May 2007.

reissued for its 40th anniversary. Many of the songs that Garland performed were written by Arlen, including 'The Man That Got Away' and, of course, 'Over The Rainbow'. After 9/11, with a government intent on war and keen to promote the possibilities of more terrorist attacks, Rufus saw these classic songs as a way of both brightening the gloom and as a reminder of a less paranoid, more joyous country.

Over one long weekend in October, Rufus worked on songs for his third, as yet untitled, album at Looking Glass Studios in New York. Marius de Vries, who had been the music director on *Moulin Rouge!* and had collaborated with both Madonna and Björk, had been suggested as a possible producer for the new record by Lenny Waronker. The sessions progressed well, with Rufus running on the artificial energy of a variety of drugs and on the natural adrenalin of realising the music that they were creating was sounding wonderful. He quickly established a rapport with de Vries and they were able to almost completely finish three songs over the weekend. One of these was 'Dinner at Eight' on which Rufus' part was recorded in virtually one immediate take and which left de Vries stunned by its simplicity and power. The decision was made to continue with the sessions as soon as possible with de Vries definitely on board as producer.

When he wasn't in the studio or playing a concert, Rufus was out partying, either to show himself at places that he thought he should be seen, acting the 'court jester' as he described it, or he was out looking for sex with strangers, a hedonistic Captain Nemo exploring the underworld loaded on crystal meth.

Alarm bells had already been ringing. His friends had begun to express concern. When Justin Bond found out about his cystal meth use he was furious, screaming at Rufus that he was on his way to 'fucking up majorly'. Even casual acquaintances felt the need to intervene. Rufus recalls one incident that demonstrated how out of touch he was becoming. 'I was at this party, I was trashed and this woman ... a photographer, a paparazzo, she said, "Rufus, Rufus, we're really worried about you, a lot of people are very worried." And of course I immediately assumed she was talking about my career. That I wasn't as famous as Ryan Adams, that I wasn't doing as well as the White Stripes. I had no idea she was talking about myself.'

A perfect example of his state of mind and generally capricious lifestyle is an anecdote he later told that begins with a visit to Yoko Ono. Rufus had decided to throw a dinner party in the apartment of one of his friends on the Upper West Side of Manhattan. Among the guests were his mother and Linda Thompson. He had also been expecting Yoko Ono but her driver called and apologised and said that she was too tired but if Rufus and his mother would like to call in to see her later on then that would be fine. After having shared innumerable bottles of wine, Kate felt that she was too drunk to go visiting but Rufus eventually convinced her and Linda to go with him. They headed over to the Dakota Building and up to Yoko's apartment. 'Yoko Ono answered the door and was a little shocked to have Linda there as well,' remembered Rufus. 'I think she was just expecting my mother and I and we were stumbling around. And stank. Probably.' Kate didn't say a word. Linda was polite. But Rufus became belligerent: 'I walked in and was like "Hey Yoko! Give us the tour. Where's the champagne?" And I cracked open a bottle. Needless to say I got the quickest tour of John Lennon's apartment that anybody has ever had. I saw the white piano and was asked to leave.'

The next day, feeling a little apologetic, Rufus sent over a bottle of champagne and some of his CDs. He was due to go back out on the road a few days later so decided to unwind by smoking a little pot in the room he had been keeping at the Roger Smith Hotel. A visit to his dealer ended in a line of coke, which led to a hit of acid, which led to a cocktail session and then some mushrooms. By the time he got back to his hotel room he was feeling a little strange. After an hour or two of staring at himself in the mirror, he moved over to the couch and started working on the song that would become 'Old Whore's Diet'. The next thing he knew was that he got a telephone call from Yoko Ono's office asking him where he was staying and telling him to expect a car. He sat and waited. No car came. Eventually he called her office and asked where the car was but nobody knew what he was talking about. He became convinced that he was going mad and that the call had been 'Death' and 'Death' was sending a car to collect him. Eventually he crashed. When he resurfaced a day or so later and headed out of his hotel room to get to the tour bus, the desk clerk called him over and gave him an envelope that had been sitting there waiting for him. Inside was a card from Yoko Ono thanking him for the champagne and CDs.

The week that he recorded his *Absolutely Fabulous* cameo was the week that everything came to a head. He found himself partying with President Bush's daughter Barbara at a fashion show, then hanging out with his mother and Marianne Faithfull. All the time his constant drug use was skewing his sense of reality and making him question his sanity.

Rufus' crystal meth use had become so extensive that his gums bled, he was constantly sweating and, on one nightmarish occasion, he found that it had sent him temporarily blind. He still didn't stop. And when he took crystal he would take other drugs too – until it became a 'big snowball of drugs'. Later he would reason that part of his problem was that he felt his schedule had been too heavy and that, although he felt he had to go out all of the time, he found it hard to cope with being the centre of attention. 'Once I did a little bit of crystal meth, I was off – I would just disappear. Especially with being gay, it just tied into all of those dark feelings that gay men have … Every time I did [speed] it was like I was taking the biggest vacation, and death would be the best vacation. In that mind frame, the closer you got to death, the better it seemed.'

In his room after yet another binge that included crystal, cocaine and mushrooms, he began to hallucinate visions of Jerry Garcia on boxes of pornography and felt that New York had become a painting that he could look at but not re-enter. He sat in his bathroom weeping for hour after hour, terrified that he might not make it back into the world.

When he finally began to come down, he realised he was in serious need of help. He called his latest manager, Barry Taylor, with whom he had recently signed, who got in touch with their friend Elton John and asked him to intervene. When Elton called him, Rufus was brutally honest about his problems. He knew that Elton had had his own battles with addiction and substance abuse and when he said that he should go to rehab, Rufus realised that he was speaking from experience. Elton recommended the Hazelden clinic as it had successfully treated some other people he had known.

Hazelden is an alcohol and drug treatment organisation that operates at a number of sites in the US. Within a couple of days of Elton's call, Rufus had checked into their residential facility at Center City, Minnesota, 50 miles north of Minneapolis. Hazelden uses the Twelve Step programme, originally devised as a means of treatment for alcohol addiction by Alcoholics Anonymous in 1939. It had subsequently been adapted as a means to deal with addictions and compulsion of all types. Although the Center City facility had successfully treated celebrities including Eric Clapton, Matthew Perry and Aaron Sorkin, its reputation was built on achieving results and not as a rehab centre for the entertainment industry. The regime was far more spartan than many of the preferred celebrity centres, with residents expected to take turns at keeping the place clean and tidy. This wasn't the kind of place that a troubled star could duck into to get out of the spotlight for a week or two before going back to their old ways. Hazelden was a functional treatment unit that expected commitment. Rufus stayed there for a month, taking part in counselling sessions and adapting to using the Twelve Steps as a guide to sober living.

Before he had agreed to go to Hazelden, Rufus had considered going to stay with Loudon instead. His father was living in Los Angeles and Rufus, in a moment of clarity (a lucid vision he put down to his drug use), had a revelation that Loudon was the key to a cycle that both of them had been caught up in that they needed to break. Later he would explain to *Paste* magazine how his experiences at Hazelden had helped him come to terms with the relationship he had with his father: 'I realised that [there] was a common thread through a lot of men. We were in all-male wards and once you get to issues with fathers, that's when [we] break down. It's odd – the love between a father and son is really volatile. Then, when I got back ... I just respected him more. I mean for all the crap that he's done to me and leaving me as a child, at least he's always been honest and always taken care of himself. My father has always been able to survive, musically and career-wise, and he's always been able to transform and better himself. So that's when I realised that I do want to be my dad, in a lot of ways. I mean, I wanna do my own thing and have my own career. But he's a survivor, and that's what I wanna be.'

Other than this, Rufus has never been prepared to discuss any specifics about his time at Hazelden and has regularly refused to comment on whether or not he still used the Twelve Step programme or whether he visited NA or AA meetings. A year or so after finishing his treatment, Elton presented him with a special silver ring that he had had commissioned to celebrate Rufus' continuing sobriety.[8]

In January 2003, Rufus expressed his gratitude to Elton by appearing in a charity concert in Anaheim, California. The 2003 NAMM Concert in aid of musical education featured numerous musicians performing Elton John songs and ended with Elton being given a lifetime achievement award after playing his own set. Rufus, who was on second and played 'Goodbye Yellow Brick Road', lined up alongside Randy Newman, Ray Charles, Jewel and Brian Wilson. All the performers signed the piano that they had played on and it was subsequently auctioned for $25,000.

It was a bright, positive start to a year that Rufus, post-rehab, intended to grasp in both hands, stating his case not just as a survivor but as a saviour for worried pop kids everywhere. 'I have to stick around for a while,' he proclaimed, 'mainly because a lot of other people – whether it's Jeff Buckley or Kurt Cobain – have gone. And this industry has become such a grinding factory that a lot of songwriters aren't even getting to come to fruition. So it's very important for me to stick around and keep my wits about me, otherwise . . . there's just not gonna be much out there for people to listen to. If I self-destruct, I do believe it's socially irresponsible because a lot of people need me right now, which I have to respect.'

Under this new work ethic, the sessions with de Vries reconvened for what was now called *Want* and Rufus found that songs were pouring out of him. In his New York apartment he would work on his piano while Andrew W.K. (at the time a major label metallic rock'n'roller who had performed with both Ozzy Osbourne and the

---

8. Rufus still wears the ring on the middle finger of his right hand. The gold signet ring that he wears is part of a male Wainwright family tradition that is mentioned in his unreleased song about Loudon, 'Two Gold Rings', and in Loudon's song about his own father, 'Surviving Twin'. Rufus also wears a ring made of labradorite, which is apparently a reminder of an ecstasy binge in Paris.

boys from *Jackass*, today an occasional motivational speaker and avant-garde musician) hammered at his own piano in an upstairs apartment. 'We didn't talk that much,' said Rufus, 'but our common whining pleas to the cosmos would collide in the back yard.'

Some of the songs had been written before he went into rehab and some were written as responses to, or reflections of, what he had seen when he decided to get clean. 'I do believe I wrote some great material in the depths of my despair,' he later explained. 'But I also had to write some answers to that despair, to accompany these melodies. And that's probably why I had so much material at the end, because a lot of these songs have their shadow images.' In a later interview he was to partly thank the quality of the songs that he had written before rehab as having given him the strength to sort himself out. 'I really do feel that when I started writing this record, I was sort of subconsciously drowning and I had to sing in a high register to pierce through the murkiness of everything. And in turn it was kind of like self-sabotage. It made me realise that if I didn't get my act together I wouldn't be able to perform this material because it's really demanding. So I think in a lot of ways my songwriting saved my life.'

In an intense burst of creativity, 30 tracks were recorded and finished in little more time than he might have spent on a handful of songs on his previous albums. One of the reasons for this was that Rufus was committed to making the record the best he had ever made and would work over his songs until he knew what he wanted to do with them before he got to the studio, rather than waiting until he got there to try out different approaches. In many ways, not least artistically, he had sharpened his focus. 'When I was in the studio for *Poses* I felt like I had the time and the luxury to just sort of extrapolate and philosophise and remix and kind of take my time, which in the end ended up being kind of tortuous,' he said. 'But certainly after September 11th and having my own personal struggles, there was just much more of a sense of urgency and of let's enjoy ourselves while we can.'

'Rufus writes very thoroughly, more so than anyone I've worked with before,' said de Vries. 'He brings his songs in very conceptualised, in terms of harmony, melody, countermelody, even orchestration. Groove-wise and feel-wise, there was more room for me to help guide the songs, especially in the more uptempo numbers. But I was always concerned to work within the spirit of the original gestures embedded in the songwriting.'

Rufus admitted to being comfortable in the studio, something he put down to having spent a lot of his childhood hanging around them while his parents worked. He hadn't bothered learning any of the technical aspects or recording though. 'I am allergic to knobs,' he told *Mix*, a technical recording journal, doubtless unaware of the double entendres lurking in his statement. 'I break out in a sweat and become dyslexic. I still say, "Could you fast-wind that please?"'

When Rufus first brought a song to de Vries, he would record a rough vocal to a click track accompanied on either a guitar or piano, depending on the song. Then the pair of them would listen to the track and decide on bass lines or synth parts, sometimes programming in drums to act as a sketch. Once they had established in which direction they wanted to take it, they would call in extra musicians to get the track really moving, overdubbing and colouring in their sketch with real instruments. Rufus described *Want* as his 'multi-city, multi-coastal' album (though in truth *Poses* had also been recorded in pretty much the same way) and sessions were spread over seven studios in New York, Los Angeles and London.

The bulk of the band sessions were held at Bearsville, Woodstock, the legendary studio that was opened in 1969 by Bob Dylan's manager, Albert Grossman. The studio was just about to close down – *Want* would be the last album to be recorded there – and Rufus' management was able to negotiate a great rate on the sessions. Out in the wilds of rural New York State, the musicians were even snowed in for a couple of days, which served to further concentrate their performances. In fact, Rufus had originally considered using Bob Dylan's touring band for the album sessions after having seen Dylan play at Newport. In the end he used Levon Helm, who had played in The Band and lived locally, and Charlie Sexton, who was Dylan's current guitarist. 'I knew that Charlie Sexton was a big fan of mine,' said Rufus, when asked how he came to use the acclaimed guitarist and one-time teenage pop pin-up, before adding, 'Needless to say he's easy on the eyes!'

Other studios included the Maid's Room in New York, where most of the early recordings were made, de Vries's own studio, The

Strongroom in London for mixing and Angel in Islington, London, where the orchestral parts were recorded. Right at the end they took the tapes to the Record Plant in Los Angeles and played them to Lenny Waronker and another Band member, Robbie Robertson. 'Their astute ears and wisdom were invaluable,' said de Vries as he signed off the sessions that had seen them create a gloriously complex and multi-layered album that would exceed the expectations of even the most imaginative Rufus Wainwright fan and all in little more than six months. 'Adrenalin and enthusiasm' is how de Vries explained their achievement. 'Working on a project as magical as this one is rare, and the body responds. There wasn't a song that didn't demand maximum care and attention – plus the support of a team of great people full of dedication and love for the endeavour.'

After the relatively restrained *Poses*, the *Want* recordings returned to the more elaborate, baroque stylings of his debut album, something that Rufus was more than happy about – he sometimes referred to the record as his *Sgt Pepper*. 'I can't deny the fact any longer that I am an opera queen, and I'm really used to dramatic gestures and full-bodied sounds in the music that I personally listen to,' he explained. 'Another thing was my relationship with my producer. A lot of producers have tried to kind of encapsulate me or edit me to make me more palatable but Marius was much more intrigued and really excited about my grandiose ambitions and really, really wanted to nurture them and help them. He thought it was different and exciting. So we went that way.'

4.4

After having gained so much exposure for his cover of 'Hallelujah' and enjoying taking part in the Harold Arlen project the previous year, Rufus needed little convincing to agree to perform in Hal Willner's latest production. 'Came So Far For Beauty' was an all-star concert of the songs of Leonard Cohen taking place at the Prospect Park Bandshell, on 28 June for the 25th year of Brooklyn's annual summer concert series. It was the first of his trademark curated events that Willner had attempted when his subject was still alive;

a tribute to Cohen's longevity and to the changing state of music-
making when an artist could have a career that spanned 30 or 40
years, something that Willner saw as a new phenomenon and worth
celebrating in itself.

Although there would be no appearance by Cohen himself, the
crowd of 11,000, a record for a concert in the park, got to see a
three-hour show by Willner's usual coterie of cult and avant-garde
musicians. As it was held a few days before Canada Day and was
partially sponsored by the Canadian Consulate, the stage was dec-
orated with the Canadian flag and the show began with the Canadian
national anthem. Fittingly, among the performers were Kate and
Anna, who had been virtual contemporaries of Cohen on the Montreal folk scene in their Mountain City Four days. Indeed, back in
the mid-1960s their friend, and the grand-mère of Canadian folk,
Penny Lang, had been offering them praise and encouragement at
the same time as she was refusing to teach Leonard Cohen how to
play guitar.[9]

There were plenty of familiar faces on stage. Alongside his mother
and aunt, Rufus performed with Martha and Linda and Teddy
Thompson. Other artists included Nick Cave, Laurie Anderson, the
Handsome Family and Julie Christensen and Perla Battalla, who had
both sung back-up for Cohen in the 1980s and 1990s.

Unsurprisingly, Rufus performed 'Hallelujah', by now a frequent
part of his own set, to rapturous applause. More unusual was his
vaudevillian take on 'Everybody Knows', turning it into something
out of Cabaret and winning over even the most cynical Cohen purists
in the process. By the time the evening had concluded with Rufus

---

9. Lang was an important figure on the Montreal folk scene right from the early 1960s.
Kate sometimes backed her on piano, along with Roma Baran on guitar, as she played the
folk circuit in the north-west. An acclaimed live performer, she somehow failed to get a
record deal in the 1960s. She once turned down the opportunity to make a record of her
version of Cohen's 'Suzanne' because the company wanted an electric version and she
would only play acoustically. Shortly afterwards it became a hit for two other artists. By
the 1970s she had been diagnosed with a bipolar disorder. In the 1990s she started making
albums and the McGarrigles appeared on a few tracks with her. Back in the mid-1960s, she
decided not to help out a musically challenged young Canadian poet. 'My manager called
saying, "There's this poet Cohen in Montreal who wants to learn to play guitar." When
Leonard called he said, "I'm Leonard Cohen. I was told you'd teach me guitar." I said, "Not
today. I'm very depressed" and I hung up on him. It was the last time we spoke. I didn't
know who he was, and I wasn't a guitar teacher. It was at the beginning of my manic-
depressive cycle.' (www.pennylang.com)

and Nick Cave howling 'Don't Go Home With Your Hard On', the
concert was already being written up as a legendary event, so much
so that it would be revived in Brighton the following year. After the
UK show, Nick Cave admitted that they had had so many offers to
restage the night that they could have toured it for a year. It was only
the allure of the Sydney Opera House that convinced everybody to
get together once more in 2005. The Australian shows would be
filmed and form the basis of the film *I'm Your Man* (dir. Lian Lunson,
2005), a documentary about Cohen interspersed with performances
by Rufus, Martha, Kate and Anna, Nick Cave, Antony Hegarty,
Jarvis Cocker et al. There was actually another staging of the show
final, at the time of writing at least, in Dublin in 2006, though
due to conflicting schedules this didn't include any Wainwright or
McGarrigle performances.

In July, Rufus found himself celebrating his 30th birthday in
Canada on the set of Martin Scorsese's Howard Hughes bio-pic *The
Aviator*, in which he had a small part as a dance-band singer in the
director's recreation of the Ambassador Hotel's Cocoanut Grove
nightclub. Back in the 1930s and 1940s, the Grove had been a
millionaire's playground where Hughes had cavorted with stars
like Errol Flynn, Clark Gable and Lana Turner. By 2003 the once-
prestigious hotel's allure had been completely eaten away as if
cursed by the murder of Robert F. Kennedy that had occurred there
in 1968. Despite various attempts to revive it, not least under Sammy
Davis Jnr steerage in the 1970s, the place had sunk to the point
where it had been closed to the public for good in 1989. The hotel's
only function had become that of a location for Hollywood films;
the last of which, with exquisite irony, was the film about the
assassination of RFK, Emilio Estevez's *Bobby*, made in 2005 as the
hotel was being demolished around the cast and crew. When Scorsese had scouted the place ahead of making his movie, the Cocoanut
Grove nightclub was still standing but over the years had been
renovated to within an inch of its life and bore no relation to how
it had looked in its heyday. It was simpler (and cheaper) to recreate
the nightclub on a soundstage in Canada.

Rufus was joined on set by Loudon and Martha. All three of them
played similar roles as singers from different periods as the film
looped to and from the ballroom as the narrative arcs through the

years. Martha and Rufus are both excellent in their blink-and-you'll-miss-them roles. Loudon, who had parlayed his *Undeclared* exposure into a mini-renaissance in his acting career having just filmed a small part in the Tim Burton film *Big Fish*, showed that experience counted and it is his grinning and slightly demented version of 'After You've Gone' that snatches the unofficial 'Best Wainwright in *The Aviator* Award'.

Rufus enjoyed his time when actually filming his routine but found all the waiting around excruciatingly boring. He did remember getting some unrequested advice from an experienced Hollywood actor, which livened things up a little. 'Harvey Keitel was hanging around the set, and he asked me how I was gonna "prepare" for my role. I said, "Um, I dunno – memorise my lines?" Harvey said he was going to look at the daily rushes, and if I wasn't any good, he was gonna take over my role, because, he said with this growl, "Marty needs a hit!"' Mr White must have been satisfied because Rufus didn't hear any more from him.

Rufus had more fun in his next film. *Heights* was a Merchant Ivory production that told an interconnecting story of five characters in Manhattan. Rufus had another small role as Jeremy, the embittered ex-boyfriend of a sleazy yet celebrated photographer. It was a small part but at least he had some lines and he did get to hang out with Glenn Close, who was as excited to be working with him as he was to be working with her and altogether friendlier than Keitel. 'She burst into the room wearing this long black wig, looking so gorgeous, just voluptuous and sexy,' recalled Rufus. 'And she ran up to me and said, "I'm so excited to work with you! Guess what, darling, there's an eclipse!" And we raced to the window to look and the moon was eclipsing. And we rehearsed our lines and it was magic.'

The director Chris Terrio says that he wrote the role especially for Rufus, confident that he'd be able to translate his stage charisma on to the screen: 'I saw him in concert and I just thought, "Somebody needs to put him in a movie." Not that I thought it would be me. But when we created the character of Jeremy, I thought, "Who could bring credibility to this, and who could bring a history to this character?" Who could do it better than Rufus? I was thrilled when he said yes. You just put the camera on him and he's naturally so smart and so interesting that I feel like there's always something going on.'

Rufus' part was filmed in 2003 but the movie wasn't released until 2005. Although perfectly watchable, *Heights* did only moderate business and wasn't given a cinema release in many territories (it didn't even get a DVD release in the UK). A shame, as Rufus holds his own among a strong cast and delivers his few lines in convincingly laconic New York slacker style.

After his cinematic diversions and with so much material recorded and ready for release, Rufus originally pushed for everything to be included on one double album. 'I was listening to it as a double album but the record company wasn't too keen,' he explained to *Rolling Stone*, and added, with his tongue firmly in his cheek, 'And also in listening to this stuff, I realised that no human mind is capable of really properly digesting that much overwrought emotion. It was just too much for one sit-down, and I realised that certain things would get lost. I tend to really demand for the listener to pay attention and I didn't want them passing out.'

Reluctantly he agreed to release the album in stages. There would be *Want One* and shortly afterwards the rest of the material would arrive as *Want Two*. In order to arrange the available material into two separate sets, Rufus decided to split the songs into a kind of diptych where one side contained the autobiographical material and the other a more esoteric, mysterious view of the world.

In an interview in the *Observer*, Rufus explained how his love of the Pre-Raphaelite Brotherhood had influenced the album and its sleeve concept. 'My music is Pre-Raphaelite in a certain way, in that it reinvents an older era and romanticises it, puts it in a gilded frame. But also I'm pretty much drenched in fairy tales and, recently, when I was making the album, a lot of those old stories and legends became very central to my recovery. In the present world, this technological, psychotic, politicised, non-sensical world, you have to believe that the good guys are going to win. That evil will be banished somehow.'

The elaborate photography session that produced the two sleeves was styled by the fashion designer Zaldy, one of Rufus' friends from his Chelsea Hotel days, and is clearly influenced by the Pre-Raphaelite Movement, a group of Victorian artists who frequently took inspiration from myths, legends and fairy stories as they sought new subjects for their paintings.

He came to think of the two albums as being equivalent to a male/female split, hence on the Arthurian-influenced sleeve of *Want One* he is fittingly portrayed as a legendary knight-errant, a solitary nobleman who has proved himself by trial and misfortune ('I'm your knight in shining armour. I'm here to save you from Linkin Park,' he joked to Alan Cumming in *Interview* magazine), and on *Want Two* he is portrayed as Sleeping Beauty, spinning and then slumbering, waiting to be rescued.[10]

On the *Want One* cover, Rufus' knight at rest is seemingly on the edge of a forest preparing to enter. He is a character out of an Edward Burne-Jones painting as though lit by Pierre et Gilles. In the inner booklet he has fallen, sword in hand, among a thicket of roses as though, like the knights in Burne-Jones' *The Briar Wood*, he has tried and failed to reach the sleeping princess.

On the front of *Want Two*, the character that Rufus is dressed as is Sleeping Beauty. In the centrefold, and most particularly in the close-up of the face and hand with the spot of blood on a fingertip pricked by a spindle, the original concept is clear. But after the cover photographs were taken, Rufus was told the Arthurian tale of the Lady of Shalott, perhaps prompted by the marked similarity of Rufus' pose to John William Waterhouse's 1888 painting of the Lady about to sing her final song. He decided that this tragic story was more appropriate to the feeling he was trying to convey and he retrospectively decided he was no longer Sleeping Beauty but the Lady of Shalott, forever spinning, face turned away so as not to look from her window.[11]

---

10. Coincidentally Kate and Anna had long been interested in the links between spinning and making music. The patron saint of spinners was St Catherine of Alexandria. They had performed at a festival in her honour back in 1983 (the poster of which featured a stunning art nouveau-style painting of Kate as the saint by Montreal artist Judy Garfin). St Catherine was a third-century martyr who had been sentenced to be tortured and broken on the wheel. She subsequently became the patron saint of all those who work with a wheel from knife-grinders, to potters, to spinners and, quite logically, Kate and Anna believed also to those who made records.

11. In Tennyson's poem, the Lady of Shalott is trapped in her tower on an island, a mythic figure, unseen; only her beautiful voice can sometimes be heard by the workers in the fields around Camelot. An unexplained curse forbids her from directly looking out and she spins and weaves a tapestry based on the sights she sees or imagines reflected in her mirror. One day she hears Sir Lancelot singing and catches a glimpse of his plumed helmet

The running order for *Want One* was deliberately designed to flow from beginning to end; Rufus wanted to make each track seamlessly move into the next. *Want Two* would be more disparate and its subject matter more contentious. Rufus suggested that the first album was like leading people to the edge of the cliff and the second would be pushing them off. Referring to the infamously censorious mega-chain store responsible for a large proportion of US CD sales, Rufus said: 'I wanted at least the first part of this project to make it into Wal-Mart and not have any major strikes against it. Mostly it has to do with subject matter. *Want Two* has a

---

as he rides towards Camelot. Tired of her imprisonment, 'half sick of shadows', and desperate for experience and love, this glimpse of the brave knight is enough for her to decide to invoke the curse and leave the tower. As a storm rises she gets into a boat where, floating towards Lancelot and singing all the way, she dies.

Rufus' experiences reflect the Lady of Shalott's perfectly – and, appropriately as we are looking at a mirror image – they are opposite but the same. A.S. Byatt has suggested that the Lady of Shalott represents any creative artist 'who makes up, pieces together, records, weaves a world – at the expense of living in it, or tasting it, or loving it directly'. When the Lady catches sight of Lancelot, she finally sees the world and wants to climb into it. When drug-induced blindness temporarily overcomes Rufus and pushes him to the edge, it is the blindness that forces him to consider his situation, to really stop and look at the world he has created with drugs, and to make the decision to try to make an escape from it.

When reality punctures a fantasy world, it is always devastating. When the real world encroaches on the artist's vision, it can all come crashing down – 'the mirror crack'd from side to side', as Tennyson puts it.

This ultimate exposure and destruction of delusion is included as part of the Twelve Step programme that Rufus had worked through at Hazelden. In the words of the *Narcotics Anonymous Step Working Guides*: 'Our addiction finally brings us to a place where we can no longer deny the nature of our problem. All the lies, all the rationalisations, all the illusions fall away as we stand face to face with what our lives have become. We realise we've been living without hope. We find we've become friendless or so completely disconnected that our relationships are a sham, a parody of love and intimacy. Although it may seem that all is lost when we find ourselves in this state, the truth is that we must pass through this place before we can embark upon our journey of recovery.' Both Rufus and the Lady of Shalott break their curses and decide to live (although of course the Lady's life is as short as that of an emerging mayfly).

The image in the *Want Two* booklet centrefold shows Rufus as Sleeping Beauty laid out on a bed of straw. His pose is a mirror of John Everett Millais' painting *Ophelia* and, despite being on dry land, the implied watery grave of Ophelia is enough to serve the interpretation of the Lady of Shalott being carried away on the water. Indeed Rufus would take the analogy further by suggesting in interviews that Jeff Buckley, another casualty of water, whom his tribute song 'Memphis Skyline' refers to as being like 'mad Ophelia', was also like the Lady of Shalott.

As a further aside, almost a footnote to a footnote, there is another uncanny, though almost certainly involuntary, reference to a Pre-Raphaelite painting that occurs every time Rufus plays and sings the piano in concert. His manner of closing his eyes and throwing back his head is an almost exact duplication of Dante Gabriel Rossetti's *Beata Beatrix*, in which the dying Beatrice is captured at the moment of rapt beatific vision.

song called "Gay Messiah" and another called "An Old Whore's Diet". So it's a little racier, a little darker. But still, all these songs were written and recorded in the same period.'

Want One begins with 'Oh What A World', the title taken from the witch's cry before she melts in the *Wizard of Oz* and it was the first vocal that Rufus recorded for the album sessions. Originally written on a Paris-London train at the end of the European tour for *Poses* when Rufus was both physically and mentally exhausted, what begins as a resigned lament for the world and his part in it: 'Why am I always on plane or a fast train/Oh what a world my parents gave me' builds into a statement of intent and post-rehab positivity. From the Dumbo-esque stomping tuba intro, the music builds to a full orchestra and explodes into a snatch of Ravel's Bolero with Rufus singing 'Life is beautiful'. It is a wonderful, life-affirming opening to the album.

The train symbolism returns on the next track, 'I Don't Know What It Is' which was inspired by a sense of confusion Rufus had felt at a party for the Strokes in New York where everybody seemed to be desperately looking for the hip and the happening but nobody quite knew where it was located. Like trying to catch the wind wherever they thought it was, it was suddenly somewhere else. Rufus realised he was searching for something too but he didn't know what. 'Everybody was just mad, rushing around, trying to be as hip as possible and all I could think was "I don't know what it is/But you gotta do it . . ."' In the song he appears on a train bound for heaven or hell, he doesn't know which, all he knows is it is out of his control. It was a moment of drug-induced satori. Very shortly after writing this song he chose to go into rehab.

The album runs in cycles: opulent, everything-at-once-and-then-add-some-more dramatic peaks, followed by the reflective descent of restrained classically influenced chamber pop songs. So 'I Don't Know What It Is' is followed by 'Vicious World' with its Wagner-referencing recorder played by Rufus. The stomping, drum heavy 'Movies of Myself', which Rufus had once considered releasing as a single and asking arch occultist Kenneth Anger to direct the video (a pity the idea was never followed through), precedes the simple, Schubertian 'Pretty Things'. The album's centrepiece, the epiphanic 'Go or Go Ahead' is in turn followed by the lovelorn 'Vibrate', featuring Rufus' 'Maria Callas moment', where he holds a note for as long as he can.

However, it is 'Go or Go Ahead' that's the real show-stopper. The song builds and builds and builds. Like an intellectual Queen (if they had had more emotion to match their masterful bombast), it is a towering achievement. The song was written during a particularly harrowing drug comedown when Rufus realised he was going to have to address the person he was becoming. This was Rufus' Rimbaud moment, his Season in Hell and he subsequently dedicated it to 'all the people who have really hit the bottom of the barrel'. He fills the lyrics with allusions to vampires and angels, daring himself to look into the face of Medusa. It's a virtual tightrope walk with the rope strung between where he has been and where he wants to get to; the rope is swaying and it's a struggle to keep his balance. 'I really do believe that when you get to that state of inebriation, you've got to pull out all the stops in terms of what's going to save you. Like mythology, and astrology . . . and mother . . .' he explained.

In fact, mother Kate does appear playing banjo on one of *Want One*'s other standout tracks. '14th Street' is Rufus' triumphant return into the world made song. A big, brassy Broadway-styled tune that evokes high-kicking dance routines, entrances on giant stage staircases and confetti falling from the ceiling. Even the words, with their puns about Bo Peep's sheep and allusions to smoking cavemen, sound like lyrics from a hit musical.

Of *Want One*'s more restrained moments, the title track is perhaps the simplest and most straightforward. 'Want' was begun on his last day in rehab and became the first song he finished when he came out. Rufus says that when he had it written, he knew he was ready to get back to work. It's a song of readjustment and fulfilment where 'want' means both what is desired and what is needed. Rufus sings 'I just want to be my dad/With a slight sprinkling of my mother/And work at the family store' and in doing so realises that he has come to terms with his place in the world and with his position within his family. A situation further evinced by the fact that felt able to include his love/hate song to Loudon, 'Dinner at Eight', as the closing track on the album. 'I've had a real yin and yang existence,' he said in a later interview. 'My mother's very bohemian and Irish

Catholic; my father is quite rigid and a disciplinarian and logical. Both of those forces have been necessary for my survival. I've had to learn to accept my parents for who they are, taking what you need, and not blaming them for it.'

Rufus maintained that he had no strong religious beliefs but he acknowledged that he had had to look for some kind of spiritual reassurance when he went through his rehab treatment. Indeed one of the crucial tenets of the Twelve Step programme is that of recognising a higher power and aiming for spiritual growth (the definition of higher power need not be a specific 'God', it can encompass a secular spirituality). When asked about his own spirituality in an interview in the *San Francisco Chronicle*, he replied: 'It's all about finding meaning. Some of the men I'm closest to – my father has a black belt in aikido, Richard Thompson is a Muslim, Leonard Cohen is a Buddhist – they all hit this kind of spiritual wall at some point. Everyone has to come to terms with their own mortality and spiritual upkeep, whether it's AA or aikido.'

This idea of searching for meaning, the fear of death and an ultimate return to innocence appears on 'Beautiful Child', a song that Rufus described as being 'happily apocalyptic'. The quasi-religious song is driven by insistent drums and rapturous gospel-tinged backing vocals. With its pounding trance-like rhythms, it comes as no surprise that Rufus claimed he had originally conceived it while high on mushrooms. The lyrics move from Rufus as child surrounded by hills (presumably the Laurentian Mountains that filled the horizon around his grandparents' house), through disillusionment and, via spiritual symbolism, wailing walls and crucifixions, to the end time of the Twilight of the Gods. It finally climaxes in a rebirth like the celestial baby in *2001* – the Kubrickian 'Star-Child' – and then returns to the opening line again, completing the circle. In essence the song is a reconnection with his pre-addiction beliefs in the power of art and creativity over all. 'I think I've been sanctioned by a higher power,' he said. 'My music doesn't just come directly from me. And also I take it as a responsibility – a need [my] audience has for truth and sincerity and real, true love.'

Rufus' stint in rehab had been a kind of lucky escape from the reality of his life in New York and although he was ready to embrace a new way of living, he was careful not to forget others who were yet to confront their own problems. A song on *Want One* was addressed to one of his close friends.

Natasha Lyonne, an actress best known at the time for parts in the *American Pie* movies, had lived in the same Manhattan apartment block as Rufus and they had spent plenty of time together. She was known to have had her own difficulties with alcohol and drugs, and Rufus' lovely song 'Natasha' is a none too cryptically coded message to her. Rufus explained that it was a song for a friend who had just gone through what he had been going through, although she was 'on the other side of the fence from me . . . There's this space between us and I really can't help [her] so all I can do is lead by example. All I can do is write a song about it.' Lyonne would continue to struggle with substance abuse until being hospitalised in 2005 and treated for heroin addiction. She has recently resumed making films.

For all of its positivism and its aura of a life stopped, assessed and restarted, to describe *Want One* as a 'recovery' album is to diminish its sophistication. Much of the material may be almost painfully personal but within Rufus' artistic candour exists a truth that is readily accessible and all too rare in contemporary music. And crucially there is no self-pity and it is never apologetic. The sheer exuberance with which the material is performed and the range of emotions that are touched upon lifts the album way above regular contemporary popular music, reaching the operatic intensities that Rufus had always promised he would one day deliver. Here are desperate lows and ecstatic highs and sometimes they are touched within the same song. He may have signed off the sleeve notes with 'This album is dedicated to me' but it also spoke directly to anybody who had ever spent time wondering about life, love and the human condition.[12]

Unlike other performers in similar situations, Rufus made no secret of the fact that he had been in rehab and in his first major interview to promote the album, he was brutally frank about the

---

12. In 2008 Echo and the Bunnymen's Ian McCulloch, a man born to blow his own trumpet at the expense of all others, actually conceded that *Want One* was the only music he had ever heard that reached the places he had gone to with his greatest ever song 'The Killing Moon'. ("Portrait of the Artist: Ian McCulloch", Laura Barnett, *Guardian*, 8 January 2008)

extent of his drug use to Anthony De Curtis of the *New York Times*. By being honest and upfront, he hoped that he would be able to get everything out into the open straight away, rather than have to skirt around the issue with other journalists only to let everything out in the end anyway. It wasn't as if he intended to keep things secret. In fact, he wanted to speak out about his experience so that he might warn others of the dangers of crystal meth.

Rufus had always had a good relationship with the *New York Times* and De Curtis, a contributing editor to *Rolling Stone*, was a serious and trusted journalist. But the sensationalised headline of the piece as it appeared in the newspaper – 'Rufus Wainwright Journeys to "Gay Hell" and Back' – would cause unwanted repercussions as it was picked up by other magazines. Although he could hardly be held responsible for the attention-grabbing skills of a sub-editor, he would have to defend himself over and over. Some members of the gay community complained that he was playing into the hands of the homophobes who were all too ready to deride and denigrate any and all aspects of gay lifestyle.

Rufus is indirectly quoted as referring to the world into which he had slipped as a 'gay hell', but it is in the context of explaining how the excessive use of crystal meth on the gay scene has seriously affected the lifestyles of its users and how there is no such thing as casual use. 'For years, and I mean thousands of years,' said Rufus, 'the gay man's mind has been treated as perverted, clandestine and dirty and speed reinforces and glamorises that as an ideal. And with drugs, what's more dangerous is more sexually exciting. I had a few of those real gay lost weekends where everything goes out the window. I mean your mind is just completely ravaged.'

Rufus admitted that his friends and fans gave him a hard time about the phrase 'gay hell' in the article and the controversy rumbled along for a few months, particularly in the gay press where he frequently had the headline thrown back at him and was asked to clarify his views. As Rufus later pointed out in an interview with the *Advocate* in 2005, there was so little coverage of the problem with crystal meth use and its impact on sexual health in the media that if he hadn't spoken about his situation, it was probable that the subject would get no coverage at all. Twenty years after the AIDS crisis had first appeared, many men were happily ignoring safe-sex advice. For the majority of readers of the *New York Times*, Rufus' description of the scene he had been involved in would be outside of anything they had experienced or even been aware of. 'Years of sexual insecurity, the low-grade discrimination you suffer, the need to belong – speed takes care of all that in one second. It was a world where people are so crazy that they're not making any sense any more. If you wanted safe sex, you were a nerd, uncool. I was one of the nerds who did have safe sex, thank God. But I'm still mentally shattered by the whole experience.'

Most disappointing perhaps is that the article inevitably focused attention away from Rufus' music and entirely on to his lifestyle and various troubles with sex, drugs and family. There is an undercurrent of latent homophobia that is implied by the headline for which both the interviewer and interviewee become unwitting proponents. Most readers would have been aware of Rufus' sexuality and to allow the details of his addiction and breakdown to be defined strictly along the lines of that sexuality was an error of judgement on both parts. Quite reasonably, many commentators pointed out that self-induced drug addiction and wanton sexual encounters were not solely the domain of homosexuals and that if Rufus had been straight, his sexuality wouldn't have made the headline.

As it was, the article set the tone for much of the press around the *Want One* album for which the music, though often lavishly praised, frequently had to take a back seat as journalists focused on Rufus' venial sins and ultimate absolution.

4.5

'I've wasted my time but had a really good time doing it,' said Martha when interviewed before playing a series of solo shows. 'But when people talk to me about why I haven't made a record, it makes me sad because I feel like I've done something wrong. Maybe I haven't always been careful, and I did some crazy things and wasn't all business, but I don't want to think that it was all for naught.'

Throughout 2003 Martha had continued working on her songs

and playing solo dates around New York. She might have shown she could handle playing in large theatres when she appeared with Rufus or her parents, but solo she was struggling to break out of the tiny venues of Brooklyn and Manhattan. Often she would appear with just her guitar and play to barely 30 people. She sometimes liked to call herself the 'most famous, un-famous' singer around. She had played all over the world, appeared on numerous records but still hadn't made an album of her own. In a way she used her lack of a recording contract as a safety net, her underachievement as a means of keeping herself separate from her family. She might have joked that there was only room for one Wainwright child to have an album out but by continually delaying making her own record after nearly seven years as a professional musician she was actually avoiding ever having to be really compared to her brother or parents. She was willingly playing a role that her family seemed to have assigned her. That of the support act, the sidekick or the stooge.

Her previous CDs had brought her to the attention of record labels and her family connections obviously didn't harm her any in getting heard, but she found it difficult to find a major label that was fully committed to her and in which she felt confident enough to sign and know that her record wouldn't get shelved halfway through. As she later admitted: 'I was really afraid of being signed and being dropped. Or, in the context of my family, I was going to be signed to a mini label and be a loser.'

It wasn't as though she didn't have offers. Joe Boyd wanted to make a folk record with her but she didn't feel comfortable working with a famous producer, or in fact anybody who she felt would take over the sessions and force her into a particular sound. When record label bosses talked about writing hit singles, it was enough to make her turn and run. Nevertheless she realised that it was really now or never. She knew she had to make a record. What else were her options? 'There's nothing else I know how to do,' she said at the time. 'I don't have a degree in anything and I'm probably not going to marry a doctor or a lawyer. I want to build a long-lasting career and know I can always tour and keep making records, and drive a car that I own, and have these simple things that you feel you need as you get older. It can be confusing being a bohemian, which

I always will be, and if I never sell a million records it doesn't matter to me. But I also want to see what I can accomplish and give myself enough of a chance.'

With a few dollars of her own but mostly on a promise that she would eventually pay back the session fees, Martha started recording at Brad Albetta's Monkey Boy Studios in Brooklyn. Working together brought Martha and Albetta closer and they would begin a relationship that resulted in them getting married in 2007. She credits Albetta with both pushing her to finish the record and giving her the confidence to do so. 'He was the only person I'd really met who took me out of the algebraic equation that is my family. You know, "If Rufus is here and Kate is here and we put you here, that equals what?" He reminded me that I exist without these people.'

Perhaps now he felt like he had enough of a head start, Rufus was generous in his praise of the recordings Martha was making. 'I'm very influenced by my sister,' he told *Salon*. 'We have an ongoing rapport partly based on jealousy, partly on love. We kind of spar with songs. I'm constantly amazed at the directions she takes and the output she has, and the wealth of ability. And it is a real shame that she's not signed.'

Between promotional dates for *Want One*, Rufus recorded a track for the charity album *Wig in a Box*, which was made to raise funds for the Harvey Milk High School in New York, an establishment that aims to provide schooling for gay and transgender youths who have been the subject of bullying at their original schools. The album was based on songs from John Cameron Mitchell's delirious rock musical *Hedwig and the Angry Inch*, which had started out as a fringe off-Broadway show before exploding into a phenomenon of *Rocky Horror Show* proportions. The album also featured Frank Black, the Breeders, Yoko Ono, Yo La Tengo and They Might Be Giants. Rufus recorded the track 'The Origin of Love' with his friend Michael Cavadias' band, Bullet. Barb Morrison, who co-produced the track, remembers the session moving very quickly, despite the song being a far more rock'n'roll tune than Rufus' usual music. 'Rufus was extremely fast at getting the performance he felt comfortable with. He didn't do takes over and over again. In fact, I think we captured that performance in the first three tries.'

In order to establish some kind of stability in his life and to have a place to return to after touring, Rufus bought his first apartment. It was also an investment in case his career collapsed around him leaving him, as he later bemoaned, 'completely empty-handed, which in the music business is what usually happens'.

The 425-square-foot studio was on the highly desirable Gramercy Park in Manhattan, the city's last private park and a neighbourhood with a great history.[13] There may not have been a view from any of the apartment's windows, other than the brick walls of his neighbours, but in psychogeographical terms it was perfectly situated to accommodate Rufus. As he walked around his new neighbourhood, he would pass the buildings where Humphrey Bogart's first wedding had taken place, where Margaret Hamilton, the Wicked Witch of the East, had regularly bought flowers, and where Oscar Wilde had temporarily taken up residence in 1883 while a play of his was running in town. More recent residents had included Julia Roberts, Donna Tartt and Deborah Harry. In the centre of the park, accessible only to those local residents prepared to pay an annual 'key fee', is a statue commemorating Edwin Booth, once America's finest Shakespearean actor and founder of the Players Club in 1888, a gentleman's club and theatre archive that still stands today.

Maybe it was as well to take care of his personal business affairs as the situation at his record label was chaotic. The DreamWorks music company had been taken over by the Universal Music Group, due in part to a general slump in music sales as the industry dinosaurs failed to react to changing times. The DreamWorks roster was to be dealt out between Universal's imprints Interscope, Geffen and A&M. For a while Rufus didn't know to which label, if any, he was currently signed. When the dust had settled, his new label (eventually the Geffen imprint would appear on the discs but for a time DreamWorks lived on in name only) continued pushing *Want*

---

13. Rufus' original idea for home decorating was to approximate James Abbott McNeill Whistler's Peacock Room, an Anglo-Japanese extravagance in gold-leaf and blue created by the artist in 1878 for a client who had bought one of his paintings but needed a room in which to best display it. In an 'At Home With' feature in Q magazine in June 2007, Rufus gave a guided tour of his apartment. He may not have created a peacock room but there is a peacock lampshade and alongside his bust of Verdi are peacock feathers on top of his piano: 'I relate to their brilliance. I am into excess and peacocks are the emblem of that. All things luxurious . . . and confusing.'

One but weren't prepared to commit to the second album, at least not in the timescale it was originally planned. The release date of *Want Two* was postponed.

In public Rufus laughed off his label difficulties. In *Interview* magazine, Elton John admitted that the fact that Rufus was having trouble getting an album as good as *Want One* properly heard upset him deeply. 'I'm a tough cookie,' replied Rufus. 'I will survive this business because in the end it boils down to whether you can entertain 10 people with your piano. I can always go out on the corner and, as Edith Piaf did, make a couple of bucks.' He had once said that even if for some reason he could no longer get records released, he would be happy just driving from town to town and playing to a different small crowd every night. He was just reflecting the work ethic that his parents had drilled in to him and his sister. If you were a musician, you were a musician for life, regardless whether you were playing a huge hall or a tiny club or if nobody was paying you any attention at all. Loudon had pretty much put the children through school by playing night after night, year after year. Kate had looked after the children and kept her music career running simultaneously, dipping in and out when the opportunity arose. Martha summed it up in an interview when she was asked what she expected from a career in music. 'I grew up in an environment in which people had long careers and it didn't really matter how many records they were selling. It ebbed and flowed, their careers changed. I'd like to try and do that.'

As if to prove that a career could be maintained successfully without anything even approaching mainstream appeal, Kate and Anna had a new French language album released on a small Canadian label in late 2003. *La Vache Qui Pleure* (the title a punning reversal of the dairy brand Laughing Cow) was a typically subdued affair with most of the lyrics written by their regular collaborator Philippe Tatartcheff (who makes a debonair debut as an ominous-sounding narrator on 'Hurle Le Vent'). An early version of the album had been privately circulated as far back as 2001 with the cover art, a black and white ink drawing of the kind of crooked shack you imagine a poor woodcutter in a fairy tale might live in, drawn by Rufus.

Musically the collection was uniformly sophisticated, more so than their previous albums, with sounds and textures designed to complement the voices and careful not to accidentally smother them as had sometimes happened before. On the beautiful 'Ce Matin', Martha and Anna's daughter Lily Lanken add another layer of melody, creating a breathtaking union of four voices that effortlessly intertwine and become one. In places the music sounds like The Waterboys ('Petite Annonce Amoureuse'), in others ('Dans Le Silence') a little like the Bad Seeds, as if Nick Cave's piano-playing had rubbed off on Kate during their London sessions. One of the best tracks, 'Ah, Sunflower', with the lyrics taken from Blake's poem (though strangely he is not credited), appears in both French and English. There is also a French language version of the Malvina Reynolds song 'Little Boxes'. This would eventually join the roll-call of versions of the song used on the credits of the TV show *Weeds* (other performers selected included Regina Spektor, Joan Baez, Angelique Kidjo and Elvis Costello).

Throughout spring 2004, Rufus continued to promote *Want One* and tantalised his fans with material from *Want Two*. Although *Want One* had performed better than *Poses* it had still failed to break into the Billboard Top 50. In March he performed 'Gay Messiah' live on the nationwide late night talk show *Jimmy Kimmel Live!*, with Rufus and his guitar, stand-up bass, drums and Joan Wasser and Shannon McNally on backing vocals. This was one of the songs that the label had foreseen a problem with, but Rufus seemed gleeful when he came to the line 'I won't be the one baptised in cum' and gave a wry smile. Although of course he might not have been paying any attention to the lyrics at all, fellow guest, boxing promoter Don King, managed to keep on waving his American flags right through to the end of the performance of one of Rufus' most provocative songs, creating an intriguing tableau for the those watching at home.

'Only in America' was King's favourite saying but Rufus' concern had been that post-9/11, post 'War on Terror', the Bush-led admin-istration had been intent on curtailing the freedom of the individual and promoting a new conservative agenda. 'Only in America' didn't have the same positive ring that it once had, even out of the mouth of perennial shock-headed hyperbolist King. The idea of a 'gay messiah' had begun as a joke song at parties but since Bush had been pushing the country ever further to the right, Rufus had begun to play it as a protest song. Later, exasperated at Bush's re-election in 2004, Rufus would refer to the song as a prayer for divine intervention.

The song itself is a tongue-in-cheek invocation to a gay superhero to come down and sort out the world. Imagine William Burroughs had written the book for *Jesus Christ Superstar*. The implication is that the hero will look like Peter Berlin in striped sports socks, be dancing to disco and that his second coming (pun intended) will be on the beaches of favoured gay resort Fire Island. By the time he was on the tour dates for *Want Two*, Rufus' performance of the song had expanded to include a theatrical mock-crucifixion with Rufus in mask and golden crown of thorns manhandled by fancy-dress-party Roman soldiers as a means to further rile the neo-cons.

In early summer Rufus, Martha and Kate and Anna embarked on a joint European tour. Prior to their joint concerts, Rufus played a low-key solo show at Camden's Dingwalls (which had temporarily been rebranded 'Lock 17'). His set encompassed material from all of his albums and previewed material from *Want Two*, which was finally set for release in November (presaged by an i-Tunes-only sampler EP to be released in June). Beth Orton joined him on stage for an ancient folk joke: 'How many folk singers does it take to change a light bulb? Two. One to change it and one to sing about how good the old one was,' plus a duet on the traditional song 'Do You Love an Apple?' He also announced a brand-new number, 'Hometown Waltz', a song of melancholic homesickness that lyrically echoes some of the early McGarrigle songs in its struggle to find meaning, safety and solace in the family. In a touching live rendition featuring Kate, Anna, Martha and Lily Lanken, it would also be squeezed in at the last minute on *Want Two*.

A couple of weeks later, after performing in the revived Leonard Cohen tribute night in Brighton, the family played a prestige concert at London's Royal Festival Hall. Billed as 'An Evening with Rufus Wainwright and Kate and Anna McGarrigle', the evening was a typically casual revue-styled performance with each friend and family member drifting on and off the stage, singing solo or in combination with each other. A mute witness to the onstage banter

as they each forgot, or pretended to forget the words, the chords,
what song was next or even where they were, was bassist Jeff Hill.

'We haven't had time to rehearse . . . obviously,' said Kate as she
called out the chords of another song to Martha. The sisters played
material from throughout their career, from 'Heart Like A Wheel',
with Rufus on lead, to the Blake song from their most recent CD.
Rufus played songs from each of his albums but concentrated on his
earlier material. It seemed that Kate had exerted her influence over
what was or was not appropriate to perform. When a fan called out
for 'Gay Messiah', Rufus shrugged and shook his head as Kate, like
a strict teacher admonishing an unruly class, told the audience that
as this was a family show 'there would be no messiah tonight'. If
not a joke (though you could almost imagine her Pythoning: 'He's
not the messiah, he's a very naughty boy!'), it was strangely contradictory prudery as Martha had already been allowed to belt out
the title track from her new self-released EP 'Bloody Mother Fucking
Asshole' (BMFA). If Rufus had summoned the spirit of the absent
Loudon into the hall with his Teddy Thompson-assisted cover of
'One Man Guy' only to taunt it with 'Dinner at Eight', then Martha's
song would have had that spirit, ears burning, thrashing around
desperately looking for an exit.[14]

Martha had included 'BMFA' in her set since early 2002. The song
was an astounding, show-stopping howl of vitriolic fury ultimately
aimed at her distant father. Strafing anger like machine-gun fire, she
takes down everybody who crosses her path, from the singers in
bars who she aspires to be, all of whom are men, to Kate, cast as the
'mother of gloom', who has been left trying to comfort a child
abandoned, holding out the phone with the absent father at the
other end.

There are echoes of Sylvia Plath's poem 'Daddy' in the sustained
and elevated level of spite that runs through the piece and the theme
of utter rejection both by, and of, the target of the words. Crucially

---

14. Actually Loudon would appear in the concert hall right next door only three weeks
later as a guest of Morrissey for the annual Meltdown festival. Morrissey's love for the
New York Dolls is well documented, but it should be noted that in his pre-fame missives
to the UK music press in the mid-1970s, he would often include Loudon Wainwright
alongside the Dolls, Patti Smith and Sparks as artistes he felt were being criminally ignored
by the mainstream.

'Daddy' and 'BMFA' depend on the fact that beneath the resentment and hurt, there is a discernible love that renders the anger more believable and therefore more touching. Plath sought to destroy both the memory of her father who had died when she was a child and her replacement for him, her husband. Both men are cast as vampires draining her, and the realisation is that without removing them she can never move on. Plath's final stanza has her driving a stake through the heart of the monstrous fiction of a father that she has created, ending in an image of villagers dancing around his body as if it were the final scene of a Hammer horror film. Plath's biographer Anne Stevenson wrote that: 'The implication is that after this exorcism her life can begin again, that she will be reborn.'[15] And the implication in 'BMFA' is that once Martha has written and sung the song she too will have destroyed everything bad that she has made Loudon represent. By exploding the politeness of pretending that she is okay and by finally speaking out, by singing her own song, by becoming one of 'those guys with guitars' she had been watching, she too will become free. At the end of 'BMFA', Martha sings 'For you, whoever you are' and it as if the mission is accomplished, Loudon is vanquished and she can now move on (and pity the next person that tries to get in her way).

Songs are not set in stone, much as Rufus' 'Dinner at Eight' gradually revealed its true meaning to him, then Martha found that 'BMFA' began to change over time. Originally she had written it as a response to a specific argument with Loudon, literally a musical 'Fuck you!', but the song soon began to evolve new interpretations: realistically how could a song with so specific a meaning exist much beyond its original passionate creation if it could not also speak of more universal truths. When Martha played it at shows and saw people mouthing the words along with her, she began to see it as an 'anthem to anyone who doesn't want to feel disregarded'. In her live set, the song would become a cri de coeur that was no longer aimed specifically at Loudon but at anybody that the listener wishes to target. The 'Bloody Mother Fucking Asshole' has become the Everyman that has ever let any of us down. And plainly, people enjoy singing (and swearing) along with it. 'I came up with that

---

15. Anne Stevenson, *Bitter Fame: A Life of Sylvia Plath* (Penguin 1989, UK).

phrase and I thought it was very funny,' said Martha later. 'I thought I should repeat it over and over and over. It makes people feel good. It's one of my sad songs that actually makes people feel good.'

In the audience at the Royal Festival Hall was Sean Adams of the UK record label Drowned In Sound. 'I was utterly blown away by her playing "BMFA",' remembers Adams. 'I went to buy the EP afterwards but the people in front of me in the queue bought the last copies. So over the next few days I went all around London trying to find a copy and nobody had it in stock. I didn't know that she didn't have a record deal.'

Drowned In Sound was building a reputation for getting in early on acts that other labels had initially ignored. They had released 'Oh My God', the first single by the soon-to-be-huge Kaiser Chiefs and it was partly the fact that Adams had discovered that the band weren't going to stick with the label for their follow-up record that freed him to look for other acts. He spent a couple of weeks trying to track down Martha's manager to see if Drowned In Sound could give the EP a proper UK release. 'We were quite a small label at the time and I assumed she already had an album deal but just hadn't got around to putting anything out,' remembers Adams. 'When I discovered that she hadn't signed anything we made her an offer. I was stunned that there weren't more people wanting to work with her. She'd played at a few conferences and been knocking around but other labels seemed to see her as Rufus' sister and not look any further than that. I think we've been proved right.'

The knock-on effect of signing with Drowned In Sound was that Martha was given the money to finish her album without any interference from the label and was then able to take the tapes to other companies for similar licensing deals in the US, Canada and Australia. By November the 'Bloody Mother Fucking Asshole' EP was out in the UK, in a sleeve featuring an anonymous 1920s nude, and plans were in place for another single and the long-awaited debut album to follow in 2005. Drowned In Sound may have been small but they had solid financial backing and a structure that meant they could compete with any major label in terms of distribution and getting their artists heard. For Martha it was an ideal situation: she retained control of her music but she had a team of people to work on getting that music into the shops and on to the radio. She would no longer have to rely on selling CDs out of a box at her shows.

4.6

After returning from Europe, Rufus joined the 'Odd Man Out' tour, which ran through late summer and saw him join Ben Folds and Guster, alternating headlining slots, on a triple-headed traipse around the US that some commentators dubbed a 'geek-rock special'.

Playing outside of the comfort zone of his regular fan base, Rufus received a mixed, if generally positive, response on the tour. Occasionally, depending on the venue and in which order the performers appeared, the headline act might find the audience gradually drifting away after their favourites had already played. To counter the problem, there was a certain amount of interaction between the bands on stage, with Guster providing back-up to the two solo acts, Folds joining Rufus for 'Crumb By Crumb', his Hansel and Gretel-inspired song of seduction, and Rufus guesting on a Folds cover of George Michael's 'Careless Whisper' that was often played for kitsch laughs. The tour was considered enough of a success to be repeated the following year with Ben Lee replacing Guster.

Rufus hoped that *Want Two* would be out before the presidential election and as he toured the country he urged people to get out and vote against the anti-gay, pro-war conservatives. He expressed his concerns to *Rolling Stone*: 'Want One very much deals with my personal battles whereas *Want Two* turns around and tries to tackle some of the earthly troubles that we're in right now. And I'd hate for the Republicans to win the election and then have that sound weird.' The record was eventually released two weeks after George W. Bush's victory in November so the 'ogre in the oval office', as Rufus had it in the song 'Waiting On A Dream', was unfortunately still very much in charge.

From the opening track 'Agnus Dei' it was clear that *Want Two* was Rufus without compromise. At nearly six minutes and sung entirely in Latin, the song begins with Middle East meets gypsy-styled violin and cimbalom (a kind of hammered dulcimer much loved by Stravinsky), before easing into traditional Western orchestration. The musical setting prompts the listener to consider the meeting and melding of worlds, the West and the East, as the lyric, more accurately the vocalising (as non-Latin speakers are dependent on appreciating what the words represent rather than what they literally mean), calls for peace. 'I wanted essentially to open the album with a bang,' said Rufus. 'One of the things that fascinates me about this time period is that with the conservative American attitude out there, it's considered that if you're not super-religious or heterosexual you have no spirituality and you don't really care about the well-being of America and the world. It's just to put my two cents in, in terms of wanting to heal what's been going on all over the world . . . I really feel that we've reached a point where we all have to look for a power above or some greater meaning to show us the way.'

Rufus still hankered after a radio hit and initial thoughts were that 'The One You Love', driven by pounding Levon Helm drums and as close to straight-down-the-line rock'n'roll as Rufus was likely to get, might be the hit in waiting. It's one of Rufus' most instantly catchy songs, including some wonderful harmonies with Martha and a vocal break that, although not exactly a sing-a-long hook, is at least compulsively hummable (and is strangely reminiscent of the Settlers singing the theme song to the children's TV show *Follyfoot*). In the UK the track would be released in 2005 as a digital single with hopeful promo CDs mailed out to radio stations featuring an edited version of the song. The label even went as far as to issue a somewhat half-hearted video cobbled together from out-takes from a documentary shoot.

The Martin Denny-flavoured ersatz exotica of 'Peach Trees', one of Rufus' loveliest songs, gives Martha's backing vocals another chance to shine before he pulls the rug from under her with 'Little Sister'. A version of this Mozartian confection had originally been recorded with Van Dyke Parks back at the sessions for the debut album but had been held back as Lenny Waronker considered it too classical for the record and too confusing in the context of the other songs ('I had to dumb down,' joked Rufus when talking about the decision).

Despite the title, it's a song that Rufus has said refers not just to

Martha, but to his half-sisters and to women in general. This seems disingenuous. Rufus has spoken about it being influenced by Mozart and an imagined altercation between the composer and his sister Maria Anna, herself a talented musician and one whose abilities were suppressed by the fact that, as a woman in the eighteenth century, her opportunities were non-existent compared to those afforded her brother. The similarities between the two sets of siblings are enough to interpret the song as blatant spoilt-child-teasing of Martha by Rufus hidden in the guise of an imagined historical event. Maria Anna saw Wolfgang become a celebrated musician and tour Europe while she stayed at home, not so very much different from Martha having to put up with Rufus being encouraged and indulged by Kate while she was always kept waiting in the background, not ignored but always second in line. 'Remember your brother is a boy,' sings Rufus none too helpfully, and 'History is on my side' as if to explain away why he was centre-stage and she was still struggling to be noticed.

To prove that his interest in classical music extended to twentieth century composers, Rufus used the repetitious style of minimalist composer Philip Glass to score his song 'The Art Teacher'. Unusually for Rufus, this self-contained vignette takes the form of a first-person narrative from the point of view of a woman remembering her schoolgirl infatuation with her teacher and dreaming of what might have been. It suffers a little from some forced and clumsy lines – John Singer Sargent is hardly a name that rolls easily off the tongue and Turner seems to have been chosen only so as to allow a half-pun on his name – but it's an interesting experiment in style that tested Rufus' songwriting in new ways. In an otherwise middling album review, *The Times* described the track as an 'intimation of genius'.

The album's closing number 'Old Whore's Diet' is Rufus operating without a safety net. Lyrically inspired by his drug days, opening the fridge in the morning and finding nothing but half-eaten Chinese takeaways, it's admirably experimental, though at nine minutes demands more from the listener than it seems able to give back. It's a loping groove that comes across like 'Tusk'-era Fleetwood Mac had been asked to soundtrack one of Wilson, Keppel and Betty's vaudeville routines from the 1930s (a comparison that makes perfect

sense in light of the mimed dance routine Rufus choreographed for
the number as the set-up to the 'Gay Messiah' crucifixion tableaux
during the *Want Two* tour). The song is complemented by a cameo
from New York musician and performance artist Antony, whose
tremulous tenor appears from nowhere to echo Rufus' verses. To the
unprepared, his eccentric warble is slightly humorous and mildly
disconcerting – like an amiable cartoon ghost has been called in to
make up the double act. In 2005 Rufus returned the favour by
appearing on Antony and the Johnsons Mercury prize-winning
album *I Am a Bird Now*.[16]

With the release of the album and the completion of the *Want
Project*, Rufus justified all his self-aggrandising and his aspirations
to high art. What he had achieved, especially when both volumes
were considered as the single body of work originally envisioned,
was one of the most remarkable suite of songs to be released in the
modern pop era. The quality of the material on *Want Two* and its
genuinely broad appeal called into question the label's decision to
split the record in two. Aside perhaps from 'Gay Messiah', which
even then was more humorous provocation than an incitement for
a gay riot, there was little here that could have caused offence to
anybody but the most small-minded reactionary. In fact, the very
worst that could have occurred was that the multitudinous musical
styles could cause confusion. But what was so wrong about an album
that left a listener a little confused?

The label's caution had been due in part to the upheavals caused
by their takeover but also due to their conviction that Rufus should
be seen as a commercially viable pop artist and not as an intelligent
(for which read *difficult*) artist that required a certain level of
engaged concentration from his listeners. By splitting the albums
the label had, albeit temporarily, delayed and derailed one of the
few successful double-album sets of the past decade.

In many of the same publications that ran reviews of *Want Two*,
there was fulsome praise for Nick Cave and the Bad Seeds' *Lyre of*

---

16. 'What Can I Do', the song that Rufus performs on the Antony and the Johnsons album
was chosen, alongside works by John Coltrane, Keith Jarrett and Richard Strauss, as one
of the favourite pieces of music of the acclaimed British abstract artist Ian McKeever on
the BBC Radio 3 show *Private Passions*: '[It's] laconic, lazy and quite beautiful. Its brevity
sucks you in and you want it to meander on but it cuts you short. . .' (16 March 2008).

Orpheus/Abattoir Blues, released as a double album the same month. Like Cave's albums, *Want One* and *Two* deserved to be heard together as a unified creative statement conceived and recorded at the peak of the artist's power rather than treated like a problem that had to be dealt with like Quentin Tarantino's bloated *Kill Bill* film and chopped in two for easy distribution.

This should have been a turning point in Rufus' music career. *Want* had shown that he was operating way above the expectations of regular rock and pop musicians. Critical acclaim was at its peak with glowing reviews in broadsheet newspapers, lifestyle magazines and the specialist music press. Barney Hoskyns in *Uncut* likened *Want* to 'Radiohead meets Mahler', which would have made a wonderful tag for an advertising campaign and a pointer to the direction that Rufus could perhaps have been heading. Artists like Radiohead, Nick Cave, Björk and to a degree Rufus' friend Antony had been pushing at the boundaries of what constituted a career in contemporary music by regularly experimenting in film soundtracks, art installations, theatre productions and classical concerts. For all his frequent talk of composing opera and writing classical pieces, Rufus seemed trapped in a maze-like search for commercial mainstream success. He frequently guested on numerous side projects and added individual tracks to film soundtracks but he didn't engage fully with anything outside of the traditional album/promotion/album/promotion cycle. Perhaps he felt driven by the reported $1 million that he was in debt to his label after his first two lavishly appointed albums failed to provide the expected hit.

It should be remembered that his albums were selling in respectable numbers. It was not as if nobody was buying them at all. But his sales figures were being judged against those of major established pop stars and not of the fringe and alternative artists with whom Rufus may have been more comfortably aligned. No matter how much Universal may have been hoping that he would turn into an Elton John-style hit machine, the realisation must have been coming that he was just too much of an acquired taste for what was left of the general music-buying public.

But the label still kept plugging away. Barbara Charone, Madonna's formidable press agent, had been hired to handle publicity and further positive coverage was virtually guaranteed. In order to push *Want Two*, it was initially issued with a bonus full-length concert DVD. Universal even bankrolled a one-hour documentary on Rufus, featuring testimonies from the likes of Elton John, Sting and Neil Tennant, all safe artists seemingly chosen to help position him within the comfortable (and lucrative) middle-aged mainstream. The same night that Rufus supported resolutely middle-of-the-road Keane in Madrid on their ongoing 'Hopes and Fears' tour, the documentary, titled *All I Want* (dir. George Scott, 2005) premiered on UK television. Although it was that curious scheduling anomaly beloved of modern commercial stations whereby an extended record company advert can be passed off as an independent programme, *All I Want* is not without its merits. Rufus is as forthcoming as ever and he gives a brief tour of New York (his lip even seems to quiver when he talks about his early failure to get any gigs there), and Kate and Martha provide their own thoughts on his career to date. Glaringly absent is Loudon, who is represented by a single tiny archive clip and by the thoughts of Tracey MacLeod, one of Loudon's former partners. By April the film had been given a DVD release packed with extra performance material.

As the Keane support slots segued into his own headlining European tour, which would in turn run into the US 'Odd Men Out Tour', Rufus settled into a routine of playing night after night through most of 2005. Along with the opera that he longed to start but never had the time for, at the back of his mind was the germ of an idea for a new kind of show, a new challenge, something that would celebrate the Great American song and in so doing celebrate America itself.

ACT 5

J'ai ce désir très pur d'une soeur éternelle,
D'une soeur d'amitié dans le règne de l'Art,
Qui me saura veillant à ma lampe très tard
Et qui me couvrira des cieux de sa prunelle;
From *Rêve d'Artiste* by Émile Nelligan, circa 1899

Question: How Do You Get To Carnegie Hall?
Answer: Practice, practice, practice.
Old musician's joke

5.1

Martha's self-titled debut album was finally released in April 2005, the culmination of a decade's worth of songwriting and a lifetime of performing. She had often spoken of her fear that once she'd made a solo record, journalists would rip her to shreds. It was one of the things that had held her back for so long. Even after she had signed a deal and been given a provisional release date, she had been dragging her heels about finishing off the album. It was with some trepidation that she finally let the album out into the world. 'I was worried when we sent it up to the press because there would be no one else to blame but me because it is kind of self-produced with someone who let me do what I wanted to do. I was worried about people shitting on it.'

Of course it didn't hurt her profile that Rufus was well known and that Loudon and Kate, although not particularly famous, provided an instant reference point for any critic who wanted to write about her. But she was quick to point out that the album should be judged on its own merits. 'I definitely think that it doesn't matter who your parents are. They can't buy you into success. Especially in music and especially with the kind of music that I'm doing, which is very honest music. So my talent will have to buy me my career and keep me going because I don't think people are stupid enough to stomach something that isn't good just because of who my parents are.'

The album was issued in a sleeve reminiscent of Joni Mitchell's *Blue*, featuring a blurred vermilion-tinted portrait of Martha by New York photographer Ken Schles who had taken the photos for Rufus' *Poses* CD (the inside of the CD booklet featured details from paintings by Anna's daughter Lily Lanken who sings backing vocals on much of the record).

It was a very personal collection of songs; Martha claimed that there was not one line on the album that wasn't actually true. She acknowledged that she didn't have a huge catalogue of material to select from and so a number of songs from her earlier releases reappeared. 'A lot of the songs were written years ago. They took a long time. I'm not a very good guitar player or a very prolific musician who writes about everything and sees everything as a song. It's all from my experience and it'll continue to be that way for a while. It makes for very unprolific songwriting.'

Martha also admitted that because some of the songs were written so long ago, she had difficulty revisiting the emotions they had originally conveyed. 'It was a challenge to me to keep myself interested,' she explained. 'You have to find a way to recreate it every time. Sometimes you have to change the person it's about. A lot of the time it's to do with acting.'

Among the new songs were some of the best work she had ever done. The opening track 'Far Away' lifts and then runs off with the melody from the Carpenters' 'Rainy Days and Mondays', setting the tone for a record that twists and turns its own route through folk, alt-country, country rock and pop. 'Ball and Chain', a song that is literally about men being ruled by their dicks, begins as an angry-feminist anthem and ends in near hysterical self-pity. And it rocks. 'There's one thing I can do which no one else in the family can do, which is rock,' she told the *Independent*. 'Rufus isn't very good at rocking out — it's like a joke when he tries to do it. But I like to get real sweaty.' Rufus does appear on backing vocals on 'The Maker' but it's no gimmick to raise the album's profile, his voice is subdued and used to blend a background harmony.

Like a mellifluous Lucinda Williams, Martha purrs her way through 'When The Day Is Short', a country rock song so well formed, so exquisitely realised, that it sounded as though it had been around for decades. It was chosen as a single with a video directed by Sara Mishara and funded by videoFACT, a Canadian agency that provided backing for fledgling Canadian musicians to make promotional films. In the video Martha appears in numerous Cindy Sherman-like guises from vamping burlesque stripper to rain-coated paparazzo to Valley of the Dolls-styled peroxide blonde rolling around in a silk dressing gown on a table top. It was probably the most commercial record that anybody in the extended Wain-wright family had ever released but it failed to become even a minor hit.

Elsewhere Martha demonstrates the full range of her voice, from coquettish whisper to full anguished howl. Lyrically the album is a triumph, not so much for the meaning of the words but in the way that she bends and shapes them, sometimes breaking words between syllables and stretching a phrase unexpectedly to wrong-foot the listener. The internal rhymes and rhythms within the lines are sophisticated, but not to the extent of Loudon's perfectly aligned lyrical vocabulary.

In fact, other than on the final track of the album where she sings Vaughan Williams' 1902 song 'Whither Must I Wander', a song suggested to her by Kate and where she comes closest to sounding like a McGarrigle, Martha maintains her own style throughout the album; earthier than her brother, more emotionally raw than her father, less restrained than her mother. Indeed in full flow Martha had a tendency to sling words around like the mad poetry of the beats like Kerouac or Ginsberg, a torrent of words sung for sound and feeling rather than clinical precision.

She needn't have worried about the press reception for the record. It immediately picked up great reviews. *Rolling Stone* praised her voice as being more expressive than her brother's and highlighted her 'lurid charisma', *Q* magazine called the album 'a thing of wonder' and *Entertainment Weekly* called her 'a briny Bridget Jones' (meant as a compliment). Even Everett True conceded the album was excellent in an otherwise comically ill-tempered interview in *Plan B* magazine during which Martha seemed bored and True took great offence to Brad Albetta's onstage gurning (he must never have seen Loudon in action). The only pleasantries passed between interviewer and interviewee was a recipe for making lemonade.

In the UK she had begun promoting the album back in February with some solo shows at small venues. At the Barfly in Camden, a tiny club above a pub, she had played to a handful of people, beginning the set with a staggeringly vicious 'BMFA' from which she and the show never really recovered. By the end of the evening she was asking audience members to call out the songs they wanted to hear because she couldn't remember what she'd already played, before engaging in long conversations with the people at the front of the stage while the rest of the crowd talked among themselves. Her usually endearingly amateurish performance style almost verged on an apologetic shambles.

By the end of the year she was playing with her band at bigger venues after supporting Wilco around the country. In November she headlined her own show at the Shepherd's Bush Empire, a 2,000-seat theatre that had once been the main location for BBC variety shows from the 1960s to the 1990s. Her confidence had risen to the point where she could disarm the crowd with a relaxed attitude to performing that, like Kate and Anna before her, would come over as casual entertainment rather than seeming like she was looking for pity if she forgot the chords to yet another song. Her album had been warmly received and she was safe in the knowledge that she hadn't turned out to be the talentless one of the family after all.

Martha had celebrated the US release of her debut album with a show at Joe's Pub, a tiny supper-bar-style venue in Manhattan. Rufus was still on tour in Europe but Kate had managed to get to the show to lend her support. Even Loudon made it to the venue, albeit a day late. He had been booked in to promote his own new album *Here Come the Choppers* the very next night.

With Rufus' success and Martha's album just released, Loudon had been asked if he felt pressure to keep up with his kids with each new record. 'There's always been generational competition,' he admitted, 'but with this album I was really competing with my peers. I wanted to show that fucker Randy Newman and that bastard

Tom Waits how you really make a record!' Loudon actually claimed never to listen to any singer-songwriters, preferring dead black jazz pianists like Art Tatum and Thelonius Monk whenever possible. 'I'm not threatened on any level: I can't play the piano, I'm not black and they can't sing,' he quipped.

His album had been recorded quickly in a Californian studio back in 2004. He had sent his guitar and voice demos to the other musicians and they had worked on the songs independently. When the band got together, aided by the organisational skills of jazz guitar legend Bill Frisell, who had worked with most of the other musicians on his own previous solo record, it only took them a day to get the songs arranged and another three days to get the whole album wrapped.

The album might not have demonstrated much to Waits and Newman that they didn't already know, or for that matter, even been vintage Loudon, but songs like 'Hank and Fred', his tribute to the children's TV presenter Fred Rogers, or 'To Be On TV', an observational piece about reflections in a TV screen conjuring ghosts into a room, showed that there were still few musicians like him who could seemingly turn to any subject and create a meaningful, and touching, song.

With a studio recording of his 9/11 song 'No Sure Way' and his commentary on the increasingly rampant American military — the title track imagines Los Angeles being overrun by army helicopters, the city a war zone under constant attack — he also demonstrated that his skills at oblique pathos and vibrant satire were undiminished.

Since appearing in *Undeclared*, Loudon's film acting career had picked up enough for him to be able to set up home in Los Angeles. He had even settled in enough to get himself a boat moored up in Ventura to take out at weekends. As well as his brief role in *The Aviator*, he had appeared in the hit show *Ally McBeal* and managed to get a part in the Cameron Crowe film *Elizabethtown* where he played Orlando Bloom's uncle. But it was the link with Judd Apatow that, over the coming years, would provide his best entry into the film world.

When *Undeclared* had been released on DVD, Apatow saw to it that the bonus features included a specially shot concert by Loudon in the hope that it would promote his music to those who may not have been aware of his work outside of his acting in the show. Apatow was an unabashed fan and hailed Loudon as being one of his biggest inspirations. 'Loudon writes bitterly funny and heart-breaking folk music, which has inspired me to be honest in my work. He is truly fearless. Commercial considerations don't seem to matter much to him. His music is gorgeous and hilarious and painful. It is everything I hope to achieve in my career. I just throw in waxing scenes, too.'

The 'waxing' comment refers to a gross-out moment in Apatow's film *The 40-Year-Old Virgin* when Steve Carell gets his body waxed. The movie premiered in August 2005 with Loudon having a small role as a priest. He would eventually play a far more significant part in Apatow's next project, *Knocked Up*, which would be released in 2007.

The plot of *Knocked Up* – what happens after a one-night stand between a high-achieving career woman and a no-good dope-smoking layout – could almost have been lifted out of one of Loudon's satirical songs. When the drunken tryst results in a preg-nancy, which the misfit couple attempt to blunder their way through for the good of the unborn child, then things are really getting Loudonesque. Apatow would be the first to admit as much. '[Lou-don's influence on my work is that] he's so brutally honest. One minute he can be comedic and the next painfully heartbreaking. He's encouraged me to go as far as I can go truth-wise in my screen-writing, to give the material a funny, sardonic edge. He certainly sees the humour in the tragedy of trying to live your life. Loudon's work is a powerful reminder to me that I must always be honest, funny and true to myself.' An example of how much Loudon's approach to confessional artistry had influenced Apatow is clear in an interview he gave to the *Daily Telegraph* in which he explained that, although it took him some time to realise it, his own experi-ences were the richest seam of comedy that he could mine. 'I realised it wasn't about the high concepts, it was about specificity. That if I really tell you how me and my wife talk in the bathroom when we're negotiating whether or not to have sex, then that's going to be funny and relatable. If I go all the way and really tell you the thing that no one would tell you.'

In *Knocked Up* Loudon plays a gooning and ultimately unreliable gynaecologist but his most important work is on the soundtrack. Apatow saw Loudon in concert as often as he could. At one show in Los Angeles, he was thinking about the music for his next film and Loudon was playing a song that reflected his feelings about his new hometown; its endless blue skies and the mixed blessing of the occasional rainstorm. 'He had a song called "Grey in LA" that I thought was fantastic,' remembered Apatow. 'He hadn't recorded it yet and I wanted it in the movie, but my music supervisor Jonathan Karp said, "Ask him to record it without lyrics because it's so pretty maybe that could be the sound for the whole movie."'

When Apatow called, Loudon was in England and he offered to record the track right there with Richard Thompson. This was even more thrilling for the director who was also a huge fan of Thompson's, particularly the soundtrack he had just done for Werner Herzog's *Grizzly Man* (2005). When they heard the recording, Apatow and Karp loved it and asked Loudon to write for the whole movie. The idea was for him to come up with new songs, record them and then take out the vocals to use just the music on the soundtrack.

'I didn't really have much experience at scoring, which is to say, none,' said Loudon. He was happy to call in some support. He had recently enjoyed working on some tracks for a charity album with Joe Henry (who coincidentally had produced Richard's son Teddy Thompson's debut album) and asked him to work on the soundtrack project with him. 'It was a very happy experience. We were given a lot of freedom, a bit of a budget and just took it from there.'

Henry praised Apatow's hands-off working methods for the success of the soundtrack. 'We approached this as songwriters, not score composers. Any germ of an idea that resonated enough to form a musical cue, we were encouraged by Judd to turn into a song. The key is he gave us a tremendous amount of freedom. You can't overestimate how much confidence that can give you. He let us do our job while he did his, largely because he wanted to be surprised at what we came up with.'

Loudon enjoyed the process of writing for films and hoped to be asked to do it more often. 'I write songs as a matter of course because I am a songwriter,' he said, 'but I do seem to respond to direction and deadline, both of which you have to do if you are working on a movie. I like the kick in the butt of that.'

The film became a huge hit, compounding the success of *The 40-Year-Old Virgin* and turning Apatow into one of the most important figures in Hollywood. The soundtrack album, billed as *Strange Weirdos – Music from and inspired by the film Knocked Up* featured the vocal versions of many of the songs from the film plus a handful of new songs. 'I am so proud that a movie I wrote in my underwear has led to this record,' wrote Apatow in the sleeve-notes. 'A completely unique piece of music and art which is both connected to our film and completely its own wonderful, heartfelt creation.'

More than the usual soundtrack CD as packaged mnemonic, the album stands as a complete Loudon Wainwright album in its own right. Apatow had certainly achieved his aim of bringing Loudon to the attention of more people as the film tie-in meant most major stores carried the album and more magazines reviewed it than any of his recent small label releases. But perversely, what turned out to be one of Loudon's most visible releases was perhaps the least personalised, least representative collection he had ever issued. His usually self-referential, self-deprecating songs of love, family, life, strife and death are replaced in part, if not in whole, by the need to express, or at least reflect, the feelings of other fictitious characters. Many of the songs are stunningly executed, the reworked 'Lullaby' from *Attempted Mustache* is sublime, indeed vocally Loudon has rarely sounded better, but the bitter depth charge of real personal experience, what Apatow highlighted as the 'specificity of situations', is mostly missing. In fact, Loudon sounds as though he is singing about people who are younger than himself; these are wistful memories not scalpel-sharp reportage. None of this is to say it's a bad album. It isn't. It's just one that betrays its roots of having been written to order.

5.2

In December 2004 Kate and Anna had arranged some recording time at a studio in Saint-Saveur in order to put down tracks for a proposed Christmas album. More a follow-up to the ensemble *McGarrigle*

Hour album than a Kate and Anna album, the sessions featured both sisters, their children and their friend Beth Orton who was staying with them for the Christmas holidays. By the time it was finished, the album also included lead vocals by Emmylou Harris, Teddy Thompson and Chaim Tannenbaum and other supporting voices.

The album comprised traditional festive folk songs alongside more contemporary cover versions and a handful of originals. Rufus performs his 'Spotlight on Christmas' and the full version of 'What Are You Doing New Year's Eve' that had served him so well on the Gap advert. Martha sings a version of Jackson Browne's 'Rebel Jesus' and a Christmas-themed original.

Although the album is as well executed as you would expect from the assembled cast, its listenability does rather depend on the season. No matter how beautifully the family harmonises on 'Seven Joys of Mary' there are only so many days of the year that you want to put on an album that makes you look out of the window and wish for snow and distant sleigh-bells.

The album was released in November 2005 as *The McGarrigle Christmas Hour* ('jingle bell pre-rock of uncommon charm', said the *Village Voice*) and a McGarrigle Family Christmas show was scheduled for Carnegie Hall in December. Both Rufus and Martha had to fly back from European tours to take part in the rehearsals at Montreal's Outremont Theatre, where they would also perform a version of the show, really a public dress rehearsal, a few days before New York.

In an interview with a local British newspaper, Rufus had joked that after the Carnegie Hall show he was going to spend Christmas alone in New York and talked about what he could expect under his Christmas tree. He complained that his mother always gave him hand-knitted sweaters – 'Useful if I was ever in an avalanche' – and Martha's gifts were nothing special. '[Martha] is not the best gift-giver, we have to honest about it – I've gotten her a guitar, a computer and a piano. She's given me a calendar and some DVDs.' For her part, Martha was looking forward to the rehearsals, noting that Kate and Anna's harmonies were enough to make her warm inside. 'The sound of people singing together is a religious experience. God is in those vibrations,' she said. The family had never been particularly religious but as Anna admitted, 'Christmas is a beautiful story. Kate and I have never been churchgoers but you really believe in it for as long as you're singing these songs.'

When it came to the performance, there were 20 musicians on stage in the extended family including Teddy Thompson, who had just released his second solo record,[1] and a rare appearance from older sister Jane McGarrigle. And although Loudon was absent, his sister Sloan, warmly introduced by Kate as her 'ex-sister-in-law', appeared to rapturous applause with her version of 'Thank God it's Christmas'. The concert was such a success that plans were made to turn it into an annual festive event.

If the Carnegie Hall show saw Rufus end the year in the metaphorical cosy embrace of his family (and yet another Christmas jumper), then the new year would offer him opportunities to really stretch himself and move into hitherto unexplored areas. His first project of 2006 saw him united with one of New York's most celebrated gay artists. For once it would be a collaboration that required an intellectual rigour and experimentation that went beyond Rufus' usual fairly comfortable guest spots on another musician's recording. This time Rufus would have to engage with another person's vision while being expected to deliver something essentially Rufusian to the work. It was a collaboration in the truest sense of the word, a fusion that writers William Burroughs and Brion Gysin had once termed the 'Third Mind[2]': when something new and vital emerges from the energy of collaborators.

The dancer and choreographer Stephen Petronio had collaborated with a veritable who's who of the avant-garde and cutting edge,

---

1. November 2005 was a busy month for related releases. Alongside the Christmas album, Teddy Thompson and Rufus appeared together on the soundtrack album for *Brokeback Mountain*, Martha issued *I Will Internalize*, a Canadian-only five-track CD compilation of songs from her previous singles, and Rufus guested on one track of Burt Bacharach's *At This Time* album. Thompson's second solo album, *Separate Ways*, was also released on Verve Records. A more successful blend of traditional folk/country than his pop-influenced debut, it was produced by Brad Albetta and featured contributions from both Rufus and Martha.

2. William Burroughs, Brion Gysin, *The Third Mind* (Viking, 1978, US). Although Burroughs/Gysin are most commonly quoted as the source for this comment on the power of collaboration, Burroughs had actually appropriated the idea from the self-help book *Think and Grow Rich* by Napoleon Hill and published in 1937: 'No two minds ever come together without, thereby, creating a third, invisible, intangible force which may be likened to a third mind.'

including Anish Kapoor, Diamanda Galas, Cindy Sherman and Lou Reed. Perhaps his most provocative work had been with one-time partner, Scottish dance-punk Michael Clark, a similarly iconoclastic and outspoken artist. The pair once conducted a live 'Bed Piece' in a London art gallery (think John and Yoko with no holds barred).

Ever since being a member of the 1990s AIDS awareness pressure group ACT UP, Petronio had not been afraid to use his art to promote sexual equality and fight against the persecution of gay men. With George W. Bush seemingly intent on rewriting the constitution to outlaw gay marriage, in effect hiding blatant homophobia with semantics, Petronio conceived a work that would celebrate same-sex union. In March 2005 he had debuted *Bud* at the Joyce Theatre, New York, using a recording of Rufus' 'Oh What A World'. The piece was a male duet in which each dancer wore a costume that was half red, half black and as they came together, the colours would unite. The idea had been to demonstrate the joyous empowerment that could arise from such a union.

Rather than merely choreograph existing pieces of music, Petronio invited Rufus to write an original score that would allow the dancers to expand on the ideas that he had been exploring in *Bud*. This was an opportunity for Rufus to work within a medium that pushed composition beyond mere song-writing, something which could perhaps help in his ultimate aim of writing classical pieces or opera.

In fact, it wasn't the first time he had been asked to work on projects for the stage. Back in January 2004 Armistead Maupin had told Rufus that he really wanted to work with him on a musical version of *Tales of the City* but nothing materialised. Rufus had also been approached by the British choreographer Matthew Bourne with a view to collaboration. Bourne is a more conventional, certainly less confrontational artist than Petronio, known for his stylish reimagining of existing works like an all-male *Swan Lake*, his dance version of the film *Edward Scissorhands* or his black and white into colour *Wizard of Oz*-influenced *Nutcracker*. He remembers Rufus appearing less than enthusiastic about the idea of working together. 'He wasn't really familiar with my work,' said Bourne, 'it was hard to pin him down. He'd been told to come see me but seemed more into opera. I love his work and thought maybe there was a collaboration there, but I felt I was selling myself to him. It was a bit one-sided and uncomfortable. I wished I hadn't arranged the lunch in the end. But his people have kept in touch with me. They think it's a good idea. Eventually something might happen.'

Petronio knew that he wanted his collaboration with Rufus to be called *Bloom*. He saw it as a transitional work from the darker post-9/11 performances he had been doing into something more positive and more obviously beautiful. When he suggested to Rufus that the work be based around existing poems, Rufus had almost automatically turned to Blake's flower poems but Petronio thought Blake too obvious and continually pushed for Walt Whitman. In the end they decided on Whitman's 'Unseen Buds' and 'One's Self I Sing' alongside Emily Dickinson's 'Hope Is The Thing With Feathers'. 'These poems say what it means to be democratic and responsible in the world and to be conscious of other people,' said Petronio. 'The floral analogy is about growing as a person.'

When he had originally agreed to work on the project, Rufus had been recording his album in New York. Little did he know that by the time he was called on to make good his promise, he would be out on a seemingly endless tour. As the deadlines rapidly approached, much of the discussion about the project, which ideally would have been developed and discussed at face-to-face meetings, ended up being conducted long distance over the telephone or via email. Petronio found himself frequently having to press his collaborator to make decisions and move the project forward. 'He'd sent me a few poems,' remembered Rufus. 'I'd loved "Unseen Buds" ... He said, "I want this poem" and I was procrastinating and not thinking about it at all. One day he called and said, "I need to know what's happening ... I need to know what's happening" and I said ... "Okay. We're going to do "Bud" into "Hope" and it means water going on youth and becoming an adult. That's it. Okay. Bye" ... So then I went into the studio with that idea and just ran with it.'

Petronio wanted Rufus to write something that related to young love, the first swoons and fluttering hearts of adolescence. 'I wanted the swell of youth, the transition from youth to adult. That moment of transformation is the inspiration,' explained Petronio. To that end, he floated the idea of incorporating a young choir. 'When

I proposed the idea of a children's choir, I thought it might drive him away. Instead he delivered an amazingly beautiful choral score. I expected him to write a song, to do the minimum. But he did the maximum.'

Although Rufus had completed his music with barely a month to go before the scheduled performance, by April 2006 the resulting work, *Bloom*, was ready to premiere at the Joyce Theatre. Petronio had extended *Bud* to now include four songs by Rufus (partly as a back-up in case Rufus had failed to get *Bloom* ready in time) and these – 'Oh What A World', 'Vibrate', 'This Love Affair', 'Agnus Dei' – served as the opener for the evening. Rufus would not appear in person but his voice was heard on a tape he had pre-prepared.

Bloom was generously received, with Rufus' contrapuntal compositions praised as being particularly effective as a dance accompaniment. In many ways, Rufus' pieces were extensions of the humming sections on songs like 'Oh What A World' and 'Tower of Learning', mini-fugues built up out of an army of tiny multi-layered Rufuses. Francisco Nunez, who led the Young People's Chorus of New York City that performed live to Rufus' recording, had had the job of transcribing Rufus' music and of creating the obbligato choral arrangement that completed it. He later joked about how long it had taken him to transcribe Rufus' music from the CD he had been sent, not least because Rufus had seemingly been unable to keep tempo during his recordings. In truth, it is Nunez's work with the choir that really flatters Rufus' somewhat hurried-sounding compositions. But what Rufus had created in the limited time that he had allowed himself demonstrated enough vision and innovation to make further excursions into the dance world a realistic possibility. The *Performing Arts Journal* had certainly seen enough potential to suggest that a new double act could be on the cards. 'What's most striking about the comparison between these artists is how wondrous vibrato and feeling for the body in Wainwright's voice is translated into Petronio's choreographic direction and costuming of the dancers' bodies. The two artists complement each other so well that they could be artistic descendants of [Merce] Cunningham and [John] Cage.'

*

Carnegie Hall is one of the most famous concert venues in the world. Since opening in 1891, with a piano recital by Tchaikovsky no less, it had hosted many important classical premieres including Dvorak's *New World Symphony* in 1893, Gershwin's *An American in Paris* in 1928 and Stravinsky's *Symphony in Three Movements* in 1946. Although it's a comparatively small venue, holding just under 3,000 people, playing Carnegie Hall adds a certain cachet to the career of any musician. For although its roots were in classical music, it has long since developed a reputation as the New York venue in which to make a statement or to receive the legitimising stamp of cultural credibility.

The tiered interior of the hall, with its all-white plaster columns and carved decoration, reminiscent of being inside a rather grand wedding cake, had seen artists as diverse as Billie Holiday, the Beatles, Buck Owens and Lenny Bruce all take advantage of the venue's inspirational ambience to perform now legendary concerts. Indeed Isaac Stern, the violin virtuoso who had fought against the proposed demolition of the building to make way for a skyscraper in the 1960s and in whose honour the main hall has been renamed, once said that the hall itself was an instrument: 'It takes what you do and makes it larger than life.'

Of course, Carnegie Hall was exactly the sort of venue that Rufus thought he should be playing. Not as part of a family folk evening either; hadn't one reviewer of the Christmas show noted that 'of all the singers of the evening, Carnegie Hall was truly built for the voice of Rufus Wainwright'? Rufus wanted to play a show there in his own right. He had already seen Antony and the Johnsons headlining in October 2005 (including a show-stopping version of Whitney Houston's 'I Wanna Dance With Somebody'). His friend Justin Bond had taken his drag cabaret show Kiki & Herb to the venue for a 'farewell' concert during which Rufus had guested alongside Sandra Bernhard, Jake Shears and Michael Cavadias on an ensemble version of 'Those Were The Days' as originally recorded by Mary Hopkin in 1968.[3]

---

3. Rufus had appeared as a guest vocalist on the same track on the Kiki & Herb album *Do You Hear What We Hear?* back in 2000. The version recorded at Carnegie Hall was also released on the album *Kiki & Herb Will Die For You: At Carnegie Hall* (2005).

Rufus was as competitive as ever. He didn't want it to seem as though he was being outstripped by the competition, especially when the competition was known to him personally. After all, even his mother and aunt had played there back in 1980. As he explained to *Time Out New York:* 'Several close friends did shows at Carnegie Hall and I was starting to feel threatened. Like, I'd better get my ass over there and do something.'

In fact, the 'something' he intended to do had its roots back in 2004 when he had appeared at Kiki & Herb's show. He had spoken to Kiki & Herb's producer, Jared Geller, in confidence about an idea he had for a show that would see him performing Judy Garland's concert at Carnegie Hall in its entirety. 'I was taken aback,' remembers Geller. 'I said, "Don't worry, I'm not going to tell anybody because that's insane." But then we kept talking about it.'

Judy at Carnegie Hall is one of the holy relics of showbusiness. The former child star captured at a moment of transcendence when all of her skills as a showman, a singer and a survivor are focused into one night of luminescent brilliance. Recorded in April 1961, the album would stay in the American charts for almost two years straight and receive numerous awards.

On the night, Garland was unaware that her label Capitol was going to try to record the show until a half-hour before the curtain rose. Even then she refused to allow any changes to be made to the set-up of her musicians to aid the taping in case it affected the way she performed. As always, she was going to be the best she could be for the people in front of her and she didn't care if they made a recording or not.

By the 1960s Garland's health was poor and she was drinking heavily and taking numerous prescription drugs. Offstage she would appear worn down and broken by the expectations that had been placed upon her and the misfortunes that had befallen her ever since her early Hollywood days when her handlers had primed her full of amphetamines so that she could keep up with her hectic schedule. On stage she would be transformed, raised high and temporarily healed by the adoration of her public. Although contemporary reviewers might liken her reception at Carnegie Hall – a rapturous standing ovation before a note was even sung – to that which might have greeted the mega-evangelist Billy Graham, it was surely the other way around. Garland came alive on stage because her audience willed her to, they had the faith that she was lacking in herself. 'I don't ever want to go home,' she would say from the stage as the applause and cheers reached a crescendo and you could believe that she was speaking a literal truth.

The acclaimed photographer William Claxton wrote quite poignantly of a contemporary assignment in which he had been sent to photograph Garland in Las Vegas.[4] The two-hour struggle to get her ready for the stage seemed quite tortuous, yet the performance was triumphant. 'She displayed such angst and fear. I felt for her, but most of the people in the room seemed used to it. I felt she was miserable, but she seemed to be enjoying it to some extent ... It seemed to me that Judy gave a very professional, yet desperate, performance. While she sang and spoke, she seemed to be crying out for help, using her performance brilliantly to express her need and her condition. I wondered how many people in the audience felt this too.' Claxton wrote that after the show, Garland's face was a mix of happiness and hysteria and that as she accepted the plaudits from those backstage, she looked ecstatic.

Musician David Was likened Garland to Kurt Cobain in that they both had an 'unmistakable fragility which made them seem more proximate to an audience than singers with more technical expertise and polish. They seemed human.' In fact, Was was on to something. The closest live album there is to approaching the sheer emotional wrench of *Judy at Carnegie Hall* is Nirvana's own spellbinding *MTV Unplugged in New York*. The ability to reach out to an audience, that indefinable almost alchemical magic that can transmute personal anguish into art that is accessible and moving to the remote, empathetic yet essentially unconnected listener is something that Garland and Cobain possessed and it's something that is captured within the 26 tracks of *Judy at Carnegie Hall*.

---

4. The full text can be found in William Claxton, *Photographic Memory* (Powerhouse Books, 2002, US). In the pair of pictures that Claxton chooses to illustrate the piece, the contrast between Garland on and offstage is startling. In a photograph of Garland getting ready she is pinned into a towel, her eyes looking up, pleading, her hands, clawed and grasping. The next shot shows her on stage in full flow; she looks a decade younger. Vibrant. Alive.

Of course Rufus had grown up with Garland, right from pretending to be Dorothy as a child, but he hadn't become acquainted with the Carnegie Hall album until its 40th anniversary reissue, which he bought not long after 9/11. In the dreadful days that followed the terrorist attacks and the subsequent march into Bush's 'War on Terror', he listened to the album over and over. 'Somehow that album, no matter how dark things seemed, made everything brighten,' he told the *New York Times*. 'She had this capacity to lighten the world through the innocence of her sound. Her anchor to the material was obviously through her devotion to music. You never feel that she didn't believe every word of every song she ever sang.'

He invested less in her role as martyr/survivor for which she was held in such high regard by members of the gay community that she could be considered canonised; to Rufus she was the consummate musician. 'I've thought a lot about this,' he continued to *The Times*, 'and I think the secret is that when she sings she is beautiful without actually being beautiful. She believed in it and you believe in it. That's the key.'

Garland was an incredible interpreter of songs. As David Was said, 'She has an actress' respect for the text and not just the notes of the song.' She chose material to reflect her situation, to play on her popular image as a troubled star and if her gestures and phrasing were taken to reflect how she was actually feeling, then her skills as an actress had probably had something to do with it. The impact was similar to somebody like 1930s crooner Al Bowlly, who could invest a song with such emotion that he could bring tears to his own eyes when he sang (an act taken to extreme, sometimes ludicrous, lengths by Johnnie Ray in the 1950s).

But Geller was right; the very notion of reproducing the Carnegie Hall concert was quite possibly insane. The Judy show was so culturally resonant that to interfere with it in any way would be an enormously risky endeavour leading to potential ridicule and/or career suicide. This could be no mere nostalgic revivalism à la Robbie Williams generic Rat Pack shows. Even Williams, in full 'ego has landed' mode, had gone for a mix-and-match pseudo-Vegas repertoire and not attempted to recreate *Sinatra at the Sands* in its entirety.[5] For Rufus, the very fact that this couldn't be seen as just another person borrowing from an old singer like Sinatra was what appealed to him. 'I don't relate much to Frank Sinatra,' explained Rufus to *Time Out New York*. 'I appreciate Frank but there are so many Frank Sinatra imitators – the kind of guys who basically want to get laid. And there's nobody being the flip side of that, which is the hungry, lonely, desperate crazy-person singer. So I wanted to pick up that mantle and try to be a little less cool.'

The idea of performing complete classic albums in note-for-note sequence had been growing more common in popular music with artists like Belle and Sebastian (*If You're Feeling Sinister*), The Stooges (*Funhouse*) and The Lemonheads (*It's a Shame About Ray*) all having taken part in the first season of the 'Don't Look Back' series of concerts instigated by London promoters ATP in 2005 and Patti Smith having played her album *Horses* as part of her Meltdown shows at the Southbank Centre. Of course, these concerts and others like them relied on performers playing albums that they had written and recorded themselves. It was more unusual for an artist to want to recreate an entire record that had been made by somebody else. Sure, once upon a time Pussy Galore had recorded all of *Exile on Main Street* and Sonic Youth had tried and failed to cover the whole of the Beatles' *White Album* (and then there was the mythical Ryan Adams version of the Strokes' album *Is This It?*, which may only have existed in Adams' head). But those were studio exercises, an exaggeration of the one-off fun cover version like blasting a thug-ugly 'Louie, Louie' or doing a disco version of a punk-rock song just to see how it sounded. It was another thing entirely to want to stage a live performance of a whole album originally recorded by somebody else and to want to take it seriously and to play it straight.

The first hurdle in getting the show up and running was convincing Carnegie Hall itself that it was a good idea. Although in

---

5. Rufus guested with Robbie Williams (and actress Frances Barber) at a special Pet Shop Boys concert at the Mermaid Theatre, London, in May 2006. Although Williams doesn't appear to have offered Rufus any tips that he may have gleaned from his successful *Swing When You're Winning* album and concert tour (the album was recorded in the same Capitol Studio that Rufus had used with Van Dyke Parks and it was a huge hit all over the world except, tellingly, in the US), he is supposed to have said that '[Rufus] is the talent I want to turn into.' (*Daily Mail*, 23 February 2008). Rufus' song from the concert, 'Casanova in Hell', was included on the Pet Shop Boys' *Concrete* album (2006).

theory the hall was available to anybody to hire out, in practice there were certain standards that had to be reached before the venue would let a performer loose on its precious boards. Geller had already shown Carnegie Hall that a riotous farewell show from a drag act made perfect sense and he quickly won them over to the Judy show. '[Carnegie Hall] really want to be artistically satisfied,' he explained. 'They wanted to know it'd be something worthy of being on their stage. Once they got it they were really supportive and excited.' In fact, the venue had already hosted a similar tribute event to the *Judy at Carnegie Hall* album back in June 1998 with various guest artists singing songs from the record; the difficulty had been in convincing them that a solo artist would be able to carry the whole show.

Geller, and co-producer David Foster, managed to secure two consecutive nights in June and liaised with the hall to ensure that the venue would be as close to how Judy had had it as the inevitable changes made over the decades would allow. Kate would later explain how strict the guardians of the hall could be. When they had been doing the McGarrigles Christmas show, she had suggested that they might like to put up some Christmas decorations: 'We had ideas for some decorations, maybe something like a shadow of a tree against the wall. Nothing huge. And they said, "Sorry. This is Carnegie Hall. You don't need anything." That's their attitude. But sometimes it works in your favour because it is so formal and beautiful.'

As the plans progressed, Rufus started talking about the show as being a great test for a singer, remarking that in structure and pacing it would be the closest he could get to actually performing in an opera. He had already made clear that although he was going to perform the original set-list, he wasn't going to be doing a Judy Garland impersonation. Nevertheless he acknowledged that he was setting himself up to be compared to one of the greatest entertainers there had ever been. 'Any singer should attempt it if they want to see how good they are,' he said, as if the concert was an Olympic endurance event.

Despite Rufus' enthusiasm, other people were less enamoured by the project. Garland's daughter Liza Minnelli was aghast, Loudon thought it was a terrible idea and Kate claimed to not even know what he was talking about when he had first told her what he was planning. The Judy album meant nothing to her. 'By 1961 I had already gotten into Pete Seeger. We were very into the Appalachian mountain stuff, people with no teeth playing banjo, stuff like that. That's the side of America we liked, so Garland wasn't even a blip on the screen.'

The sheer scale of the performance, entailing more than two dozen numbers accompanied by a full orchestra, was prohibitively expensive and meant that rehearsals had to be arranged piecemeal. It was far too costly to set up the whole orchestra and work on the show from scratch. Stephen Oremus, who had arranged and conducted the music for the Broadway hit *Wicked* (another show that in its own way wouldn't have existed without Garland), was hired as the musical director and put in charge of reassembling the album's original arrangements. 'Some of these arrangements are just amazing,' he would enthuse as the project moved forward. 'The things going on musically were so sophisticated and so absolutely thrilling and you don't hear that much any more. We use the same size orchestra and the same orchestrations.'

Oremus had to transcribe certain songs because Rufus couldn't physically sing them in the same key as Garland. 'Rufus isn't singing as Judy Garland,' he explained. 'He's doing his own interpretation of the songs. But everything he's singing over is as exact a replica as we can muster.'

Rehearsals started with just Rufus, piano, bass and drums. Gradually more musicians were added and the rehearsal venues grew larger until, at Rufus' insistence, they held a couple of run-throughs in a 600-seat theatre. 'That was just two days of rehearsals in which I did whatever I wanted and attempted to exorcise the little showbiz demons spinning around my brain,' he said. 'I basically was silly and childish which was really good because there were certain things that worked. I've been refining my vaudevillian sensibility without becoming a parody of showbusiness.' Even so, rehearsals with the full orchestra were expensive and they would have to make do with just a couple of days immediately prior to the show to get it right and last-minute fixing on the day of the concert in Carnegie Hall itself.

In order to get back as much money as they could from what

looked like becoming a loss-making endeavour (even if the concert sold out both nights it would still lose money), Geffen had inevitably opted to release the show as a CD and DVD. Oscar-winning film director Sam Mendes came on board to film the concerts (apparently after some persuasion from his wife, and huge Rufus fan, Kate Winslet) and he began to attend rehearsals to help Rufus block out his moves.[6]

To add the requisite glamour to the staging, Rufus asked flamboyant Dutch designers Viktor & Rolf to provide the clothes for the event. They were a suitably decadent pair with the required propensity for outrageous fashions that set apart the best designers. They once described their clothes, with a nod to Lautréamont, as 'a chance encounter of a tuxedo with an atom bomb on a catwalk'. Rufus had met them at a photo-shoot when they were both featured in the Dutch gay magazine *Butt*, and after the designers had seen Rufus play, they became mutual admirers. Later he would repay them by writing and recording a song especially for use in the launch of their fragrance Antidote.

As both Martha and Kate had been called in to perform on the show, Viktor & Rolf were to clothe them too. The thrill of being dressed by internationally acclaimed designers was lost on Kate; instead of a personal consultation with Viktor & Rolf, she chose to just measure herself, send them the details and hope for the best. 'I don't know what I am going to wear yet,' she said a fortnight before the shows. 'I hope they turn up all right because you know how it goes when you have to put your foot on the tape measure and pull it up to your waist or the inside of the thigh.'

By the time the concerts came around, Rufus' pre-show hyperbole had grown to Don King proportions. He was no longer just talking about the inherent difficulty in taking on Judy's set-list, he was proclaiming that his performance would finally prove to his doubters that he was as much a singer as he was a songwriter. 'I have always considered myself equally a songwriter and a singer,' he

---

6. Although the Judy concert was released on DVD, it was the later London Palladium show and the footage was not directed by Sam Mendes. The proposed Mendes documentary, which would also have featured the recording sessions for what would become *Release the Stars* as well as rehearsal and backstage footage from the Carnegie Hall performances, was eventually completely scrapped in November 2007.

explained. 'Not to be arrogant, but I feel pretty confident in both fields. I have a tremendous reverence for that era when certain people wrote and certain people sang. But in doing this concert I am trying to establish myself as one of the voices of the twenty-first century. Maybe some people will tell me to stop writing songs and go on singing standards. But I do feel like I have established a signature sound and perspective that is really needed by a public so I will continue both things.'

The week before the concert, on what would have been the star's 84th birthday, Rufus and Kate took part in a special launch event for a new Judy Garland commemorative postage stamp that was also held at Carnegie Hall. One of the other performers was Judy's daughter Lorna Luft, who gave her seal of approval to Rufus' show (an opinion possibly coloured by the fact that she had been secretly asked to take part in the show herself as a surprise guest). 'I think he's coming from all the right places. He's coming out of love, and he's coming out of doing it as a tribute. He's coming out of respect, and he's wanting to do this the right way. I have no problem with anybody who comes out and does something with love and respect. It's the people who mock and come out of disrespect I have a problem with. She was everybody's legend, but she was my mother.'[7]

There is a quote attributed to Judy Garland, a little motherly advice she is once supposed to have conveyed to Liza Minnelli: 'Always be a first-rate version of yourself, instead of a second-rate version of somebody else.' Rufus was so convinced of his own ability that he believed he could be a first-rate songwriter and performer in his own right and also a first-rate version of somebody else too if he so chose. He was going to tackle Judy head-on. He was setting himself up to be judged alongside her as her equal, not as a tribute, not as the medium for the 'gay seance' that one critic worried it

---

7. After her contributions to Rufus' Judy Garland shows ended with the Hollywood Bowl performance, Luft reprised and toured her own tribute concert to her mother, Songs My Mother Taught Me which featured most of the same tracks as the Carnegie Hall album. Luft has always been completely overshadowed by the success of her half-sister Liza and has often found it hard to fight for her own place in the world of showbusiness with critics seemingly ever ready to dig at her. Indeed one such reviewer is supposed to have spiked a piece on her show which he had retitled Songs My Mother Taught My Sister (While I Was In The Room).

would turn into and certainly not for him the knowing camp of the
Garland drag act. It could almost be viewed as Rufus vs. Judy. Even
the posters for the event were laid out in blocked two-colour and
text like an old-time boxing poster. They were close facsimiles of
Garland's original 1961 design. The same colour orange, the half
silhouette in black and the name big and bold, three times. 'Rufus
Rufus Rufus' replaced 'Judy Judy Judy', but the subtitle remained
the same – 'World's Greatest Entertainer'.

Before the publicity drive for the concerts had really even started,
the tickets had almost sold out. These would be shows for the
dedicated Rufus fans who had scooped up seats in pre-sale, those
with the connections or celebrity status to get themselves guest-
listed or those who were prepared to pony up whatever the scalpers
wanted to get themselves inside. Premium VIP tickets, with an
invite to an after-show meet-and-greet had originally cost $1,000
each, but by the time the curtain rose, even regular seats had been
changing hands for close to that figure. 'Rufus does Judy' had
become as much a must-see-must-be-seen-at social event as it was a
music concert. Even so, a number of his early New York supporters
had been alienated, having been invited to the show, only to be
expected to pay for their own tickets.

The New York gossiping classes had dubbed it the 'gayest event
of the season'. At least it would be the campest. As Susan Sontag
had it, a definition of camp was 'the triumph of epicene style'.[8]
With the expectation that Rufus and Judy would somehow fuse
into an all-conquering male/female showbiz monster, how much
camper could you get?

As the crowd gathered on 57th and 7th and bustled and chatted
and filed their way inside, the buzz of anticipation was tempered
by a frisson of anxiety felt by the dedicated Judy Garland fans who
were attending, not so much to see Rufus, but to symbolically run
to the aid of Judy's ghost if this upstart pop-singing New Yorker
somehow sullied her memory by ruining or ridiculing her holiest
of nights.

When the lights finally came down, putting a stop to the craning

8. Susan Sontag, 'Notes on Camp', essay in *Against Interpretation*, Farrar, Strauss & Giroux, 1966, US.

necks of those audience members who were as desperate to see which celebrities they were sharing the show with as they were to hear Rufus sing, the chatter and hum of the packed house subsided and with a flick of the baton, Oremus had the orchestra working through the introductory instrumental. The overture was one section at least that sounded exactly as it had back in Judy's day. A time machine, superbly played yet oddly quaint in the twenty-first century, a fanfare of brass, an instrumental tease of ancient half-buried, almost forgotten songs ready to be disinterred and reborn. There was an audible gasp as a trumpet played and the hook to 'Over The Rainbow' swelled and then faded, bringing the audience to its feet. Maybe, for just one second, with the overture so perfectly replicated, it wouldn't have been altogether impossible to imagine that it was Judy herself who would be coming out on to the stage. But of course it was Rufus who bounded up to the microphone in his Viktor & Rolf suit, grinned and then belted, 'When you're smiling, the whole world smiles with you'. The Judy fans relaxed, they were smiling too. Rufus was serious, the show was no joke.

As the show progressed, Rufus struggled with some of the mater-ial. The demanding uptempo numbers that Garland had been able to wrestle to the ground and throw over her shoulder as she marched through the set were not the kind of songs that were best suited to Rufus' voice or approach. Indeed, he had rarely been successful when attempting anything above mid-tempo even on his own records. His legato phrasing, brilliantly utilised in the sliding vocal lines of his own songs, was inappropriate for the more hurried and precisely placed lyrics of some of the show tunes – his diction on 'Puttin' on the Ritz' threatened to push the song into *Young Frankenstein* territory and 'San Francisco' had dipped into pure 'jazz hands' pastiche by the song's climax. If he had been compiling the set from scratch, he would probably have jettisoned these in favour of more smouldering torch numbers like 'Do It Again' that he effortlessly turned from Garland's needy pleading into a lascivious, knowing come-on.

Before the concert, Rufus had warned a radio interviewer that people should prepare for things to go wrong because there were a lot of lyrics to try to remember. He was true to his word. There were mistakes, both deliberate (the lyrical fluff in 'You Go to My Head' mirrored Garland's own recorded mistake and was met with knowing cheers by the Garland aficionados) and unintentional. Fortunately both nights were recorded and producer Phil Ramone was able to mix and match between the sets to create a near word-perfect collection for the eventual CD release.

The fact that Rufus was forgiven for not having memorised all of the songs and for occasionally having to rely on hamming it up to get through material that called for skills which he had not mastered – a brief, embarrassed 'tap dance' was about as far as the stage choreography went – was the combined result of playing to an enthusiastic 'home crowd', of which such a high proportion were gay and middle-aged that it became a point of comment in almost every newspaper review, and his undoubted charisma as a stage performer in his own right.

During the concert, Rufus replaced Garland's showbusiness anecdotes with his own. Where Garland's stories were somewhat incoherent, including one about her hairdresser in which she meanders like a proto-Eddie Izzard, Rufus' were concise, practised and timed for laughs. The anecdotal rambling introduction was something that he had long incorporated into his own shows with great success. Rufus could be quick-witted and funny, but he wasn't afraid to hone a successful off-the-cuff joke into a prepared ad-lib for later use.[9]

---

9. The showbusiness onstage anecdote is a thesis in waiting in itself. By the 1950s, performers who were appearing in one-person shows, as opposed to variety nights, had incorporated the meandering gag used by the comedians who would once have been sharing the bill with them into their own act. It gave them a breather between songs, padded out their running time and gave them an opportunity to extend an empathetic hand to the crowd by revealing a personal story, or at least a carefully scripted tale that would seem plausible and press the required buttons. And they could use the same story over and over again and pretend that they were remembering it on the spot.

Since his very early shows in Montreal, Rufus had understood the power of engaging the audience with a funny story, which would in turn make them more receptive to his own material. It's something that Martha has also adopted. In the Judy show, Rufus told apt stories of his pretending to be both Dorothy and the Wicked Witch when he was a child and also of Loudon's own childhood crush on Liza Minnelli.

In fact Minnelli herself is a master of the onstage anecdote. In her 2008 London shows, she told a wonderfully paced story about her mother and Kay Thompson, the acclaimed choreographer and vocal coach and close family friend, going to watch her as a child in a dancing contest. The pair was so moved by Liza's dancing that they both began sobbing and all they had to mop up the tears was the powder puff from Thompson's compact. After the show Liza ran up to her mother and asked if she had enjoyed her dancing. Judy said she had and handed her daughter the sodden pad as some odd kind of evidence. 'And you

Rufus was true to his promise of not trying to impersonate Garland. In fact, he went so far the other way that the very crux of the whole show could justifiably be called into question. Rather than remain 'in character' while performing the set, Rufus in effect stepped aside and made so many knowing comments relating to gay pride and the inherent 'gayness' of his endeavour that he was in danger of turning what could have been a career-defining 'performance art meets showbusiness' happening into a rainbow flag-waving self-indulgent love-in.

None of which would have mattered so much had he been more consistent in his criteria for how the evening should run. The show was sold as Rufus does *Judy at Carnegie Hall*; in fact, the Garland recreation was the concert's very raison d'etre. But as the evening progressed, the non-partisan viewer (of which there were precious few in the hall) would have begun to wonder whether it was really Rufus gets to Carnegie Hall *via* Judy Garland. He didn't help himself with his contradictory approach to Garland's actual set. While struggling to come to terms with the archaic minstrel numbers 'Swanee' and 'Rock-A-Bye Your Baby with a Dixie Melody', but allowing them to stand because they were part of the original concert, showed Rufus' commitment to historical accuracy as evinced by the work Oremus had put in to arranging and transposing the original scores. But this rigorous approach to the staging did not extend to prohibiting the inclusion of guest artists. When asked why he was handing songs out to other people, Rufus explained, rather unconvincingly, 'I wouldn't want to listen to myself for that long.'

Martha's rendition of 'Stormy Weather' was a revelation in terms of her ability to wrench the heart out of a song and hold its essence out in front of her – pulsing, beating, bleeding. As impressive as she was when appearing in front of her own band of rock musicians, at Carnegie Hall she truly sounded as if she was born to sing in front

---

know what?' said Liza from the stage of the London Coliseum, a gulp, choking back the tears, 'I still have it. I still have it now.' . . . And into the next song.

When Rufus discussed Garland's Carnegie Hall show with hx.com he also spoke fondly of Minnelli's concert film *Liza With a Z* as an example of how performers should work: 'I'd like to help promote a renaissance of stagecraft and performance excellence that both of those projects exemplify.' While he was never going to be able to hoof it like a Garland/Minnelli, he has at least been successful in resurrecting the anecdote.

of a full orchestra. Throughout the evening Rufus had received applause and adoration that ranged from enthusiastic clapping to staggered standing ovations, but when Martha finished singing it was like the roof had been blown off the building. In fact, so spectacular was the response to her – a standing ovation so instantly attained it was as if the seats had been wired to the mains – that at least one reviewer suggested that should Rufus ever stage the show again he would be as well to leave his sister out of it. It was undoubtedly an awesome performance, but perhaps not one necessarily in the context of the show. Where Garland sounded broken and dejected (her oft-quoted quip 'Behind every cloud there's another cloud' sums up her version of the song), Martha sounded strident and histrionic – like Patsy Cline having a meltdown.

What had begun as a unique take on a historic event, which could have succeeded or failed but always remained valid by existing within its own parameters, lurched precariously close to standard tribute-night fare with the wholly unnecessary duet 'After You've Gone' sung with Garland's daughter Lorna Luft, whose lusty vibrato clashed horribly with Rufus' reedy tenor and then an appearance by Kate to reprise the mother/son party piece of 'Over The Rainbow', which was introduced by Rufus mock-grumbling about how often Kate had made him sing it to her friends when he was a child ('And look where you ended up,' said Kate, gesturing around the room).

In fact, Rufus' best performance of the night was with a song that was not part of the original concert at all. He had considered holding back one of his own songs for the encore but wisely realised that that wouldn't make any sense. Instead he prepared a version of Cole Porter's 'Every Time We Say Goodbye', and in so doing demonstrated that, after all, the show had in fact always been more about Rufus Wainwright than it had been about Judy Garland. Perhaps it was because there was no possibility of a straight comparison being made; perhaps it was that the song came as a release after the restrictions of Garland's set; more likely he just revelled in the perverse fact that he had awarded himself an extra encore, in effect going one more than Garland. Whatever the reason, Rufus truly nailed the song and shone brighter than he had throughout the preceding two-and-a-half hour show. If there was one moment where he truly could stake a claim to being the current 'world's greatest entertainer', it was during a song that had not even been part of the original plan.[10]

To further enrage the Garland purists and all those critics who

---

10. My criticisms here are based on the fact that I was perhaps prepared to read more into the Judy concerts than Rufus was willing to concede and that its potential, in the end, far exceeded its execution. My own take on the project held that the closest antecedents to 'Rufus Does Judy' could be found not in the growing wave of live track-by-track concerts but in film and contemporary art practices. For example, artists Iain Forsyth and Jane Pollard have, since the late 1990s, created work using seminal musical events as their starting point. David Bowie's *Ziggy Stardust* concert 'Farewell', The Smiths on *The Queen is Dead* tour and an infamous live Cramps bootleg video tape have all been lovingly recreated with stand-ins playing the parts of the musicians in carefully stage-managed productions that operate beyond the realm of nostalgia by connecting directly with the viewer to allow new experiences to envelop any residual expectations of what an historical event had represented. Forsyth and Pollard identify and acknowledge that a recreation can never replicate an original event and that it is the creation of the imitation and the watching of it play out that is important: 'The copy never reproduces the original completely. This shortfall is where the real emerges and where understanding can begin. Good art always, at some level, fails.'

Likewise Gus Van Sant's much misunderstood literal remake of *Psycho* (1998) sought to give viewers the opportunity to revisit the classic movie by representing, that is *re-presenting* (or more properly *reiterating*) it as a new film and subject to 1998 critical and cultural values and not forever frozen in 1960. Many a cineaste got their knickers in a twist in debates ranging from whether the casting of the recently out Anne Heche in the Janet Leigh role and the bullishly hetero Vince Vaughan in place of Anthony Perkins' confused effeminate Bates meant that Van Sant was revealing a new queer take on the film or whether the remake was just an elaborately raised middle finger to the studio system. Whether Van Sant's film was a success was the least interesting thing about it.

But Rufus' personal approach to the Judy performances removed the possibility of failure, in its critical sense, by shifting the emphasis as far away from the original event as was possible so that the show's title became virtually meaningless. Hence, my assertion that it was really Rufus *gets* to Carnegie Hall *via* Judy Garland, and the name and supposed premise became an extravagant marketing trick.

My impression of the project from listening to the Carnegie Hall tapes and attending the London, Paris and Los Angeles shows was that Rufus had fallen in love with the idea of the show but was only prepared to take it so far. Certainly by the time he was doing the press and publicity for the European shows, he was announcing them as being 'The ultimate American song-cycle. It doesn't matter whether it's me or Judy singing – this is just the best collection of popular songs ever recorded.' By which he was implying that the set-list was the only important thing and the context in which he chose to showcase it was secondary, merely a gimmick.

But by choosing to perform not just a Judy Garland-style set but to select an actual documented live recording and make this the unique selling point of your concert anchors the project to a specific time and place and requires a certain commitment on the part of the artist to follow that through. You pack the baggage, the least you can do is carry it yourself.

Taking the already inexact Carnegie Hall set on the road resulted in the Judy project diminishing with each retelling. Rufus does Judy does Carnegie Hall at the London Palladium or the Paris Olympia (the Hollywood Bowl show featured slight adjustments to the set-list) is a dilution of the original concept to the point where it becomes an unnecessarily restrictive cabaret show. We are left with a spectacle no more authentic than those had questioned his motives in taking on the show at all, by the time he appeared on the cover of December's *Out* magazine as their 'Entertainer of the Year', he was hinting that his performance had actually outshone the original: 'I would never say I was better than her, because I don't want to die. But I've had a chance to listen to the recording of my performance, and while I think her belts are bigger than mine, when I got to those belts, they are a little more thought out.'

Rufus may have been grabbing all the media coverage with his Judy Garland extravaganza but it was Martha who would end up singing on what was undoubtedly the most commercially successful record a Wainwright had ever appeared on.

Martha once joked that she was a 'musical whore', meaning that she was more than happy to offer her vocal talents to any interesting project that came along. It was an attitude borne of a combination of just loving to make music and of having a work ethic, shared with Rufus and shaped by Loudon and Kate, of being a working musician who loved any opportunity to keep playing. Back in February 2006, she had performed with classical violinist Sophie Solomon and the London Symphony Orchestra at the Barbican in London. Solomon had played on *Want Two* and both Rufus and Kate attended the concert. During the afternoon an interviewer mentioned to Martha that Richard Hawley had had to cancel a show that night at the *Mojo* magazine-sponsored evening at the tiny Barfly venue in Camden. Martha volunteered to take his place and, after her performance with the LSO in a packed concert hall, jumped into a cab with Rufus and Kate and crossed town to play to a handful of people. Unsurprisingly both Kate and Rufus joined Martha on stage, who gave what Sean Adams of Drowned In Sound described as a 'simply breathtaking performance'. Indeed Adams relates that a singer-songwriter of his acquaintance had been so stunned by

---

touring multi-media concerts where Elvis, Sinatra or, more recently even Garland herself, sing in archive clips on a screen above some live musicians. Rufus may shrug and say that his intention was only ever to entertain (as those kinds of shows inevitably will and there is nothing wrong with that) but to paraphrase Barthes: 'What does the artist know about anything?' The fact that 'Rufus Does Judy' raised questions of artistic experimentation, re-enactment and role-playing beyond merely discussing the performance as if he were a tribute act justifies the resulting criticism. And the fact that his work can wear these kinds of critical approaches, at the very least, tests his potential as an artist.

Martha's performance that she couldn't write a song for three months afterwards.

But it was her guest performance with an earnestly emotional Northern Irish indie band that would bring her to the attention of millions of record buyers. While working on what would become *Eyes Open*, their fourth album, Snow Patrol had been listening to Martha's debut album so often that their producer suggested that it might be interesting if the band asked her to sing on a song with them. After vocalist Gary Lightbody approached her with the idea and she had agreed in principle, he set about writing something that would work for both of their voices. In the end Lightbody said that the song he had composed was actually 'a love song to Martha's voice' – no wonder she adored it. As she was already due to appear in Dublin where they were recording, it was simple enough to schedule a recording session. 'Set the Fire to the Third Bar' is not really a traditional duet as both vocalists sing simultaneously, offering a male/female perspective to the song's theme of lovers wanting to be together but kept apart by events or emotions unknown.

The track was one of the highlights of an album that became the best-selling British album of the year (as well as going platinum all over the world, including the US) and it was released as a single in November 2006, accompanied by a simple yet effective promo video in which Martha and Lightbody sing in an interrogation room separated by a one-way mirror echoing the song's theme of isolation. Whenever their schedules allowed, Martha would support Snow Patrol on tour allowing her to perform the song with them live.

After the success at Carnegie Hall, plans were in place for Rufus to take the concert to the London Palladium, where Garland had played many times and then on to Paris in early 2007. But he would be back at Carnegie Hall before 2006 was out, performing at The Wainwright Family and Friends Christmas Show. Originally intended to be a reprise of the previous year's family show and part of a longer Christmas tour, Kate fell ill and the tour had to be cancelled. Rufus and Martha called in as many favours as they could and put together a bill that included guests Lou Reed, David Byrne and Laurie Anderson. On the other side of the country, Loudon stepped in to take over the Los Angeles date and performed with Suzzy Roche and his sister Sloan.

5.3

'I was a fool to think that when finally given the reins of my own carriage I would all of a sudden turn into a Seventies minimalist and be able to completely edit myself. I went to Berlin thinking I would be this Lou Reed-Bowie character, wear mascara, stand in dark doorways and come out with this Kurt Weillian hatchet job. But what happened was I ended up wearing lederhosen, visiting palaces, taking little trips to the Alps, eating sausages and turning into this heavy-duty German romantic.' Rufus Wainwright (*Sydney Morning Herald*, 5 May 2007).

After enveloping himself in the old-school showbusiness excesses of his Judy show, Rufus had to get back to work recording a new album. He felt that he might have gone as far as he could in building albums as ornate musical cathedrals, a tactic which had reached its apogee with the magnificent *Want* project, joking that if he tried to make music any grander, the whole thing could collapse. *Want One* had sold well. *Want Two* had entered the British charts just outside the Top 20 but had still sold less than 90,000 copies in the US. Although he would not admit to being under pressure to deliver a successful album, the nagging worry of his seemingly unrecoupable record company debt still concerned him. 'I wish I could sell out,' he would later tell the *Sunday Times*. 'I do try to make my music more commercial but only within the boundaries of my own mind. If I put in a chorus, that's a big move for me. Of course I want to sell well but I could never write a straight pop song. It just doesn't interest me.'

Early indications were that Rufus intended to record a back-to-basics album, provisionally entitled *The Black and White Album*. It was to be a minimalist solo record, predominantly voice and piano (which is of course what Loudon had suggested he should have done on his debut album). He went so far as to describe his intention of making the kind of transition Hitchcock made moving from the big-budget thrills of *Vertigo* (1958) and *North By Northwest* (1959) to the downmarket shrieks of *Psycho* (1960).

One of the first songs he wrote for the album was 'Going To A Town'. It was his most overtly political song since 'Liberty Cabbage' and one in which he railed against the way that America had been tarnished in the eyes of the world by its leader's relentless war-mongering, hateful attitude to homosexuality and its inability, as demonstrated post-Hurricane Katrina, to look after its own while seemingly able to instantly interfere internationally at the whim of its president. Rufus said that the song came to him fully formed within a few spare minutes spent at the piano while he was waiting to go out to dinner. As much as the song attacked America, it was also an exasperated lament for a country that he admitted he still loved. Although the song didn't set the agenda in terms of subject matter for his forthcoming album, it was instrumental in Rufus deciding to record some of the album away from his home city.

The city that Rufus chose was Berlin, long associated with artistic freedom and a cultural vitality that has been driven by a history of destruction, restriction and eventual rebirth and, tellingly, the city that enabled musicians like David Bowie, Iggy Pop, Nick Cave and even U2 to deliver key works that reinvented their careers. 'One of the main reasons I went to Berlin, although New York is the greatest city on earth and I still love it, [was] I was sick of this victim dance that they took after 9/11,' explained Rufus to *Outlook* magazine. 'People were saying, "We've been through so much horrible stuff and our city is destroyed and we're beaten" and stuff. I wanted to go somewhere that had really experienced that several times and, in a weird way, become wiser and stronger because of it, even though they are always grappling with their past. So, I just needed a little bit of that grounding perspective of what real destruction is all about.'

Another more pressing reason that Rufus had for choosing Berlin was that he was going out with a new boyfriend who had become his first serious partner. Jörn Weisbrodt worked at the Berlin Opera and in his role as 'Head of Special Projects' had met with Rufus in the summer of 2005 to discuss the 'Soccer Opera' that Robert Wilson and Herbert Groenemeyer were collaborating on to coincide with Germany's hosting of the 2006 World Cup. Wilson had wanted to include Rufus in the performance but in the end nothing came of the project as the plans for staging it escalated and it became financially unworkable. 'The first big scene will be a soccer match with dinosaurs. The second scene will show cavewomen and dinosaurs. It will be an event for the family,' Wilson had announced at the original press conference for the project, giving a hint as to the scale on which he had been planning. Rufus may not have got to share a stage with a footballing brontosaurus but he did stay in touch with Jörn and over time they became close. After the album was finished, Jörn would move to New York, move in with Rufus and take charge of Robert Wilson's American office.

The Berlin sojourn was the perfect opportunity for Rufus to reposition himself after the baroque *Want* project and the Judy concerts. He was to be in charge of production and was able to push the project in any way he wished. It could have been a bold move into the unknown, enabling him to create a thrilling, brittle album that would confound those who had looked upon his previous albums as overwrought and self-indulgent.

The studio in Berlin-Köpenick was housed in a crumbling former East German state-run broadcasting complex built in the mid-1950s. Since the fall of the Wall, it had been taken over by artists and musicians and housed numerous studios, workshops and offices. Eventually it would almost certainly go the way of so many of the artistic quarters of the new Berlin and be turned into apartment-hotels and uniform open-plan offices, but for now, with its worn-out functionalist fittings and unreliable plumbing, it represented the kind of edgy, wildflowers-growing-out-of-the-rubble Berlin that Rufus had come looking for. In short, a perfect base from which to shift his music from *Want*'s saturated Hollywood Technicolor to the drizzling monochrome of a European arthouse album.

But within a short time of entering the studio, Rufus was calling in session musicians and building tracks that were even more ornate than those on *Want*. The new minimalist Rufus' head had been turned by the romantic possibilities of the German and Austrian countryside and the visits to mountains and castles that he had been making with Jörn. Germany was the land of the great romantic composers and he was always more in thrall to soaring Wagnerian towers than he was to Bowie and Eno's concrete bunkers and broken glass. He might have imagined hunkering down in the studio with an asymmetrical haircut, heavy eyeliner and tight jeans, programming motorik patterns into a drum machine, but he ended up in made-to-measure lederhosen arranging string quartets and vocal harmonies.

Another key to Rufus' change of heart lay in the fact that Peter Gelb, the new head of the Metropolitan Opera in New York, had approached him with the idea that he might like to try to develop an opera as part of a new programme to revitalise the Met and reach out to younger audiences by working with composers from outside of the traditional opera world (others invited to participate included film-music composer Rachel Portman, jazz musician Wynton Marsalis and playwright Romulus Linney).

Gelb was a controversial character in classical music circles. In his previous job as head of Sony Classical, he had shown he was an unashamed populist who had invested more in film soundtrack recordings and crossover artists than he had in new recordings of acknowledged classical works. The plan was exactly the kind of thing that riled traditionalists and at the same time achieved maximum publicity for the opera house. Many opera lovers whispered that Gelb was more interested in getting people through the door than he was in maintaining any kind of quality control, not that they were convinced that Gelb had the critical ability to exercise quality control in the first place.

The proposal allowed Rufus the time to create his own opera, which would be work-shopped and, if successful, eventually performed, if not at the Met itself then at least at one of its associated theatres. Each commission would eventually amount to $50,000 by the time the opera was ready to be put into production. There was no exact timescale, just a general agreement that the participants would begin the work and keep the opera house informed of their progress. This was the sort of project that Rufus had always dreamed of. Ever since Papa Verdi's *Requiem* had smothered him and smuggled him away into opera-land, his long-term aim had always been to write an opera for the Met, one of the most prestigious opera houses in the world. It was an incredible opportunity. It was as if the Metropolitan Museum of Art had bought your first painting and put it on permanent display or the Royal Shakespeare Company had offered to produce your first play. And it certainly impacted on the way that Rufus approached his new album.

Rufus used the recording sessions to develop ideas that he had, with one eye (and both ears) on the pending opera. He admitted that now he had been left to produce alone, he wanted to figure out his musical language and try to establish a solid base for his musical flights of fancy, as he would later explain: 'If anyone can accuse me of anything in my past albums [it] is that occasionally they are unbalanced. There are these big gestures but they are not quite sitting on something because I was still searching. I think with this album I finally built this proper foundation and it doesn't seem to topple over too much.'

One of the benefits of recording in Berlin was the ability to tap into a talented pool of classical musicians and Rufus found them thrilled to be working on a pop record with its more experimental recording techniques than those that they had been used to. 'They'll double, triple, quadruple themselves in the studio,' Rufus enthused. 'They'll improvise if they have to. They're just so hungry and desperate to be doing something new.' One of the musicians that Rufus called in had never played anything other than scored classical compositions before. He found the sessions so liberating that he soon began to compose work, eventually forming an experimental group of his own.

'I wanted to strip back and investigate the inner recesses of Rufus,' he would later say when asked to explain the shift from minimal to maximum. 'What ended up happening – I think due to this intersection occurring of my prime age, my being allowed to write this opera for the Met, being in very good health, having all my family around me – it feels like, no, this is the time when you have to lay it all out on the line, and just make it as fabulous as possible. And that is sort of what happened. The record was definitely officially the "New Me". I'm approaching songwriting and stardom and showbusiness and my thirties with a kind of prime coating. Meaning, this is as strong and magnificent and young as I'm ever gonna be all at one time.'

Even though Rufus had complete control of how the album would sound, he had opted to bring in Tom Schick, an experienced engineer, to guide him through the recording process. He also chose to enlist the services of Neil Tennant from the Pet Shop Boys as executive producer. Rufus believed that Tennant would be a useful sounding board for the songs and a means of testing whether they had commercial appeal. He would come in for a week towards the end of the sessions, listen to all the tracks and make suggestions. 'He could come into the studio and see what I was doing intellectually and tell me flat out nobody would get it or everyone would get it,' said Rufus. He looked upon Tennant as an expert in the pop world which was now, ultimately, where he envisaged the album heading.

'I would argue that Neil is probably the foremost professor of both high and low culture,' Rufus said. 'He has a real firm grip on both ideas. And that is something that is really essential in my musical world. Because I know very little about low culture. And when I say low culture I'm not being derogatory – popular culture is a better way to put it. So, I'm kind of in the dark, but knowing about it is necessary for me to work with the hoity-toity shit that I do know about. And Neil's a good way to bring me out of the heavens a little bit.'[11]

As the recordings progressed, the tracks became more involved, more complicated. By the time Tennant arrived, Rufus had long since abandoned any pretence of stripping down the music. Like an ambitious stylist buzzing around a model, adjusting one exquisite item of clothing on top of another, he was determined to dress them up. He was planning layers – layers – layers!

Tennant recalled his initial impression of the material. 'Nearly every song on it, I said: "Don't you think the tempo could be faster and don't you think it could be shorter?" Rufus works like a composer. He'd written all of the arrangements and at one point I thought he was overegging the album. There were lots of brass

---

11. The only logical reason to call in Tennant was in the hope that he could help find the hit single that Rufus had long been searching for. Tennant's ability to ascertain what might have general appeal could well have been questioned by anybody who had studied the steady commercial decline of the Pet Shop Boys since their early 1990s peak. If the ultimate aim was to have a hit, even if it meant shaving off a little bit of credibility, how much better would it have been had Rufus been steered towards somebody like production wizards Brian Higgins and Xenomania, who had proved that they could achieve success with a string of hits (most notably with manufactured pop acts Girls Aloud) while being artistically respected enough for the likes of Franz Ferdinand to seek them out to work with (and, ironically enough, for the Pet Shop Boys themselves to call them in to help on their 2009 album).

arrangements which I thought might be heavy-handed but, in the end, they worked. But he knew that because he had the whole thing in his head.'

One of the strongest tracks on the album, a beautiful song that concerned Rufus and Jörn ambling through the city's famous sprawling gardens, was one of the first to be addressed by Tennant. 'Originally "Tiergarten" was a slow, slow, slow ballad,' remembered Rufus. 'It was gonna be with harps only and no drums, this languid thing. Neil immediately told me he was bored. And I said, well, I don't want Neil to be bored. Vicious When Bored: Neil Tennant. We pushed it up and tried another approach.'[12]

With much of the recording completed in Germany, Rufus spent a few months finishing up and overdubbing material in the US and England, including a stint with *Want* producer Marius de Vries mixing tracks in his London studio in early 2007. The completed album featured many of the usual guest artists – Martha, Kate and Teddy Thompson – with a sprinkling of new faces. Richard Thompson, who Rufus admitted to being musically afraid of ('He's so fierce and heterosexual,' he told one journalist), played guitar on a couple of tracks, Tennant played keyboards on one track and provided backing vocals, and Welsh actress Siân Phillips was plucked from Rufus' fond memory of the 1976 BBC series *I, Claudius* to provide an apocalyptic narration on the song 'Between My Legs'. *I, Claudius* would later become a favourite DVD on the tour bus, at least for Rufus, who also insisted the band watch episodes of *Upstairs, Downstairs* with him.

The entire project, by now titled *Release the Stars* had taken the best part of a year to complete. Rufus was proud of his work but the thrill of finally completing an album as both producer and performer and of falling happily in love with Jörn was overshadowed by his

---

12. There would also be a dance remix of 'Tiergarten' issued in 2007. Although it was only ever available as a one-sided white label that was presented as if it was an unofficial release, it was actually officially sanctioned by Rufus' label in the UK. The remix by German electronica duo Supermayer runs over 13 minutes long, uses lots of harp, snatches of Rufus' vocal harmonies isolated like they were Beach Boys samples and mixes rain sound-effects with a throbbing deep house bass line. As is often the case with extended remixes, there is very little of the original track left but it was certainly a bold move and one that took at least a little essence of Rufus on to the dance-floors of some of the hipper clubs in Europe (where he certainly would never otherwise have been heard).

mother's ongoing illness that had forced the cancellation of the 2006 McGarrigle Christmas shows. After being diagnosed with a rare form of cancer, Kate had had to have an operation in August and another in the spring of 2007. Understandably both Rufus and Martha, who was recording tracks for her second album in Brooklyn, were devastated with worry.

'The time surrounding the making of the album was the best of times and the worst of times,' Rufus later said. 'On one hand I was falling in love and I was at the height of my powers artistically and still looking the part and all that, but on the other hand my mother had a very serious operation during that process. That tore a hole through any kind of security that I might feel.'

Rufus later reflected that Kate's illness had seriously changed the way he looked at the world. 'It definitely put a flame under my butt in terms of emotional antics. When I made *Want One* and *Want Two* I was very much involved in my own reconstruction, personal growth and purging of demons. But when my mom had this operation it became Herculean all of a sudden. The emotion and intensity dwarfed any personal things that had happened in the past.'

And in an *Interview* feature, he movingly related the moment that he knew something had changed, when he reacted to some bad news during Kate's treatment. 'The minute I saw my mom, and showed her my fear, there was this weird transmission that occurred. When I saw the fear in her eyes, my entire life changed. I became a total man. I was like "We're going to get through this. I'm going to be strong for you."'

5.4

Prior to the *Release the Stars* launch, Rufus appeared on a couple of movie soundtracks, including a pleasant version of the Rogers and Hart song 'Bewitched' for *The History Boys*, the rather flat film version of Alan Bennett's hit play. The other commission was more interesting and resulted in three songs for the Walt Disney space flick *Meet the Robinsons*. It was an opportunity for Rufus to try his hand at writing movie songs to order rather than simply covering a song that somebody had chosen for him. And it would be for a film for which he would not have been the most obvious or automatic choice. Like Randy Newman, Elton John, Peggy Lee and dozens more before him, he could say he had written songs for a Disney movie. He didn't need to mention that the *New York Times* and others had suggested it was one of the worst Disney films of all time.

In the end, one of his cartoon tunes, 'Another Believer', would be (very) long-listed in the early nominations for the Academy Award for the Best Original Song (the Oscar ultimately went to 'Falling Slowly' from the film *Once* but by awards night, Rufus had been cast aside like the 54 other songs on the long list that didn't make the final nominations).

Rufus reprised the Judy shows at the London Palladium in February 2007. If anything, it was a venue that figured more prominently in Garland folklore than Carnegie Hall. Garland had made her British stage debut at a variety night at the theatre in 1951 (when she was so nervous she tripped over the hem of her dress and fell over on stage) and performed her first solo concerts in 1960, when she trialled most of the set that would eventually become enshrined as the Carnegie Hall album. She appeared on the same bill as the Beatles in 1964 and stole the show, and in her last movie *I Could Go on Singing* she can be seen performing numerous songs on the Palladium stage. It was also the venue for her debut performance with her daughter Liza for a television special in 1964 and where she appeared at one of her last ever concerts before she died at her London home in June 1969.[13]

Although he could have altered the set to fit any one of the documented shows that Judy had performed at the venue, Rufus kept the main show to the same songs he had performed in New York. There were guest spots again from Lorna Luft and from Martha, who very nearly missed the whole thing. After having

---

13. That her memorial in New York on 28 June 1969 occurred on the same day as the Stonewall Riots would forever link Judy Garland to the modern gay rights movement. Indeed some claim that the emotional charge of her funeral, which was observed by thousands of gay men, was a catalyst for a section of the rioters. It was not so much that Garland's spirit itself had inspired the rioters but the fact that so many obviously gay individuals had gathered together to pay tribute to her that it became apparent that sheer strength of numbers could have a positive effect in fighting back at the victimisation that the gay community had been suffering at the hands of a bigoted police force. When yet another police raid occurred at the Stonewall Inn in Greenwich Village, a riot ensued.

failed to make her original flight due to a hangover, her rescheduled flight had been cancelled, forcing her to plane hop from city to city with long layovers in between, finally making it into London with only hours to spare. 'I sang my ass off that night – all the pain to get there was put into that one song,' she would later tell a journalist. Kate, who was still recuperating in Montreal, appeared for the second night only, which was filmed for a DVD release and an edited television show.

'This is insane, right?' Rufus announced by way of introduction. The sheer oddness of the idea of channelling Judy Garland at what was her traditional London home and the positive reports from the New York shows was enough to ensure that the concerts had been instant sell-outs. Unfortunately, on the first night there were swathes of empty seats in the stalls (which were filled at the interval by willing recruits from the balcony who had gone outside for a cigarette), perhaps indicating that many of the invited celebrity guests had either declined or chosen to go the following week when the cameras would be rolling. Nevertheless, the reviews of the first night were uniformly excellent, with even those who inevitably gasped at Martha's immense 'Stormy Weather' acknowledging that a night of sister Wainwright singing standards might have grated, whereas Rufus' charisma had sustained two hours of innuendo, kitsch and old-fashioned entertainment.

That Rufus found the material as difficult to perform as he said he did was evidenced in a close to disastrous concert at L'Olympia in Paris that was sandwiched between the two London dates. Under the weather and visibly tired, it seemed to be a show too far. Rufus' voice was hopelessly shot by the first couple of numbers and he resorted to speaking the lyrics, larking about and generally trying to make light of the situation by overindulging in the knowing camp winks that had blighted the project from its inception. Far worse than the croakiness that would appear during the Hollywood Bowl show, there was little excuse for continuing such a below-par performance beyond the intermission. Rufus or his management should have cancelled and offered a refund, partly out of self-preservation (the second Palladium show was looming and the film crews had already been booked), but mostly out of respect for the fans who had paid handsomely to attend. That the show still ended with a standing ovation speaks volumes of the warmth with which Rufus' fans hold him, unconsciously echoing the often slavishly indulgent approbation Judy herself received in some of her frail final shows, but said precious little about his actual performance on the night.

Rufus had recovered sufficiently to perform the second London date, when the combination of the presence of the cameras and a determination to overcome the disappointment of Paris resulted in a triumphal performance, which would probably rate as the best of all of his Judy concerts.

The concert DVD would be released at the end of 2007 alongside the live album from Carnegie Hall. Even on the eve of the launch of his new album, Rufus seemed convinced that the Judy Garland shows would somehow be seen as his greatest achievement, telling *Attitude* that it saddened him that he could end up scoring his biggest commercial success with an album of other people's songs. Whereas he knew that other similar projects, including Rod Stewart's *Great American Songbook* series, had been considered artistically questionable and was keen to distance himself from them ('It's ten steps away from that,' he snapped when asked if he was approaching Stewart's territory), he had also seen them achieve huge success. Was it too much of a stretch to think that *Rufus Does Judy at Carnegie Hall* would follow Rod the Mod's path to platinum discs? In the end it was. Not helped by a pair of unforgivably dire sleeves – the DVD looks like it is a bad Seventies rock opera and the album cover features a photograph of Rufus by Jack Pierson that captures him looking so despondent it's as if he's reacting to the news that Miss Gulch actually had succeeded in getting Toto put to sleep – and put back to December from the originally planned September release, the album was lost in the pre-Christmas product glut and barely brushed the charts.

By contrast, the sleeve to *Release the Stars* extended the attention to detail that had been put into the creation of the music. The cover and booklet featured a detail of Athena attacking the giants from one of the friezes of the Great Altar of Zeus that Rufus had photographed when he had visited the Pergamon Museum with Jörn on one of their frequent trips around Berlin's Museum Island. The booklet also featured photographs of Rufus resplendent in his monogrammed lederhosen taken by acclaimed artist Sam Taylor-Wood[14] as well as photos by Jörn and half-sister Lucy Roche. And to demonstrate that Rufus had seen the album through to absolute completion, he had even designed the lettering on the front cover.

The first push for *Release the Stars* came with the release of the 'Going To A Town' single, with an accompanying promotional video that saw Rufus again directed by Sophie Muller. The sombre film features Rufus trapped in a concrete cell with a rosebush with golden leaves and a laurel crown hanging on the wall. As the song progresses, a cascade of falling rose petals is projected into the room, looking like splattering blood, and then three veiled women hold him as if crucified and place the laurel wreath on his head. Heavy with symbolism – the laurel crown of the Roman poet becoming Jesus' crown of thorns, the red rose as an allusion to martyrdom and to the Passion of Christ – Muller's treatment is a fitting accompaniment to one of Rufus' most accomplished songs.

The lyrics may have been highly critical of America but despite Rufus' fears (or perhaps secret hopes) that he might end up 'doing a Dixie Chicks' and cause controversy by speaking out against the government, it was never really likely to happen. When in 2003 the Dixie Chicks had infamously admitted that they were ashamed that George Bush was a fellow Texan, the controversy they caused was fuelled by the fact that their traditional country fan base was predominantly Republican. Rufus' fans were more likely to cheer a song promoting tolerance and forgiveness than to rush to throw his CDs under a bulldozer as Dixie Chicks fans had been encouraged to do at the height of the protest against them. And as Rufus rightly stated: 'Part of being a good American right now is exercising your right to free speech – that's what this country is all about, supposedly.'

The meaning of the song was clear and there could be no mistaking what he was singing about. Although it wouldn't change his style of singing completely, this song in particular demonstrated

14. Sam Taylor-Wood, a Turner Prize nominee, has herself made recordings with the Pet Shop Boys under the pseudonym Kiki Kokova. Her former partner Jay Jopling is one of the most influential art dealers in the world and in 2005 flew Rufus to the Venice Biennale to play at the private party of Gilbert and George, who were Britain's representatives at the event.

some slight alterations to his approach to phrasing: less vibrato, less melismatic wandering around the syllables. It was something that directly related to his previous project. Rufus was asked whether he had taken anything from the Judy Garland concerts into his own music. 'I was drenched in some of the greatest lyrics ever written,' he replied. 'I just realised the importance of having the audience understand what you're saying, and that your diction should really be the centre of your singing style and that every word should be crystal clear – and I haven't always done that. I've been accused of slurring my words – and it's probably true, but I don't think it's the case with this album.'

Helped by some healthy airplay for the single, the album debuted in the UK chart at number two and would become his best-selling album around the world. Despite his best efforts, it was not necessarily any more commercial than his earlier albums but he had gradually been picking up fans as his career progressed and his easy way with television, press and radio and his predilection for a pithy soundbite meant that whenever he had something to promote, he could find his way into the press or the airwaves whether it was through taking bitchy swipes at Madonna or cosying up to the future British prime minister on a breakfast television show.

Rufus looked upon his decade-long climb up the chart as an ongoing battle to achieve the recognition and the sales that he had always felt he deserved. He explained to *Attitude* how he had been striving towards this point from the beginning: '[I have worked] on this like a pyramid structure, building it up stone by stone. I've spent years being aloof and mysterious in my ivory tower. I think if you are going to do what you want to do and be as challenging as you want to be in this day and age and not completely suck everybody's penis, you have to treat the music industry as a type of war.'

If the ultimate aim of 'Rufus versus the music industry' was higher chart placing and higher sales, then his decision to have his Pet Shop Boy mentor vet *Release the Stars* for commercial appeal was vindicated. For Rufus, the UK chart success of the album was confirmation that what he had described as 'going for the sound of cash registers' had been the correct thing to do. But although the album was a comparative success by his own sales standards, it was by no means a huge smash. After its debut at number two in the UK chart, it was out of the Top 20 the following week and soon dropping away from the chart altogether. It was a sales pattern similar to an artist like Morrissey, whose loyal fan base would ensure high chart placings in the first week of sales but whose limited general appeal would see subsequent weekly sales plummet. Nevertheless, in the UK at least, it did give Rufus his first certified gold record, selling over 100,000 copies. Despite his UK success, when it became clear that the album had not provided the crossover hit that he had been looking for and the tills of the world weren't ringing in quite the way he had hoped, Rufus would joke that in fact he'd been mis-quoted and had actually said that the album *had* the 'sound of cash registers' on it, hidden among the brass, strings and layered voices.

Release the Stars is a good album that could have been a great one. Songs like 'Leaving For Paris', almost Cole Porter sings Satie, 'Nobody's Off The Hook', a sweet song about Teddy Thompson and 'Not Ready To Love', which is Radiohead meets Bread via 10cc, show just how exhilarating the proposed minimalist album could have been. This is not to say that the baroque flashes and com-plicated arrangements in many of the other numbers fail in them-selves, just that for the most part, they never soar to the heights of some of the biggest *Want* songs.

The opening song, 'Do I Disappoint You' has everything but the proverbial kitchen sink thrown at it – it could be the song written specifically to prove his mother's suggestion that his songs were 'somewhere over the top'. But for all its bluster and portentous backing vocals, it never really convinces and teeters on the brink of sounding like something from a Disney parade. The title may be rhetorical but it's easy to imagine many first-time listeners lured in by radio plays of the single, tentatively thinking, 'Well yes, I think you do.' At least the scheduling of 'Going To A Town' as the following song puts everything back on track.

'Rules and Regulations' was a song that had originally been planned for Robert Wilson's soccer opera. It was released as a down-load-only single in the UK and was even given a video in which Rufus and a variety of moustachioed men in Edwardian-era long johns do synchronised exercises in the assembly hall of a north London boarding school. Amusing though the video was, the song was not really single material. A far better choice would have been the sublime 'Sanssouci' with its fairy-tale harp and spiralling vocal hook. This was Rufus' ode to Frederick the Great's rococo palace outside Berlin (although at the time he wrote the song, he hadn't actually visited it), where the king would play without a care. In his famous children's story Oscar Wilde reveals that the Happy Prince is so called because he used to live at Sanssouci, 'where sorrow is not allowed to enter'. In Rufus' version, the palace exists as a bittersweet reminder of his wilder times, with lines referencing his debauched New York period. He wistfully imagines going back to those days before the vision gutters and the carefree princes of Sanssouci disappear like ghosts.

'Tulsa', a song about a night spent drinking with Killers front man Brandon Flowers, is almost turned into slash-fiction by Rufus' opening line 'You taste of potato chips in the morning' and its shameless hint of (imagined) intimacy.

If the elegantly coutured verses of 'Slideshow' are unfortunately bludgeoned by a bombastic and overpowering chorus – when the verse moves into the chorus, it's as if an immaculately tailored suit had been ripped off to reveal a Day-Glo jumpsuit with 'Look At Me' spray-painted across the chest – then at least Rufus showed in the languid, high-kicking title track that he was capable of creating his own big show-tune to rival the songs he had been singing in his Judy concerts. It's easy to imagine Garland belting out the line 'old Hollywood is over' in a Busby Berkeley version of 'Release The Stars', leading a troupe of movie stars through the gates of Paramount Studios and dancing along Melrose Avenue ready to save the world.

The reviews of the album, which Rufus had taken to calling his 'accidental masterpiece', because it had turned out so different from how he had first envisaged it, were encouraging. *Uncut* called it an 'opulent masterpiece' and *Mojo* likened it to the Beach Boys *SMiLE*: 'It extends the language of pop, setting a fearsome standard for anyone equal to the challenge of matching [its] limitless invention.' Even the *New York Post*, in a one-star review that sought to maul the disc, called it 'musically elitist ... out of step with everything mainstream' which by most rational criteria, at least outside the pages of a lurid tabloid, would have been considered a recommendation.

In order to capitalise on the positive response to *Release the Stars* and determined to push himself as hard as he could in what he was calling his 'Jesus' year, Rufus soon found himself committed to a seemingly endless tour. Beginning at the Coachella Festival in April 2007, he would play more than 150 shows within a 12-month period travelling across Europe, the US, Australia and the Far East.

Aside, of course, from the final Judy show at the Hollywood Bowl, the vast majority of the shows were with a full band and entailed a complicated two-part set that contained most of the new album mixed with a few earlier songs. There would be no support and Rufus and his musicians would carry the entire evening's entertainment in a show that ran for almost three hours. The first section of the night would end with the comparatively rocking 'Between My Legs', on which a member of the audience who had been pre-selected via an online fan competition to take on Sian Phillips' narration, joined the band on stage (occasionally a celebrity would be roped in, including a bewildered-looking Phillips herself in London and a bearded Jake Gyllenhaal preposterously hamming it up like it was cod-Shakespeare in New York). But this was nothing compared to the number that Rufus had worked up for the grand finale. After returning for the first encore solo at the piano enveloped in a towelling bath robe, Rufus would begin to apply make-up and earrings and slip into a pair of high heels before throwing off his gown and revealing a Judy Garland signature look of jacket, stockings and hat and embarking on a (mimed) rendition of 'Get Happy', complete with comically chaotic choreography from his band members. In all of the time that Rufus played with being Judy, he never looked as comfortable (and never nearly so happy) as he did during these tour dates dressed as a woman who was dressed as a man. It was guaranteed to bring the house down.

His current band was the largest he had ever toured with and moving them around from town to town, from hotel to hotel, was expensive. Not to mention all the little extras that Rufus deemed necessary for putting on a good show. Before the tour started, he had even gone so far as spending $1,000 on brooches to jazz up the band's stage outfits. Almost every night was a sell-out but the books only just about balanced. The *Release the Stars* tour certainly didn't yield the kind of income that Rufus was hoping to grow accustomed to. In order to generate some money, almost as soon as the band tour was over he found himself back on the road returning to many of the same cities he had earlier visited. This time he performed alone, just a piano and his acoustic guitar. On the solo shows he was sometimes supported by friends or relations. Teddy Thompson, who was promoting his album of country cover versions *Up Front and Down Low*,[15] was a frequent opener, as was Loudon's sister Sloan and Lucy Roche, Rufus' half-sister, who was beginning to make a name for herself as the latest member of the Wainwright clan to pick up a guitar.[16]

If the grinding tour schedule was beginning to take its toll, then for the most part Rufus managed to grin and bear it. At a time when perhaps artistically he may have been better served being able to take the time out to seriously work on his opera commission, he found himself pinballing from the US to Europe and back again and slotting in radio sessions, television appearances and even a small role as a singing prince in the Canadian arthouse film *L'Âge des Ténèbres* (dir. Denys Arcand 2007) as he went. His gruelling work schedule didn't go unnoticed and if a journalist enquired as to why he was touring so hard, he admitted to the difficulties of maintaining the lifestyle he wanted through playing music. In a podcast recorded for *The Times* newspaper in May 2007, Peter Paphides pertinently enquired as to whether Rufus had recouped the money that had

---

15. Rufus contributed a string arrangement to the album which was recorded at Brad Albetta's studio in Brooklyn. It went some way to realign Thompson's musical direction, or at least the public perception of it. It sold so poorly that when asked what he had learned in making it, Thompson replied, 'Mostly that people don't like country music.' But Thompson had always seemed more confident when playing country material rather than folk or pop. He continued opening for Rufus on a number of shows right through to the release of his own excellent 2008 album *A Piece of What You Need*. This was produced by Marius de Vries, who he had met when he had guested on the *Want* album sessions. Rufus has a cameo as a roller-skating, drape-suited organist in the entertaining video for Thompson's 2008 single 'In My Arms', a song that had a hint of Dire Straits about it and the kind of catchy chorus that once would have guaranteed it enough radio play for a nation of builders and delivery drivers to have learned to cheerfully whistle along to the chorus.

16. Lucy Wainwright Roche had been working as a teacher of second- and third-grade pupils in New York. Although she had sung backing vocals for Rufus, she hadn't considered a career in music. In 2007 she took time out to investigate her songwriting and after releasing a well-received debut EP, *8 Songs*, decided to play music full time. She has toured extensively with Loudon and the release of her follow-up CD, *8 More*, in 2008, showed that she was another remarkable musician in her own right.

been invested in him. The response was couched in humour but beneath his usual good-natured media banter, Rufus was being brutally honest about the root of his ongoing financial struggle. 'Oh no, I'm a long way from that event. When I was very young I was signed to DreamWorks. And God bless Lenny Waronker and Mo Ostin, all those big record moguls of the time that signed me and had the guts to do so. But really they are from hell and they're representatives of Satan. Truly. [laughs] 'Cause they slipped me into this contractual jungle which I think happens to everyone that doesn't have a proper lawyer or manager, which I had neither . . . So, whatever, it's just the way it is . . . And I also love making very expensive records.'

When Paphides asked whether there was anything that could be done about the situation, Rufus initially suggested that if his label would like to drop him (thereby freeing him of his obligation and allowing him to sign with another label and, importantly, a clean slate), then they should 'feel free', before he backtracked and some-what unconvincingly thanked the label for having allowed him to concentrate on his music without worrying about the accounting.

In the years since Rufus had first signed his deal, the music industry had changed completely. DreamWorks itself had long since been bought out and over the years the subsequent companies had been resized and restructured as the industry as a whole tried to come to terms with changes in technology and with the public's evolving tastes of how it wanted to own and acquire music (and especially whether it actually wanted to pay for any of it). With more emphasis on downloading and the increased opportunity for direct interactivity between fans and bands via the internet, many of the roles that record companies had traditionally carved out for themselves seemed increasingly redundant. A number of major artists who were coming to the end of traditional contracts could see the labels as nothing more than glorified marketing inter-mediaries and demanded a fairer slice of the pie.

If more and more albums were being downloaded rather than pur-chased over the counter, why couldn't the artists themselves control this new means of distribution? Of course many small independent bands did just that, but it wasn't until the pioneering pay-what-you-like online release of Radiohead's *In Rainbows* in October 2007 grabbed news headlines that the mainstream cottoned on.

Rufus may have been one of the last musicians to have benefited from the nurturing of an old-fashioned record label. It's highly unlikely that any future artist would receive such continued financial backing without delivering a bona fide hit. In the current climate, a band could record an album and find themselves dropped, with the album permanently shelved if the record company considered that what they had recorded was not commercial enough. Why throw good money after bad? Why wait and see if an artist can develop when it's easier and cheaper to try somebody else? Or, if you are the band, why bother looking for a label in the first place? It's a problem highlighted by many insiders who see the industry as being in a state of turmoil, if not terminal decline.

Nic Harcourt, music director of KCRW, the influential Californian radio station that has long supported marginal artists like Rufus and Martha[17] throughout their careers by playing their records and bringing them in for live sessions, identifies a change in attitude coming from the bands themselves. 'Many of the bands that we play, or that come in and record sessions for us, might not even have record deals. Perhaps the smart ones are not even looking for a deal any more. There are new ways to work.'

Harcourt is of the opinion that this shake-up is no bad thing. 'Artists like Rufus, and Martha for that matter, are talented enough to move with the times. And Rufus has matured. He's more interesting now than he was ten years ago and he is still developing. If his record label thinks he is going to sell a million records well . . . he's not going to sell a million records, but then nobody is going to sell a million records any more . . .'

The old-style record contract was certainly a mixed blessing. If you were an aspiring musician, the opportunity for almost unlimited funds for recording would be enough to turn your head. If you were commercially successful then the hundreds of thousands of dollars

---

17. In fact, as producer of their flagship music show *Morning Becomes Eclectic* Ariana Morgenstern was pleased to tell me when I visited the station in August 2008 that KCRW must be the only radio station to have hosted live sessions by the whole family. As well as more recent performances by Rufus and Martha, Kate and Anna appeared (with Rufus on backing vocals) in February 1997, playing songs from *Matapedia* and Loudon has visited the station a number of times.

invested in you would eventually be recouped and everybody would start earning. But if you spent a decade waiting and waiting for the hit that would invigorate the back catalogue, waiting for the commercial success that never came, you could be buried by a debt that grew with each release.

The reality is that most artists don't turn a profit. As an example, EMI, another major label, had 14,000 artists under contract through the first seven years of the millennium and 85 per cent of these made no money at all. Was it any wonder that one of EMI's regular annual expenses was a multi-million-dollar bill for disposing of unsold CDs?[18] If you were permanently playing catch-up on the costs of albums from years before, perhaps you too would be not so secretly hoping that you might get dropped so that you could start from scratch somewhere else.

Despite the increasing frequency of his gripes to the press about having no money, for better or worse Rufus was tied to his ongoing contract, remaining indebted to the label and seemingly on a never-ending tour.

5.5

Throughout 2007 Martha was recording her second album. The deal she had struck with Drowned In Sound allowed her to license her albums to different labels in different territories so that each label would provide a portion of her costs. She might not have had access to the type of funds that Rufus had been able to call on, but in many ways her frugal budgeting allowed her more independence and freedom to call her own shots. And if the album actually made some money she would get a share of the profits. The original plan was for the album to appear at some point in 2007 but commitments to

---

18. The disposal of unsold CDs as industrial waste is an illuminating example of how the music industry should be considered an 'industry' just like any other and stripped of its pretensions to be somehow elevated to 'art'. In 2007 the UK press gleefully reported how millions of copies of Robbie Williams' much unloved *Rudebox* album had been sent to China to be crushed and used as aggregate for the country's new building projects. Ironically, back in the 1990s the labels used to send unsold CDs to China to be sold cheaply in Chinese stores to avoid having to pay for their disposal as industrial waste. These days they literally can't give flop CDs away.

other projects, not least her wedding to Brad Albetta[19] in September, and the fact that she had chosen to record the songs in a variety of studios with different producers rather than in one sustained session, resulted in the release date being pushed back.

In April she had appeared in a new version of Kurt Weill's *The Seven Deadly Sins* at the Royal Opera House. The short ballet chanté tells the story of Anna and her encounters with each of the deadly sins in turn. It is performed as a schizophrenic double act as Anna 1 (the singer) shadows Anna 2 (the dancer) through a series of choreographed tableaux. The new staging, by Will Tuckett, featured most of the female dancers in lingerie, leading UK tabloid newspaper the *Sun* to froth that it was the 'most shocking ballet ever', the headline blaring that it was 'Tutu Much!' In truth, the costuming was perhaps as much to distract from the clunking Bertolt Brecht script, partially rescued by using W.H. Auden's English translation, as it was to titillate the regular staid opera house crowd.

Vaguely recalling the ballet lessons she had taken as a child and now certain that she had made the right decision to drop out of acting classes to concentrate on music, Martha admitted that the rehearsal process for the ballet had been difficult. 'This show has really called upon my showbiz chops,' she told the *Independent* during one of her rehearsals, where she was surrounded by ballet dancers who would arrive early and work cripplingly long hours, day after day. 'I wouldn't do this as a full-time career. As a singer-songwriter you keep your own hours. I like the freedom of that existence. I don't really do what the record company tells me. This experience has certainly taught me to enjoy the weekends.'

Martha was generally praised for her performance; what criticism the show received revolved around the difficulties in performing *The Seven Deadly Sins* at all. Earlier stagings of the piece by choreographers as varied, and as talented, as George Balanchine and Kenneth MacMillan have rarely, if ever, been revisited, leading to

---

19. Unsurprisingly there was no shortage of friends and family prepared to sing at the wedding. Teddy Thompson and Jenni Muldaur serenaded the newlyweds with a version of 'Viva Las Vegas' before a reception that evolved into an all-night open mike with Ed Harcourt, Emmylou Harris, Joe Boyd, Jimmy Fallon, Linda Thompson and all of the immediate family among the performers. 'I could have sold tickets,' Martha later joked to the *Sunday Times*, 'but the evening was actually stolen by Brad's dad who was a Sinatra-style crooner in New York. He sang some big standard and everyone was up dancing in couples.'

the general opinion that the work itself is flawed and should only be performed, if at all, as a concert piece. So it was testament to the success of the show that it was revived in 2009 with Martha invited to reprise her role.

If her wedding was the personal highlight of the year, then her musical highlight could well have been the unusual collaborative work she embarked upon alongside Teddy Thompson in December. It was one thing to join in with a fellow folk or rock musician but quite another to agree to perform live, after only two afternoons' rehearsal, with a 'human beatboxer' at the high-profile, all-sold-out Queen Elizabeth Hall in London. It demonstrated how she had shaken off her earlier insecurities and how she was now unafraid to take chances, even if she had no idea whether the experiment would work or if she was going to be left exposed in front of an audience.

Shlomo was Artist in Residence at the Southbank Centre and ran a series of events called 'Music Through Unconventional Means', where he collaborated live with guest musicians using his remarkable ability to create rhythms and sound-effects using only his mouth. After playing short introductory solo sets, a nervous-looking Martha and Teddy shuffled out with Shlomo and he explained how they had only got together two days earlier and weren't sure if everything was going to work out first time. 'We're going to surprise you. It's something nobody will be expecting,' said Shlomo. 'There's no music,' said Teddy Thompson. 'He's going to take a big shit on stage,' laughed Martha, pointing at Shlomo, beaming in his baggy jeans and Drool Skool T-shirt. The three worked together and as duos playing their own songs and cover versions. Teddy sang 'Walk Like An Egyptian', Martha sang 'Don't Think Twice, It's All Right', reading the words from a sheet of paper. At one point, with Shlomo dropping slow beats like Bristol trip-hop, Martha vamped her way through an improvised song, revealing a hitherto undisclosed ability to perform as a pure wailing soul diva. The concert was a triumph.

From her much delayed start as a solo performer, Martha was gradually creeping into the public's consciousness and, as well as her ever-increasing confidence and charisma in her own solo concerts, it was left-field choices like the Shlomo collaboration, the Royal Opera House shows and the slow-burning idea she had of an album and

concert series of Edith Piaf songs (that she would begin publicly
with a trial performance at the tiny, and temporary, Spiegelworld
cabaret tent in New York in September 2008) that clearly demonstrated how far her gradual evolution into an artist in her own
right had come. Her name would appear in a newspaper and increasingly it wouldn't immediately be followed by Rufus' as a means of
explaining who she was.

By the time her eagerly awaited second album was released in
May 2008, she had reached the stage where she could sell out the
2,500 seats of the Southbank's larger venue, the Royal Festival Hall,
weeks before show time and be booked to headline ever more
prestigious venues in other countries around the world.

In the unspoken race for success that the family had been privately engaged in since Loudon and Kate first traded verses, and
which ramped up after Rufus started writing songs, Martha was
gaining ground on her brother. It seemed that, commercially at least,
it was inevitable that Martha would eventually take the lead. Loudon
was by now somewhat grudgingly resigned to coming in a distant
third with Kate and Anna having more or less withdrawn from
competition.[20]

It was close to 40 years in the business for Loudon. And in spite
of having inadvertently instigated a seismic shift in mainstream
Hollywood comedy by sparking the early creative inventions of
Judd Apatow, what he still hankered after was respect as an original
songwriter and musician. While other artists who had begun in the
1960s had been rediscovered and reinvestigated – indeed, over the
decades some had even been rediscovered, forgotten again and then
rediscovered once more – Loudon still undeservedly languished as
a somewhat marginal figure, never successful enough to appear as

20. The sisters still received awards, however. In February 2008, Anna's song 'Heart Like
A Wheel' had been inducted into the Canadian Songwriters Hall of Fame. Since Linda
Ronstadt had brought the song to public attention in 1974, it had been covered by more
than a dozen artists and had even been used, albeit rather inappropriately, for the title of
the 1983 biopic about the drag racer Shirley Muldowney. Rufus suggested that the song
was the reason that he was in music today. 'On several levels [the song] is responsible for
Kate and Anna's careers in music as well as mine and Martha's,' he explained to a Canadian
newspaper. 'My mother and aunt hadn't planned on being professional songwriters but
when Ronstadt picked up the song it altered their paths and accidentally led us all to a life
in showbusiness.' ('McGarrigle Family Reunites At Songwriters Gala', Greg Quill, the *Sun*,
28 February 2008.)

an established mainstream entertainer nor cool enough to be seen as an underground hero. As he grumbled to his friend and producer Joe Henry, there wasn't even a Loudon Wainwright retrospective box-set available. And surely the box-set was the mark of a truly important artist, one whose work, even in the download age, deserved to be archived – multiple compact discs, box, book and all. It seemed an obvious way to celebrate what would be the ruby anniversary of his first hitting the stages of New York in 1968. Loudon had even gone so far as to pencil in the tracks that he would include on it: three discs of old material and then an extra disc of new versions of old songs using the musicians with whom he had recorded *Strange Weirdos*.

After asking around, Loudon was dismayed to find that there were no takers for the box-set idea but he decided to record the 'bonus' disc in any case. With Henry producing, he recorded new versions of songs from his first four records, songs like 'The Man Who Couldn't Cry', 'Motel Blues' and 'Be Careful There's a Baby in the House'. Some of the songs he could hardly remember and found himself having to listen to the original LPs in order to learn the material. He was often surprised by what he heard. 'I wondered "What happened? I used to be so cute!"' he told *Uncut*. 'Listening to them was even more unsettling. The high, keening vocals put me off – sounds like a strange young man I'm not sure I'd care to hang out with. Good writer, though.'

Loudon chose to release the album as it was, without the hoped for retrospective box, on the independent label Yep Roc in late summer 2008. He called the album *Recovery*, likening the recording process to recovering bones at an archaeological dig. But the songs he had disinterred were certainly not curious fossilised relics to be dusted down and rearranged for display. In some ways it was ironic that Loudon was now recording songs with a band that he had originally fought so hard to be allowed to play sparse and solo on his early records. It was also typically perverse that while other artists had received acclaim by reinvestigating their earlier material by stripping it away and performing it 'unplugged', Loudon had chosen to 'plug in' and flesh out the bones. The choice of material – songs that now resonated in new ways with the passage of time and the gaining of age and wisdom – meant that this was no dewy-eyed nostalgia trip but a serious re-evaluation of his songwriting and a meditation on change and on ageing itself.

It was certainly difficult to listen to the rendering of *Album II*'s meditation on the perils of fame, 'Saw Your Name In The Paper', without thinking of Rufus and Martha and familial rivalry.

The May release of Martha's second album had gone some way to cementing her position as the Wainwright most likely to achieve sustained commercial success. The album featured guest slots from older musicians like Donald Fagen and Garth Hudson – both of whom she claims to have turned to so that she could sound out whether her songs were actually any good – and Pete Townshend, who she had met after being asked to perform on Townshend's partner Rachel Fuller's internet radio show. Rufus also appeared, but Martha claimed that her 'secret weapon' was the backing vocals of Anna's daughter Lily Lanken.

The album had almost been named after its opening track and first single, 'Bleeding All Over You', a pulsing dissection of an obsessive love affair. 'Too menstrual,' decided Martha, 'I'd have to give away a tampon with every copy.' Instead, she chose the song's Loudon-esque lyrical hook 'I know you're married but I've got feelings too' as the album's title.

For the second single, 'You Cheated Me', a video was directed by Canadian film-maker Maxime Giroux that hinted at the duality of the Anna character in *The Seven Deadly Sins* and reflected the new glamorous Martha, photographed reclining on a sofa or rolling on a bed, on the album sleeve and in promotional shots. The video itself was risqué enough to have to have some shots of Martha 'making out', edited to make it appropriate for all ages broadcasts. The song, sounding somewhere between Blondie, Fleetwood Mac and Shania Twain, was an unabashed attempt at writing a straight pop song: 'I purposely set out to write a pop song and was finished in 20 minutes,' said Martha. 'Then, having written it so quickly, I couldn't work out how to sing it. It just didn't feel like one of my songs. I considered sending it to someone else. Madonna maybe.'

Whereas her debut was the result of years of introspection and what she would term 'navel gazing', the follow-up was more varied, taking its subject matter from beyond the confines of her personal life. 'With this album, I've looked outside myself, to show that the

world is a vast, scary, dark place,' she explained to the *Guardian*.
'There's more to life than your own problems. There's more to sing
about.'

That may be so, but the best songs on the album are still haunted
by personal experience, from the oppressive doom march of 'In The
Middle of the Night', a response to Kate's cancer, to the odd country
number 'The George Song' about the suicide of a former lover. 'Niger
River' is an intense love song to her husband composed while
she was visiting Mali as part of Damon Albarn's Africa Express
educational charity project that sought to bridge the gap between
African and Western musicians. Even the weakest original song
'Hearts Club Band' is partially rescued by a stanza about Loudon's
relentless songwriting and how it always made her want to tell him
to shut up. Considering the song that she had sung for him on
Martha Wainwright, he got off lightly.

Martha saw the new album as having evolved out of her debut.
'This record is more complicated,' she explained. 'It's dramatic and
intense like the first, but not as desperately so. It has more of a sense
of humour. There's more of a pop-rock feel, more joy – all the things
that I feel. It's a real honest representation of who I am.'

Overall it was an understandably slicker affair than her debut,
but it perhaps lacks the first album's warmth and cohesion. It is
more a compilation of songs than an album constructed to be listened
to as a whole. One of the strengths of the debut was the way that
the tracks flowed. Here the songs flit between sounds and styles.
Indeed, things almost grind to a complete halt with a pleasant but
pointless cover version of 'See Emily Play' (featuring Kate and Anna
and the result of them having played the song at a Joe Boyd-arranged
Syd Barrett tribute concert at the Barbican in 2007) and a dreadful,
plodding Eurythmics cover. (Wisely, the latter was left off the UK
version of the album, reportedly at the request of the UK label.)
Nevertheless, the record garnered the best reviews of her career
from both the music press and mainstream newspapers and she
found herself on the covers of magazines and newspaper sup-
plements and invited onto the kind of television talk shows that she
would usually have only appeared on as part of Rufus' band. Even
that most populist of UK tabloids, the *Sun*, perhaps alerted to her
by the previous year's 'explicit' ballet, ran a full-page interview and

named her as a 'fast emerging, wonderful, expressive artist'.

By the summer of 2008, Rufus' tour schedule had eased off to the point where he was playing only short strings of dates, appearing at festivals or headlining one-off special events. One of these was an appearance at a fundraising concert at Robert Wilson's Watermill Center on Long Island where he topped a bill that included opera legend Jessye Norman and which turned into a mini-family show with the appearance of Kate, Anna and Martha, who all played solo songs.

Over his summer concerts he had begun to introduce new work into his solo set, based on Shakespearean sonnets. He had already recorded one sonnet for a compilation album *When Love Speaks* back in 2002 but these new settings were written to form part of a major Robert Wilson production that he had agreed to score, undoubtedly without requiring too much encouragement from his boyfriend Jörn, who remained Wilson's assistant.

Although he had originally planned to devote a block of time to concentrate solely on the composition of his opera, Rufus found himself having to work on it between the sonnets project and all of the other side projects to which he regularly committed.[21] Extra-curricular activity since *Release the Stars* had already included guest slots on albums by Joan As Police Woman, Linda Thompson, Ann Wilson and Marianne Faithfull; an appearance on a Judy Collins tribute album; and a live performance as part of the *Plague Songs* event at London's Barbican.

---

21. Aside from the sonnets, another project that had bubbled along since earlier in the year was Blackout Sabbath, Rufus' eco-friendly idea for everybody to turn off their power for a day every summer solstice. He had been inspired by the sense of community that he had experienced during the New York blackouts in 2003 and by an increasing concern about the environment. Although undoubtedly well intentioned, the project seemed ill-defined, if not somehow half-hearted, perhaps due to his inability to fully commit time to it. It was launched on 19 March 2008 with a special candle lit acoustic performance at New York's Angel Orensanz Center, a beautiful artist's space that had previously been a synagogue, at which Rufus appeared with Martha and friends, including Beth Orton and Paul Simon's son Harper, and played a short set of solo songs and cover versions (including the Bee Gees' 'Stayin' Alive'). The performance was filmed by Albert Maysles, which led some cynics, especially those sat back from the first couple of rows and who could neither hear anything nor see anything in the gloom, to suggest that far from kick-starting a new eco-movement (after all, the show was months in advance of the proposed date for the Blackout Sabbath on which the live show would have made more sense), the ticket-holders had in effect funded a video shoot.

None of this would have mattered had he been working to the original open-ended schedule of the Met's commission. Back in 2006 when he had first begun composing, he had stated that he hoped to get the opera finished within five years, realising there was no particular rush and citing the example of Janáček, who he admitted to be using as a template, who had been almost 50 before he had achieved operatic success. But Rufus seemed determined to push his work along as quickly as he could. Perhaps he was too used to working to a pop musician's timescale, when idea, execution and (hopeful) approbation could be achieved within a year or two to be able to shift to the decelerated expectations of the opera world. Opera moves incredibly slowly, with even revivals of classic tried-and-tested productions taking years of planning before they reach the stage of the opera house.

When the *New York Times* had checked in with Peter Gelb in July 2007, the Met's manager had been unconcerned that little progress seemed to have been made by the majority of the musicians he had asked to take part; indeed, many had not even started on their compositions some 18 months on. 'It's hard to put a deadline on creativity in the world of opera,' admitted Gelb. 'The deadline is when they get the job done.'

Rufus had certainly been furthest along with his work and had already prepared a short extract to be played at a private preview for Gelb and other officials at a rehearsal hall at the Met as early as June 2007. He had long since announced the opera was to be called *Prima Donna* and was to be about a day in the life of an elderly singer who falls in love with a journalist. Rufus was the only musician in the group who had been commissioned who had chosen to write the libretto himself.

Although he was experienced enough in writing song lyrics, the construction of a libretto was at another level entirely. As far back as 1999, he had suggested that whereas a melody would come to him as if it had arrived from another planet, a lyric was something that he had to consciously work on. 'When you write a melody, it's not necessarily you writing it – it's like you're channelling some type of music that already exists . . . Any great composer is just taking from God . . . or something. But the words, for me personally, are the most difficult, challenging part.' In many of his songs, he had achieved a near-perfect balance between the sound and emotional intensity of the words by ignoring explicit meaning by mixing short descriptive passages with enigmatic images and oblique phrasing, letting the vocal lines flow, becoming something other than just words on a page. The poet C. Day Lewis likened successful lyrics for music as being like water-weed, which comes fully alive only in the 'streams and eddies of melody'.[22] A good libretto had to achieve this and more. It would also need to carry a story and Rufus had rarely attempted narrative songwriting. He had once described opera as being 'like a laser beam of Western culture', when story, voice, music and design come together and exist in perfect harmony. The design and the casting for voices would be out of his hands but Rufus needed to ensure that the story, the words and the music were unified, a task so exacting that the esteemed opera critic Peter Conrad had once suggested that the balance of words and music was so antagonistic that 'Opera is the continuation of their warfare by other means.'

It would have been difficult enough even to adapt an already existing plot from another writer, but to work alone and completely from scratch was a daunting task that was further complicated by Rufus' decision to compose the work in French. He reasoned that the French language held a greater musicality. This raised a few eyebrows as, although he had been brought up in Montreal, he was far from fluent in French; in concert in France and Canada his pronouncements to the audience would occasionally slip into what the late satirist Miles Kington would have dubbed 'Franglais'.

Throughout 2007 and early 2008, Rufus had frequently spoken about 'the opera [he] was writing for the Met' and how it was 'a dream come true' to have been asked and was happy to tell every-body that he was enjoying frequent free tickets to any Met show he chose to attend, so it came as some surprise when he let slip in a Brazilian television interview in August 2008 that the premiere of the opera would no longer be taking place in New York at all, but at the 2009 Manchester International Festival.

Within weeks the Met were forced to make an announcement confirming that they were no longer interested in producing Rufus' opera. The official reason given was that the agreement had been

---

22. C. Day Lewis, *The Poetic Image*, Cape, 1947, UK.

that the opera was to be in English but Rufus was insisting that it had to be in French. It had certainly been no secret that it was being written in French. Although Gelb claimed that he had tried and failed to get Rufus to agree to translate the libretto into English, unofficial sources close to the opera house suggested this was merely an expedient excuse concocted by the Met's PR department that allowed both parties to walk away from the contract with reputations intact. The implication was that the early extracts of the work had fallen some way below what the opera house had expected.

In an interview with the *New York Times*, Rufus claimed that a further stumbling block had been that the Met had given him a provisional production date of 2014 as the earliest available slot which, even by opera standards, seemed excessively cautious for a project that they were truly committed to. 'I wanted to get it out as soon as possible,' said Rufus, 'because I'm an impatient pop star.'

Even if Rufus' confidence had not been bruised by the collapse of the Met commission, the availability of Manchester as an alternative location was fortuitous. Although he joked that Manchester was ideal because it was 'somewhere small so that if it's a complete failure, nobody knows about it', he would've been more than aware of the success of another pop musician's debut opera at the same festival in 2007. Damon Albarn's *Monkey: Journey to the West* proved to be hugely popular with audiences (despite being performed in Mandarin and being almost tuneless). That the critics' reception was lukewarm at best was overlooked or ignored by the public and it eventually had a sold-out season at London's Royal Opera House and an extended run in its own custom-built theatre within the O2 Arena in London's Docklands.

Whether Rufus had hurried the work to completion remained to be seen but whatever the reception *Prima Donna* eventually received, he would do well to remember his mentor Janáček, who was not only almost 50 before *Jenufa* provided him with his first successful opera but who had worked on that opera for nine years having already tried and failed twice before. These were merely the difficult first steps on what would undoubtedly be a long slow climb towards the rarefied heights of operatic success.

If Rufus was looking for a way to win over the doubters, outrage the opera snobs and slay what he would later refer to as 'the dragon of expectation', then his entrance into the lobby of Manchester's Palace Theatre[1] for the *Prima Donna* premiere on July 10th 2009 dressed as Verdi, complete with top hat and cane, and with Jörn at his side as a dapper Puccini look-a-like could not have been more effective. Of course, this moment of pure Rufusian camp delighted his fans and the family and friends who were gathered at the event (so much so that he actually restaged his entrance so that they could get another look at him) as much as it surely irritated the critics who were ready to dig their sharpened pencils into the upstart composer without even hearing a note.

The dressing-up was a masterstroke. A secret plan, long hatched and hinted at only by Rufus rubbing and pulling on his newly sprouting beard through the numerous press photo-shoots and publicity appearances he had done as the opening night drew closer. Did this pop singer really think he could compare himself to Verdi? The contemporary opera world expects a little conservative eccentricity and even accepts a certain amount of flamboyance, but fancy dress? On opening night? Before the critics had taken their seats Rufus had already wrong-footed them.

The germ of the idea for *Prima Donna* had originally come when Rufus had been watching archive footage of Maria Callas talking about her life and art to Lord Harewood. Callas defined the role of the great female singers as being the driving force behind all opera, not just as a voice but as the main instrument of the orchestra – the Prima Donna. 'The minute I heard that, the whole story just fell into my lap', Rufus explained. 'I was like, "Of course that's it. An opera about an opera singer." I can relate to it. As a singer, I know that world.'

Rufus' opera singer became Régine Saint Laurent – a reclusive soprano in Paris on Bastille Day in 1970 who is preparing to meet a

---

1. If Rufus had been looking for help from above he might have prayed to Judy Garland who'd made her first and only appearance in Manchester at the same theatre back in June 1951 as she rebuilt her career, after being dropped by MGM, with a series of comeback concerts in the United Kingdom.

journalist to discuss her distinguished career. Part Callas, part Norma Desmond, Rufus would guide St Laurent through a day-in-the-life where she would have to deal with her past and come to terms with her future. As the opera progresses we discover that this prima donna has not performed for six years and the arrival of the somewhat sycophantic journalist is the key to unlocking the mystery that drove her into self-imposed operatic exile.

As with many operas the story is slight and when written down just a little hokey. St Laurent, one of the biggest stars of her day, has sensationally quit singing after an opening night performance of her signature role in the opera *Aliénor d'Aquitaine* in which she played a queen, and her then lover, an equally celebrated tenor, played the king. The journalist, who himself happens to be an aspiring tenor and a long-time fan of St Laurent, persuades her to sing an extract of this opera with him and their singing reminds her of the passion she had once felt for her lover and sparks an instantaneous infatuation with the visiting writer. As their duet reaches its climax St Laurent's voice breaks down and once again she becomes mute.

The interview is abandoned only to be later rescheduled by the devoted butler Philippe. St Laurent listens to a recording of her legendary performance in *Aliénor d'Aquitaine* and prepares to meet the journalist for dinner. We discover that the reason she can no longer sing is that her heart was broken by her lover's infidelity with a member of the chorus but she feels a glimmer of hope has been rekindled by her meeting with the journalist. When he reappears he is in the company of his previously unmentioned fiancée, and for St Laurent all is lost once more. The prima donna announces that she will never sing again.

After the debacle of the Met's decision to drop the opera, The Manchester Festival's intervention and resurrection of *Prima Donna* benefited both Rufus and, more importantly, the work itself. The libretto as originally rejected by the Met had been overhauled with the assistance of Bernardette Colomine, a long-time friend of Rufus — who had once provided backing vocals on *Poses*. The most important contribution to the successful staging of the work came when Rufus was hooked up with Opera North and the young American director Daniel Kramer.

Kramer had made a name for himself as an innovative and experimental director and had won an award for his ominously creepy revival of Harrison Birtwhistle's *Punch and Judy* for English National Opera in 2008. The director's brief was to develop the opera as presented to him into a production that would maximise the drama of the story while allowing Rufus' vision to shine through. In the end this meant that the director helped to restructure the libretto, introduced flashbacks and reordered scenes for maximum impact, changes which, initially at least, Rufus found hard to accept. So used to making all of the important decisions himself, Rufus found that the compromises needed to be made in order to get a major production ready for the stage could be frustrating. 'Once I got to (dealing with) the singers and the producer it was a war in itself,' he would later recall. 'In opera everyone's a star. The pop world is very delineated – there's the pop star and everyone else. In opera you have the conductor, the composer . . . you have to battle it out. It's fantastic, but exhausting.'

After handing over the work to Kramer, Rufus sat in on some early rehearsals where he was initially resistant to allow the director to change anything. He likened the process to going through the pain of childbirth only to immediately hand over the baby to somebody else. In the spirit of compromise, and at Kramer's request, Rufus stepped aside as the staging was developed only coming back to the rehearsals a month or so ahead of the premiere. From mid-June Rufus was involved in the production on a daily basis, renting a cottage in Yorkshire so as to be permanently on hand as the opening night loomed closer.

The lead role of St Laurent had been given to Janis Kelly, a well-respected soprano who had a reputation for dependability and versatility. Kelly had long been an admirer of Rufus and had actually written a letter of encouragement to him when she had first heard he was writing an opera. Little did she expect that she would eventually become his Prima Donna. In interviews Kelly praised Rufus' commitment and vision and spoke about how hard everybody had worked to get the opera up and running: 'The opera is very close to Rufus' heart. Sometimes it was a bit difficult in that respect when those of us who'd worked all our lives in opera could see that little things would be difficult to do but in the end he did

compromise very well. To achieve what he's achieved is fantastic –
I'm so full of admiration for him. I threw my heart and soul into it
as well – we all did.'

Of course Rufus had been talking himself up for months before
Prima Donna finally opened, telling everybody that he was about
to breathe new life into the world of opera, explaining that he could,
single-handedly, revive a moribund art form. In reality much of this
was bluster and hyperbole and, as had often been the case in the
past, Rufus' rampant egomania and self-aggrandising proclamations
were a form of attack as self-defence, epitomised by the effrontery
of the Verdi costume, an impudence that disguised a genuine
concern that he might have bitten off more than he could chew.

When the reviews came in, many of them were very harsh but
almost all of them held at least a kernel of positive encouragement.
Janis Kelly's performance as St Laurent was universally praised as
were the innovative set design and lavish costumes. In fact, though
the received wisdom is that the opera was poorly received, there
were many more positive reviews than there were negative. Nobody
was calling it an unequivocal triumph but almost everybody agreed
that it was an entertaining work that hinted at a promising future.
By the time the opera had finished its run, even Rufus was prepared
to compromise his high opinion of himself and admit to some of the
work's shortcomings.

Much of the criticism stemmed from the flimsy plot. The set-up
would have made an exquisite pop song, indeed the idea of hope,
hopelessness and heartbreak had been used by Rufus to create
dramatic vignettes in earlier songs, but stretched over two hours
the story seemed inconsequential and the libretto awkward and
lacking insight and depth. The *Independent* called it 'at best banal,
at worst boring' and the *Daily Telegraph*'s Rupert Christiansen[2]
called the plot and characters 'the most awful hokum' and stated
that the opera was 'hammy and camp without being theatrically
exciting or grandly emotional' but even then he made it clear there
were plenty of positives and enough evidence to suggest that the
composer's next opera could be 'a real success'.

---

2. Christiansen wrote a superb book about the myth and majesty of the opera singer which
Rufus had mentioned in numerous interviews when talking about his concepts for his
opera. (Rupert Christiansen, *Prima Donna: A History*. Penguin Books, 1985)

While many of the critics honed in on the plot, others took umbrage at Rufus' seemingly dilettantish delight in referencing everybody from Berlioz to Verdi to Massenet to Mahler which seems to somehow miss the point. Rufus had hinted that *Prima Donna* was a love letter to opera itself and the passages that played tribute to great composers of the past were neither supposed to sneak in unidentified as if he was claiming them as his own nor be strewn liberally about the work as so much decorative pastiche. These were knowing winks and loving homage to past composers that were designed to put the opera into its proper context in the same way that the Puccini-esque reveal of a previously hidden romantic partner at the opera's climax was not meant to suggest that *Prima Donna* was to be directly compared to *Madam Butterfly*, but was merely to acknowledge an operatic convention. The stylistic shifts and self-aware references reflect that in the rarefied and fanciful un-reality of the *Prima Donna* universe in which his characters lived their lives other operas would happily co-exist.[3]

Before the Manchester run had ended it was announced that the show would be restaged in London and then later in 2010 in Canada and Australia. There would be time and opportunity for the work to mature and develop. And time for Rufus to consider his next move as an opera composer.

'I'm still trembling from the drama of opera,' he told the *Montreal Gazette* when he returned home from England. 'It was amazing. Most of the reviews were positive. Some were ecstatic, some were negative . . . The general consensus was that I survived the dragon. I haven't slain the dragon, but I survived. I fared very well. I got the piece up, people enjoyed it. Now other theatres are interested.

---

3. A number of critics picked up on a line in the libretto – 'It's like being in an opera' – and used it as evidence that Rufus was merely playing with the form, perhaps actually trapped within it, while not truly understanding it. While there are weak points in the work (and the pacing of the libretto is perhaps the weakest link of all) this self-referencing doesn't seem to me to be one of them. Indeed the fact that Rufus had knowingly created a work that tipped its hat to so many other composers whilst still retaining a uniquely Rufusian sonic architecture is actually quite remarkable. Like the world depicted in the video for the song *April Fools*, *Prima Donna* seems to exist in a parallel universe where life is defined by and created from opera rather than the other way around. Rufus has created a work that is so indebted to the romantic operas of the past that the way he has used elements of their sound and structure moves his own work into the realms of the post-modern.

I don't think by any means it's a masterpiece. It's a long journey. Most composers – when you look at their first opera and mine, I'm doing amazingly well.'

While Rufus prepared his opera, Martha was continuing work on her Edith Piaf project. The idea was instigated by Hal Willner and Martha had been initially reluctant to commit to an album of Piaf songs. Mindful of the success of the film *La Vie En Rose* and the fact that it had introduced so many people to the original songs Martha feared that any new recordings would be redundant. Willner's reputation was enough to convince her that the project could be artistically viable. After the successful trial at Spiegelworld in 2008 she agreed to play a handful of shows at the tiny Dixon Place Theatre in New York to be recorded as a live album. From the start Martha was more interested in getting at the truth of the songs rather than giving any kind of impersonation. 'I didn't do too much research into Piaf's life before making the album,' she would later explain. 'I don't look like her and I'm not an actor. She became the ghost behind all that I sang and hopefully I conjure something of her. I have a great amount of respect for Piaf. The power of her music, the crackling emotion of it, is rooted in our knowledge that these songs of longing and pain are from her own life. Her story is told in those lyrics. That's why, as an icon, she endures today.'

Martha and a small band played and recorded three concerts and the best of the material was released as the album *Sans Fusils, Ni Souliers, A Paris – Martha Wainwright's Piaf Record* in late 2009. Both Willner and Martha had decided to steer clear of the best known Piaf songs so there is no 'La Vie En Rose' or 'Non, Je Ne Regrette Rien'[4] on the disc (undoubtedly much to the chagrin of the record label). In truth the unfamiliarity of much of the material and the freewheeling nature of the recordings, captured without resorting to retakes or overdubs, allows Martha to trigger a frisson from her sometimes ragged but always intense performances. Compared to the planned pomp and circumstance of Rufus' Judy

---

4. At the concert recording Martha did actually sing 'La Vie En Rose' with Kate as something of a crowd-pleaser but the song was not included on the album.

Garland shows, Martha's Piaf project is altogether less formal. '[Piaf's] complete abandon as a singer and person inspired me to put all of myself into these performances,' said Martha. 'When you are singing songs that have been so well sung and recorded there is a great want to rise to the occasion and honour the writers as well as Piaf. I wanted the way in which we recorded it to mirror Piaf's off-the-cuff style.'

If Martha and Rufus were intent on paying tribute to their musical idols it was no surprise that Loudon had been planning a tribute album of his own. *High Wide & Handsome: The Charlie Poole Project* had appeared in August and was the culmination of almost two years of work by Loudon and musician/producer Dick Connette. Poole was an old-time banjo player and the leader of a band called the North Carolina Ramblers who had been remarkably successful in the early part of the century selling hundreds of thousands of records. Poole led a wild drink-sodden life, drifting from town to town to play dancehalls, barn dances and speakeasies but had died aged 39 in 1931. Though he didn't write many of his own songs his genius lay in his interpretation of others' material and in his unique way of playing his instrument. Loudon had long been a fan: he'd listened to Poole 78s since the early 1970s when Patrick Sky, a fellow traveller on the folk circuit had played him 'Hungry Hash House' and inspired him to track down more material from this intriguing old singer. There were obvious similarities between the ancient songs, full of humour and humanity, and Loudon's own approach to writing songs and singing stories. Loudon identified with Poole, he had lived the life of the travelling musician and the legend of the rambling man resonated with him – at one stage he had even considered trying to get a movie made so that he could play Poole on the screen. The *High Wide & Handsome* project, consisting of a double CD and accompanying filmed concert was more modest than a motion picture but was still a labour of love. Loudon curated an impressive roster of guest stars and family members – the album features contributions from both Martha and Rufus alongside their half-sister Lucy as well as Sloan Wainwright and Suzzy Roche and her sisters – singing Poole material as well as crafting some bio-graphical songs of his own to set the scene and fill out Poole's story. The album was a triumph: like Kate and Anna's *McGarrigle Hour* recordings, Loudon had succeeded in breathing new life, relevance and vitality into songs that were generations old.

With so much time having been devoted to side-projects like Loudon's album and the completion of *Prima Donna*, the writing and recording of Rufus' follow-up to *Release The Stars* to be titled, in a nod to Shakespeare and Louise Brooks, *All Days Are Nights: Songs for Lulu* was put on the backburner. At the end of 2009 Rufus released a CD/DVD package that celebrated the live band show he had toured so extensively. *Milwaukee At Last!!!* captured a performance at the historic Pabst Theatre in Milwaukee. Rufus saw the performances on the tour as reaching the peak of what he had been trying to achieve with full band presentations of his songs as he explained to *American Songwriter* magazine: 'After years of hiring and firing, I came up with a band that I was one hundred percent satisfied with. I'd always had great musicians and I'd always gone out on a limb, but it wasn't always spot on. But this tour I finally got there and so I wanted to capture that.'

While the CD contained edited highlights of the show, mostly versions of the tracks from the *Release The Stars* album, the DVD was a more expansive look at Rufus in concert from his rapturously received entrance in the Jean Charles de Castelbajac dazzle-suit, seemingly stitched from an avalanche of deckchairs to his coy lederhosen interlude and the drag finale of *Get Happy*.

Unfortunately the film, even with camera work provided by Albert and Philip Maysles amongst others, was a wasted opportunity. It was a rather flat and slipshod edit of strangely framed performance footage and extended sequences showing the rapt faces of the audience rather than the performers, all inter-cut with repetitive backstage footage that inexplicably featured nothing more interesting than extended discussions about brooches with members of the touring party. For fans that had seen Rufus on the *Release The Stars* tour the CD/DVD served as a functional, if uninspiring, souvenir of some excellent shows. The odd choice of tracks for the CD resulted in it essentially becoming just a live rendition of Rufus' previous album rather than a sampler of his best material from all of his records and the lacklustre quality of a concert film poorly represented what would surely have been another exceptional night on the tour. It was unlikely to attract many new converts.

By November 2009 Rufus was back in the studio in New York working on the long promised *All Days Are Nights: Songs for Lulu* record — a stripped down piano/vocal album that he suggested would act as a refreshing sorbet between the lushness of the opera, the extravagance of *Release The Stars* and his promise of a return to lavish pop in the future. Early solo live performances of new songs like 'Who Are You New York?' and 'Sad With What I Have' hinted at sophisticated and complicated piano parts in the vein of 'The Art Teacher' as if for Rufus, a back-to-basics album couldn't just mean simple songs with sparse accompaniment but required him to push his performing and arranging skills into still new areas. For Rufus, the magic of the songs could exist in widescreen and Technicolor no matter how many layers of orchestration he peeled away. He likened this new phase to *The Wizard of Oz*, a chance for his fans 'to look behind the curtain and see the little fat guy working the knobs'.

CODA

Walking back down the hill towards Hollywood and Highland, the guy in the blue T-shirt tells me he has seen Rufus play maybe 'two dozen' times. The guy in the rainbow T-shirt thinks that the Hollywood Bowl is the best concert he has ever seen in his life. I tell them that my aunt saw Judy Garland perform at the Talk of the Town in London and she was still talking about it 40 years later, and I ask them if they think they will still be talking about tonight's show when they're old men.

We are outside the Kodak Theatre where the Oscars are held and there are people dressed in home-made costumes, hopscotching their way among the brass letters and pink terrazzo stars set in the pavement, trying to get tourists to pay them as they pose for a photograph. There are so many of them that even obscure, unloved characters get a look-in. After all, it's better to be the only Rocketeer than it is to be the third Captain Jack Sparrow.

The guy in the blue T-shirt tells me about the film director D.W. Griffith. Back in 1916 he put everything he had into the spectacular movie *Intolerance*. It cost a staggering amount of money to make and returned very little, eventually leading to him losing his studio. But Griffith was obsessed by the film and constantly tinkered with it, even going so far as to try to sneak into the projection booth and re-edit the print that he had given to MoMA in New York before they held his first-ever retrospective in 1940. Today, few people will have heard of the film, even fewer will have watched it, but up above the shopping arcade at the Hollywood and Highland Center are replicas of the immense Babylonian pillars and huge stone elephants that he conceived for its opening scenes. The guy in the blue T-shirt points them out to me and shows me the replica of Griffith's giant archway that now frames the distant HOLLYWOOD sign. 'More people will see these than are ever going to watch

Intolerance,' he explains. 'It doesn't matter how hard you try to protect your legacy, in the end it's out of your hands. Your greatest moment could be reduced to kitsch decorations on top of a shopping mall. Rufus might just be remembered as the man who pretended to be Judy Garland instead of for his own songs. The future is in other people's hands. You just have to hope that the future has good taste.'

ACKNOWLEDGEMENTS

Thanks to Josh Holden for translation services in Montreal, Jan Hughes for help in New York and Paul Lamont for accommodation and hospitality in Los Angeles, and to Ian Preece and Jane Sturrock at Orion and my agent Neil Taylor.

Thanks to the following people for interviews, information, the loan of rare material, good intentions, advice and assistance: Sean Adams, Joe Ambrose, Penny Arcade, Jon Carin, the late Bill Claxton, Shaun Connon, Clive Davis, Rock Demers, Thierry Demont, Gene Denonovich, Danny Fields, Iain Forsyth and Jane Pollard, Nic Harcourt, Ethan Johns, Osman Koulenovitch, Caroline Leaf, Roger Liptrot, Zoe Miller, Ariana Morgenstern, Barb Morrison, David Nichtern, Gillian Parry, Sybilla Poortman, Anthony Reynolds, Rachel Reynolds, John Ross, Mike Rubbo, Steve Popovich, Lois Siegel, Allan Taylor, Nick Terzo. Thanks also to those who consented to be interviewed but asked to remain anonymous. The guy in the blue T-shirt was called Tom, the guy in the rainbow T-shirt was called Carlos. Thanks for inadvertently giving me the name of the book and if I'd known I was definitely going to write the book when I met you, I'd have asked for your surnames. Thanks also to the National Film Board of Canada, KCRW in Santa Monica and the London Palladium and the ever enthusiastic and supportive members of the Rufus Wainwright message board.

BIBLIOGRAPHY

Newspapers, Magazines, Journals

Adams, Tim. 'Rufus Wainwright', *Observer Music Monthly*, February 2005.

Anderson, Ian. 'Joe Boyd: The Producer's Tale', *Folk Roots*, February 1986.

Apatow, Judd. 'Judd Apatow's Diary', *slate.com*, 29 September 2005.

Applefeld Olso, Catherine. 'Artists now proud to pitch', *Brandweek*, 24 May 1999.

Aquilante, Dan. 'Release The Stars' review, *New York Post*, 13 May 2007.

Arnum, Eric. 'Orton, Crenshaw Sing Some of Century's Best', VH1.com, 8 December 1999.

Aronowitz, Al. *The Gaslight and the Greenwich Village Scene*, Column 6, 1 February 1996. www.theblacklistedjournalist.com.

Azzopardi, Chris. 'Run, Run Rufus', *Between the Lines*, 18 January 2007.

Babcock, Jay. 'Cigarettes And Chocolate Milk', *LA Weekly*, 18 July 2001.

Baker, Spencer. 'Two Muses', *Performing Arts Journal*, no.84, 2006.

Bambarger, Bradley. 'Christmas with a Canadian Accent', *Star Ledger*, 20 December 2005.

Barrett, Amy. 'The Way We Live Now', *New York Times*, 14 March 2004.

Barrett ,Jon. 'Entertainer of the Year: Rufus Wainwright', *Out*, December 2006.

Bartlett, Thomas. 'Songwriting Saved My Life', Salon.com, 7 October 2003.

Bartlett Thomas. 'Pete's Candy Store', Popmatters.com, 23 February 2003..

Barton, Laura. 'In Her Own Right', *Guardian*, 22 May 2006.

Berg, Karin. *Loudon Wainwright III record review, Rolling Stone*, 5 August 1971.

Blackman, Guy. 'He's Their Man', *Age*, 2 January 2005.

Blevins, Brian. 'Loudon Wainwright III', *Time Out*, 14 May 1972.

Bliss, Karen. 'Rufus Sings With Elton', *Rolling Stone*, 20 June 2001.

Boehlert, Eric. 'Nike Experience Bittersweet For Verve', *Rolling Stone*, 16 February 1998.

Bowman, Kate. 'Odd Man Out Tour', *Paste* magazine, 29 June 2004.

Broome, Eric. 'Pride of the Clan', yahoomusic.com, 26 August 1998.

Browne, David. 'Loudon Wainwright', *Rolling Stone*, 23 April 1987.

Bunn, Austin. 'Rufus On The Couch', *Nerve*, August 2001.

Butler, Tray. 'Friend of Dorothy', hx.com, May 2006.

Byatt, A.S. 'Twisted Yarns', *Guardian*, 21 June 2008.

Cairns, Dan. *Want Two* review, *Sunday Times*, 6 March 2005.

Carlson, Amy. 'The Second Coming', AE:Online, 17 July 1998.

Carman, Joseph. 'Fresh Moves', *The Advocate*, 25 April 2006.

Charlesworth, Chris. Everly Brothers, Albert Hall, live review, *Melody Maker*, 23 October 1971.

Charlesworth, Chris. 'Whimsical Wainwright', *Melody Maker*, 24 July 1976.

Chonin, Neva. Rufus Wainwright review, *Rolling Stone*, June 1998.

Chupnick, Steve. 'Judd Apatow on Knocked Up', latinoreview.com, 25 May 2007.

Christgau, Georgia. The McGarrigle Hour, *Village Voice*, 10 November 1998.

Ciabattoni, Steve. Rufus Wainwright interview, *CMJ*, April 1998.

Clegg, Rachael. 'Interview with Martha Wainwright', manchestermusic.co.uk, 28 February 2005.

Colley, Claire. 'Chip Off the Old Block', musicohm.com, Feb 2006.

Colville, Peter. 'Record Breaker', *ES Magazine*, 5 September 2008.

Cosyns, Simon. 'Bleeding Wonderful', *Sun*, 7 May 2008.

Cripps, Charlotte. 'Song and Dance Girl', *Independent*, 19 April 2007.

Cromelin, Richard. 'Rufus Wainwright Branches Out To Stay In Place', *LA Times*, 24 May 2007.

Crompton, Sarah. 'On Seas of Unreality', *Daily Telegraph*, 8 May 2007.

Cumming, Alan. 'Bucking Convention with his Grand Talent . . .' Interview, October 2003.

Cumming, Tim. 'Shepherds Bush Empire – Martha Wainwright', *Independent*, 16 November 2005.

Dallas, Karl. 'Loudon Alone', *Melody Maker*, 1 June 1974.

Dalton, Stephen. 'Rufus Wainwright London Palladium', *The Times*, 20 February 2007.

Dansby, Andrew. 'Universal Acquires DreamWorks', *Rolling Stone*, 11 November 2003.

Dansby, Andrew, and Scaggs, Austin. 'Wainwright Has More Want', *Rolling Stone*, 13 October 2003.

Davis, Hazel. 'Martha Wainwright', *Word*, July 2006.

DeCurtis, Anthony. 'Rufus Wainwright Journeys To Gay Hell and Back', *New York Times*, 31 August 2003.

Denberg, Jody. *Fame and Wealth* album review, *Rolling Stone*, 12 May 1983.

Devenish, Colin. 'An interview with Linda Ronstadt', *Rolling Stone*, 23 October 2002.

Deziel, Shanda. 'Rufus Wainwright on Becoming Judy Garland', *Macleans*, 5 June 2006.

Dix, Noel. 'Rufus Wainwright', exclaim.ca, October 2003.

Doggett, Peter. 'Grand Designs', *Mojo*, June 2007.

Dolech, Marc. 'Wainwright, Folds to Tour', *Rolling Stone*, 4 May 2004.

Duerden, Nick. 'How We Met: Martha Wainwright and Beth Orton', *Independent on Sunday*, 27 March 2005.

Dunlevy, T'cha. 'Wainwright Reaches Cruising Altitude in New Album', *Gazette*, 2 June 2008.

Dunlevy, T'Cha. 'Rufus Comes Home', *Montreal Gazette*, 12 May 2007.

Eldridge, Jackie. 'Getting Intimate with Rufus Wainwright', *Outlook*, April 2007.

Ellen, Mark. 'A Night at the Soap Opera', *Word*, March 2005.

Empire, Kitty. 'Nowt as Queer as Folk', *Observer*, 12 October 2003.

Errigo, Angie. New Victoria Theatre live review, *New Musical Express*, 26 February 1977.

Eyre, Hermione. 'Why Do I get All the Nerds?', *Independent*, 8 June 2008.

Farbcr, Jim. 'Rufus Wainwright, Bowery Ballroom', *New York Daily News*, 17 December 1998.

Farinella, David John. 'Rufus Wainwright', *Mix*, 1 February 2004.

Feldman, Adam. 'Judy Blooms', *Time Out* New York, 8 June 2006.

Feliciano, Kristina. *Martha Wainwright* review, *Entertainment Weekly*, 18 April 2005.

Flynn, Paul. 'Rufus Exclusive', *Attitude*, June 2007.

Frei, Darren. 'Rufus of Montreal', *Advocate*, 26 October 2004.

Fricke, David. *Want One* review, *Rolling Stone*, 16 October 2003.

Funke, Lewis. 'Judy Garland in Concert', *New York Times*, 24 April 1961.

Galliano, Joseph. 'Justin Bond and Rufus Wainwright', *Gay Times*, July 2007.

Ganahl, Jane. 'Rufus the Baptist', *San Francisco Chronicle*, 9 January 2004.

Garcia, Gilbert. 'Rebel Prince', *Phoenix New Times*, 15 November 2001.

Geary, Tim. 'Over The Rainbow and Away With the Fairies', *Daily Telegraph*, 16 June 2006.

Ghorbani, Lisa. 'Q&A: Rufus Wainwright', *Rolling Stone*, 31 March 1999.

Gilbert, Jerry. 'Sisters In Song', *Sounds*, 10 April 1976.

Grotte, Nathaniel. 'Rufus Wainwright Strikes A Pose', *Daily Cardinal*, 25 February 2002.

Guarino, Mark. 'Rufus Wainwright: Stars in His Eyes', *Harp* magazine, May 2007.

Guzmon, Rafer. 'Garland He's Not – But Oh How He Tries', *Newsday*, 16 June 2006.

Hannah, JD. The McGarrigle Hour, salon.com, 4 November 1998.

Harris, Will. 'Interview With Judd Apatow', Bullz-eye.com, 6 August 2005.

Harrity, Christopher. 'Judy's Stamp of Approval', advocate.com, 9 June 2006.

Hattenstone, Simon. 'Verdi and Me', *Guardian*, 14 April 2007.

Hayes, David. 'The Chosen One', *Saturday Night*, May 1999.

Hilburn, Robert. 'LW III's LA Debut', *LA Times*, 1974.

Hilburn, Robert. 'Zip Off The Old Block', *Los Angeles Times*, 11 April 1999.

Hodgkinson, Will. 'They fuck you up, your mum and dad', *Guardian*, 18 March 2005.

Holden, Stephen. The McGarrigle Hour, *New York Times*, 27 November 1998.

Holden, Stephen. Album III record review, *Rolling Stone*, 26 October 1972.

Holden, Stephen. 'Kate and Anna McGarrigle album review', *Rolling Stone*, 26 February 1976.

Holden, Stephen. 'Heartbeats Accelerating', *New York Times*, 28 October 1990.

Holden, Stephen. 'Rufus Wainwright Pays Tribute to Judy Garland at Carnegie Hall', *New York Times*, 16 June 2006.

Hollingsworth, Ray. 'The Man Who Made The Speakeasy Listen', *Melody Maker*, September 1971.

Hoskyns, Barney. 'The Backpages Interview: Rufus Wainwright', *Rock's Backpages*, 2 June 2001.

Hoskyns, Barney. *Want Two* review, *Uncut*, April 2005.

Hughes, Rob. Van Dyke Parks, *Uncut*, April 2008.

Irwin, Colin. 'Waking Up To Chorley', *Melody Maker*, 31 July 1976.

Irwin, Colin. 'The Third Man', *Folk Roots*, June 1986.

Irwin, Colin. 'Loudon is a Tuft Man', *New Musical Express*, 29 September 1979.

Irwin, Colin. 'Such Devoted Sisters', *Folk Roots*, February 1986.

Irwin, Dave. 'Raising The Rufus', *Tucson Weekly*, 23 July 1998.

Jesperson, Peter. 'Review of 1999', *Crawdaddy*, no. 23, Spring 2000.

Jinman, Richard. 'Guardian Profile: The Wainwrights', *Guardian*, 15 April 2005.

John, Elton. 'Rufus Wainwright', *Interview*, April 2004.

Jones, Chad. 'Bourne To Boogie', *Oakland Tribune*, 17 March 2006.

Kahn, Brenda. 'Coffee With Martha', womanrock.com, Spring 2000.

Kaye, Lenny. 'Loudon Wainwright', *Rolling Stone*, 29 April 1971.

Kelly, Katherine. 'Tori Amos Live', *St Paul Pioneer Press Minneapolis*, 23 October 2001.

Koepke, Melora. 'Genetic Composition', *Hour*, 22 January 2004.

Landau, John. Maria Muldaur: *Waitress In The Donut Shop* album review, *Rolling Stone*, 19 December 1974.

Lanham, Tom. 'Rufus Wainwright', *Flaunt*, May 2001.

Leonard, John. 'Evil Comes To Suburbia', John Cheever, review, *New York Times*, 29 April 1969.

Lichtenstein, Grace. 'They Won't Boo Loudon Any Longer', *New York Times*, 3 February 1974.

Lynskey, Dorian. 'I'm Getting Out From The Shadows', *Guardian*, 6 May 2008.

McCormick, Brian. 'Please Don't Eat The Daisies', *Gay City News*, April 2006.

McCormick, Neil. 'How Martha Melted Snow Patrol', *Daily Telegraph*, 25 November 2006.

McGrath, T.J. 'Linda Ronstadt Interview', *Dirty Linen*, 2003.

McInnes, Gavin. Live review – Roxy Music/Rufus Wainwright, Madison Square Garden, New York, NME.com, 25 July 2001.

McKenna, Brittney. Rufus Wainwright Q&A, *American Songwriter*, October 2009.

Maclean, Craig. 'The Boy's As Bold as Brass', *Scotsman*, 29 April 2007.

McLeod, Rodd. Rufus Wainwright, Bowery Ballroom, *Rolling Stone*, 18 December 1998.

McNair, James. 'Son Arise', *Mojo*, September 2008.

McNair, James. 'Rufus Loves You', *Independent*, 9 May 2003.

Miles, Barry. *Kate and Anna McGarrigle* album review, *New Musical Express*, 6 March 1976.

Miller, Jim. Van Dyke Parks: album review Song Cycle, *Rolling Stone*, 24 February 1968.

Miller, Sienna and Poehler, Amy. 'Two Sides of Rufus', *Interview*, June 2007.

Mulvey, John. *Release the Stars* review, *Uncut*, June 2007.

Murray Winters, Pamela. 'Loudon Wainwright III', *Dirty Linen*, February 2002.

Murphy, Kerry. 'Selling Out The Jingle', *Seattle Weekly*, 17 March 1999.

Orloff, Brian. 'Rufus' Sleeping Beauty', *Rolling Stone*, 16 November 2004.

Pareles, John. Rufus Wainwright, Bowery Ballroom, *New York Times*, 18 December 1998.

Pemberton, Andy. 'At Home With Rufus Wainwright' *Q*, June 2007.

Petridis, Alexis. *Want Two* review, *Guardian*, 25 February 2005.

Petridis, Alexis. 'Rufus Wainwright, London Palladium', *Guardian*, 20 February 2007.

Phipps, Keith. 'Judd Apatow', *A.V. Club*, 3 October 2001.

Powers, Ann. 'Following his Troubadour Lineage. . .', *New York Times*, 13 March 1998.

Powers, Ann. Martha Wainwright, live review: Required Listening Series, *New York Times*, 9 December 1997.

Powers, Ann. 'Poses' *New York Times*, 1 July 2001.

Ratliff, Ben. Poses, *Rolling Stone*, 21 June 2001.

Regenstreif, Mike. 'On Their Own Terms', *Sing Out!* Vol. 41/4 February 1997.

Ridenour, Shelly. 'Rufus on Top', *Nylon*, May 2001.

Robinson, John. 'Up Close and Personal', *Uncut*, June 2007.

Rockwell, John. 'They Sing Honest Songs of Love', *New York Times*, 10 April 1977.

Rockwell, John. 'Magical McGarrigles: Live Bottom Line', *New York Times*, 13 April 1977.

Roderick, Stephen. 'Jon Brion', *New York Times*, 17 August 2003.

Ross, Mike. 'Rootin' For Rufus', *Edmonton Sun*, 24 April 1999.

Rudis, Al. 'Loudon Wainwright: The New Dylan?', *Melody Maker*, 26 December 1970.

Saroyan, Strawberry. 'Nerdy But Nice', *Daily Telegraph*, 12 January 2008.

Scaggs, Austin. 'Rufus' New World', *Rolling Stone*, 24 September 2003.

Schinder, Scott. The McGarrigle Hour, *Entertainment Weekly*, 16 October 1998.

Schwartz, Mara. 'Rufus Drops His Poses', CDNow.com, January 2002.

Sculley, Alan. 'Singer Faces His Demons', *Press Enterprise*, 27 February 2004.

Shapiro, Gregg. 'Interview with Chris Terrio', afterelton.com, 27 June 2005.

Shenton, Mark. 'Somewhere Over The Rainbow (Coloured Flag) with Rufus Wainwright', *Stage*, 26 February 2007.

Shulman, Randy. 'The Wainwright Stuff', *Metro Weekly*, 3 November 1999.

Simpson, Mark. 'Ban The Folk Mass!', *Pride*, 2005.

Sinagra, Laura. 'An Extended Family Holiday Outing, Onstage', *New York Times*, 23 December 2005.

Sisario, Ben. 'Arts, Briefly: Soccer Opera Cancelled', *New York Times*, 14 March 2006.

Smith, Rupert. 'Passing The Torch', *Gay Times*, January 2007.

Spencer, Neil. 'Loudon Wainwright Q+A', *Uncut*, September 2008.

Straub, Dick. 'Came So Far For Beauty', www.leonardcohenfiles.com, June 2003.

Sutcliffe, Phil. 'Do It Again?', *Mojo*, September 2006.

Taylor, Graham. 'Busy Being Born', *Let It Rock*, November 1975.

Todd, Bella. 'Rufus Wainwright Dome Concert Hall', *Argus*, 30 November 2005.

Tommasini, Anthony. 'Rufus Wainwright', *New York Times*, 7 September 2005.

Trebay, Guy. 'Rufus Wainwright Plays Judy Garland', *New York Times*, 4 June 2006.

Tucker, Ken. 'Rufus, Son of Loudon, and his take on love', *New York Times*, 19 April 1998.

Tucker, Ken. 'Oedipus Wreck', *Entertainment Weekly*, 19 October 2001.

True, Everett. 'Method Actress', *Plan B*, June 2005.

Udovitch, Mim. 'The Importance of Being Rufus', *Rolling Stone*, 10 June 1999.

Vary, Adam B. 'Pose Guardin', *Entertainment Weekly*, 28 August 2001.

Verrico, Lisa. 'Somewhere Over The Rainbow, He Struck Gold', *Sunday Times*, 9 September 2007.

Verrico, Lisa. 'Stop Your Sobbing', *Sunday Times*, 13 April 2008.

Viktor & Rolf. 'Stop Making Sense', *V&A* Magazine, Spring 2007.

Vincentelli, Elisabeth. 'Countdown to Judy Week 1', *Time Out* New York, 20 April 2006.

Vincentelli, Elisabeth. 'Countdown to Judy Week 2', *Time Out* New York, 27 April 2006.

Vincentelli, Elisabeth. 'Countdown to Judy Week 3', *Time Out* New York, 4 May 2006.

Vincentelli, Elisabeth. 'Countdown to Judy Week 4', *Time Out* New York, 11 May 2006.

Vincentelli, Elisabeth. 'Countdown to Judy Week 5', *Time Out* New York, 18 May 2006.

Vincentelli, Elisabeth. 'Countdown to Judy Week 6', *Time Out* New York, 27 May 2006.

Vincentelli, Elisabeth. 'Countdown to Judy Week 7', *Time Out* New York, 1 June 2006.

Wainwright, Loudon III. Identity Crisis, *Mojo*, December 1995.

Wainwright, Loudon III. 'Loudon Wainwright III', *Word*, June 2005.

Wainwright, Martha. 'My Life In Travel', *Independent*, 23 August 2008.

Wainwright, Martha. 'Edith Piaf Became The Ghost Behind All I Sang', *The Times*, 30 October 2009.

Wainwright, Rufus/Thompson Teddy, 'How We Met: Rufus Wainwright and Teddy Thompson', *Independent on Sunday*, 12 December 2005.

Wakin, Daniel J. 'Met Opera's Commissions Show Signs of Progress', *New York Times*, 3 July 2007.

Walsh, Ben. 'Rufus Wainwright London Palladium', *Independent*, 20 February 2007.

Walsh, Jeff. 'Rufus Wainwright Strikes Impressive Poses', *Oasis* magazine, June 2001.

Walsh, John. 'Success is Relative', *Independent*, 4 March 2005.

Walters, Barry. 'Talkin' 'bout his Generation', *Advocate*, 1 September 1998.

Walters, Barry. 'Rufus Wainwright', *Advocate*, 12 May 1998.

Walters, Barry. *Want Two* review, *Rolling Stone*, 15 December 2004.

Walters, Barry. Martha Wainwright review, *Rolling Stone*, 21 April 2005.

Waters, Juliet. 'Dreamboy', *Montreal Mirror*, 18 January 1996.

Watts, Michael. 'Shattering McGarrigles', *Melody Maker*, 31 July 1976.

Widerhorn, Jon. Elton: 'Elton John Bags Technology', MTV.com, 5 October 2001.

Williams, Richard. Victoria Palace Theatre live review, *The Times*, 26 July 1976.

Williamson, Nigel. 'Family Albums: Q + A Loudon Wainwright', *Uncut*, May 2005.

Willner, Hal. Sleevenotes, *Stormy Weather: The Music of Harold Arlen* CD release, Sony, 2002.

Wilson, John S. 'Allison Blues Band Reigns at Festival', *New York Times*, 31 August 1970.

Wilton, Lisa. 'Rufus Wainwright', jam.canoe.ca, 23 October 1998.

Windolf, Jim. 'Songs in the Key of Lacerating', *Vanity Fair*, May 2007.

Woffinden, Bob. 'Dancer With Bruises', *New Musical Express*, 9 April 1977.

Woffinden, Bob. 'Dancer With Bruised Knees', *New Musical Express*, 12 February 1977.

Wolfson, Julie. 'LAist Interview: Loudon Wainwright III', *LAist*, 5 November 2007.

Wood, Mikael. 'Tending To Yuletide Tradition', *Village Voice*, 6 December 2005.

Wright, Ian. 'Interview with Martha Wainwright', cluas.com, June 2005.

Writes, Arjan. 'Interview With Rufus Wainwright', arjanwrites.com, 15 November 2004.

Zahora, George. Nick Cave 'No More Shall We Part' review, splendidezine.com, March 2001.

Zuel, Bernard. 'Who's A Pretty Boy', *Sydney Morning Herald*, 5 May 2007.

Uncredited: 'Hot Dad', *Rolling Stone*, 30 August 2001.

Uncredited: 'Making a Ruckus Over Rufus', *Newsweek*, 18 January 1999.

Uncredited: 'Martha Wainwright', *Observer*, 12 March 2006.

Uncredited: 'Night writer', *Empire*, June 2001.

Uncredited: 'Rufus Wainwright', exclaim.ca, October 2003.

Uncredited: 'The Year In Music', *Crawdaddy* #23, Spring 2000.

Uncredited: 'Tori Amos Helped Me Get Over My Rape Ordeal', me-me-me.tv, 15 May 2007.

Transcripts/Radio/ Television/Audio

Adams, Noah interviews – Kate and Anna McGarrigle: radio transcript – *All Things Considered*, NPR, 22 November 1996.

Gross, Terri – *Fresh Air*, NPR, 24 July 1999.

Gross, Terry – *Fresh Air*, NPR, 19 October 2001.

Harcourt, Nic – radio transcript – *Morning Becomes Eclectic*, KCRW, 21 October 2003.

Paphides, Peter – 'Times Podcast: Interview Rufus Wainwright', *The Times*, 11 May 2007.

Simon, Scott – 'Wainwright to Channel Judy Garland', NPR radio transcript, 10 June 2006.

Wainwright, Loudon – Lecture: 'My Cool Life', Ohio University Spring Festival 2004.

Waronker, Lenny: www.artistshousemusic.org 'Industry Legends' video interview series, September 2006.

Was, David – 'A Lot to Learn from "Judy at Carnegie Hall"', NPR radio transcript, 14 June 2006.

Millbrook School Alumni 75th Anniversary Film – Episode 7.

Winterson, Jeanette: *The South Bank Show,* Granada Television, 2004, UK.

Uncredited radio interview transcript – 'Off The Record With Rufus Wainwright', Triple R FM, Melbourne, 6 February 2005.

'Bloom Project – Soundcheck', WNYC radio recording, 19 April 2005.

Uncredited – Rufus Wainwright interview transcript, *MTV News,* 2 March 1999.

Hoffman, Kristian interview – radio transcript – 'Queer Music Heritage', April 2008. KPFT 90.1FM Houston.

Muller, Sophie video shoot diary: http://hole.b5.net/rufus/aprilfools _video.html

TV show – *Lance Loud! A Death In An American Family* – dir. Alan and Susan Raymond, 2002.

Wainwright, Martha, *Loose Ends,* BBC Radio 4, 29 December 2007.

Books

Ambrose, Joe. *Chelsea Hotel Manhattan,* Headpress, 2007, UK.

Barnes, Ken. *Sinatra and the Great Song Stylists,* Ian Allan Books, 1973, UK.

Barthelme, Donald. *The Dead Father,* Farrar, Strauss and Giroux, 1975, US.

Barthes, Roland. 'Death of the Author' essay in *Image-Music-Text*, 1977. (Flamingo, reprinted, 1982 UK.)

Browning, Robert. Poems, Penguin, 2001, UK

Burroughs, William, Gysin, Brion. *The Third Mind,* Viking, 1978, US.

Claxton, William. *Photographic Memory*, Powerhouse Books, 2002, US.

Connolly, Cyril. *Enemies of Promise,* Routledge, London, 1938.

Conrad, Peter. *Romantic Opera and Literary Form,* University of California Press, 1977.

Crisp, Quentin. *The Naked Civil Servant,* Cape, 1968, UK.

Dickinson, Emily. *The Complete Poems,* Faber and Faber, 1970, UK.

Du Maurier, Daphne. *The Infernal World of Branwell Brontë*, Victor Gollancz, London, 1960.

Dyson, Jeremy, Gatiss, Mark, Pemberton, Steve, Shearsmith, Reece. *The League of Gentlemen's Book of Precious Things*, Prion, 2007, UK.

Holden, Stephen. *The Rolling Stone Record Guide*, Rolling Stone Press, 1979, US.

Hopkins, Jerry. *Bowie,* Macmillan, 1985, UK.

Hornby, Nick. *31 Songs,* Penguin, 2003, UK.

Hughes, Ted. *The Letters of Ted Hughes,* ed. Christopher Read, Faber, 2007.

Jarman, Derek. *At Your Own Risk,* Hutchinson 1992, UK.

Kramer, Larry. *The Normal Heart,* Plume, 1987, US.

Lanken, Dane. *Kate and Anna McGarrigle: Songs and Stories*, Penumbra, 2007, Canada.

Larkin, Philip. *Selected Letters of Philip Larkin*, ed. Anthony Thwaite, Faber 1992, UK.

Larkin, Philip. *High Windows*, Faber, 1974, UK.

Lewis, C. Day. *The Poetic Image*, Cape, 1947, UK.

McDarrah, Fred. *Kerouac and Friends: A Beat Generation Album*, Avalon Publishing, 2002.

Marcus, Greil. *Mystery Train*, E.P Dutton, 1975, US.

Nelligan, Emile. *Selected Poems*, Ryerson Press, 1960, Canada.

Pattison, Robert. *The Triumph of Vulgarity*, Oxford University Press, 1987, UK.

Peel, John. *Margrave of the Marshes*, Bantam, 2005, UK.

Pilton, Patrick. *Every Night at the London Palladium*, Robson Books, 1976, UK.

Poe, Edgar Allan. *The Complete Stories and Poems of Edgar Allan Poe*, Doubleday, 1984, US.

Poe, Edgar Allan, *The Poetic Principle, Sartain's* Magazine 1850, reprinted in *The Works of Edgar Allan Poe Vol. III*, Arcadia House, 1950, US.

Silverstein, Richard. *Folk and Blues Encyclopedia*, St Martin's Press, 2001, US.

Sontag, Susan. 'Notes on Camp', essay in *Against Interpretation*, Farrar, Strauss and Giroux, 1966, US.

Stevenson, Anne. *Bitter Fame: A Life of Sylvia Plath*, Penguin, 1989, UK.

Tennyson, Alfred Lord. *Alfred Lord Tennyson: Selected Poems*, Penguin, 1991, UK.

Wetzsteon, Ross. *Republic of Dreams: Greenwich Village: the American Bohemia, 1910–1960*, Simon & Schuster, 2002, US.

Whitman, Walt. *The Complete Poems*, reprinted Penguin 1975, UK.

Wilde, Oscar. *The Happy Prince and Other Stories*, 1888, reprinted Puffin Books 1962, UK.

Wilde, Oscar. *The Soul of Man Under Socialism*, 1891 (reprinted 2001, Penguin, UK).

Woliver, Robbie. *Hoot! A 25-Year History of the Greenwich Village Music Scene*, St Martin's Press, 1986, US.

The Narcotics Anonymous Step Working Guides, Narcotics Anonymous World Services inc, 1998, US.

Discography

This is a selected discography for albums only, listing the original labels and release dates. Almost all of these recordings are still available, although many have been subsequently repackaged and issued by other labels.

In addition to these official releases, through the course of my research

I have listened to and watched many hours of live recordings, out-takes, demos and archive material featuring the family and spanning the past four decades. For those wishing to delve deeper, many live shows and radio broadcasts are now available online and can be easily accessed with a little careful searching.

There are also dozens of songs that have been recorded specifically for film soundtrack work as well as guest appearances on other people's recordings. For reasons of space, these have been omitted from this discography.

Rufus Wainwright

Rufus Wainwright	(DreamWorks 1998)
Poses	(DreamWorks 2001)
Want One	(DreamWorks 2003)
Want Two	(Geffen 2004)
Release the Stars	(Geffen 2007)
Rufus Does Judy at Carnegie Hall	(Geffen 2007)
Milwaukee At Last!!!	(Decca/Universal)

Loudon Wainwright

Loudon Wainwright III	(Atlantic, 1970)
Album II	(Atlantic 1971)
Album III	(Columbia 1972)
Attempted Mustache	(Columbia 1973)
Unrequited	(Columbia 1975)
T-Shirt	(Arista 1976)
Final Exam	(Arista 1978)
A Live One	(Rounder/Radar 1979)
Fame and Wealth	(Rounder 1983)
I'm Alright	(Rounder 1985)
More Love Songs	(Rounder 1986)
Therapy	(Silvertone 1989)
History	(Charisma 1992)
Career Moves	(Virgin 1993)
Grown Man	(Virgin 1995)
Little Ship	(Virgin 1997)
BBC Sessions	(Strange Fruit 1998)
Social Studies	(Hannibal 1999)
Last Man on Earth	(Red House 2001)
So Damn Happy	(Sanctuary 2003)
Here Come the Choppers	(Sovereign 2005)
Strange Weirdos	(Concord 2007)

Recovery	(Yep Roc 2008)
Hide Wide & Handsome: The Charlie Poole Project	(Proper/2nd Story Sound)

Kate and Anna McGarrigle

Kate and Anna McGarrigle	(Warner Brothers 1976)
Dancer With Bruised Knees	(Warner Brothers 1977)
Pronto Monto	(Warner Brothers 1978)
The French Record	(Hannibal 1980)
Love Over and Over	(Hannibal 1983)
Heartbeats Accelerating	(Private Music 1990)
Matapedia	(Hannibal 1996)
The McGarrigle Hour	(Hannibal 1998)
La Vache Qui Pleure	(La Tribu 2003)
The McGarrigle Christmas Hour	(Nonesuch 2005)

Martha Wainwright

Ground Floor	(self-released, cassette only 1997)
Martha Wainwright	(Drowned In Sound/Zoe 2005)
I Know You're Married But I've Got Feelings Too	(Drowned In Sound/Zoe 2008)
Sans Fusils, Ni Souliers, A Paris — Martha Wainwright's Piaf Record	(Drowned In Sound)

Filmography

(as performers only, not including soundtrack work)

The Slugger's Wife – dir. Hal Ashby 1985
(features Loudon Wainwright)

Tommy Tricker and the Stamp Traveller – dir. Mike Rubbo 1988
(features Rufus Wainwright)

Jacknife – dir. David Hugh Jones 1989
(features Loudon Wainwright)

28 Days – dir. Betty Thomas
(features Loudon Wainwright)

Big Fish – dir. Tim Burton 2003
(features Loudon Wainwright)

The Aviator – dir. Martin Scorsese 2004
(features Loudon, Rufus and Martha Wainwright)

Heights – dir. Chris Terrio 2005
(features Rufus Wainwright)

The 40-Year-Old Virgin – dir. Judd Apatow 2005
(features Loudon Wainwright)

Elizabethtown – dir. Cameron Crowe 2005
(features Loudon Wainwright)

For Your Consideration – dir. Christopher Guest 2006
(features Loudon Wainwright)

Knocked Up – dir. Judd Apatow 2007
(features Loudon Wainwright)

L'Âge des ténèbres – dir. Denys Arcand 2007
(features Rufus Wainwright)

INDEX